Video Gamers

Video gaming is economically, educationally, culturally, socially and theoretically important, and has, in a relatively short period of time, firmly cemented its place within contemporary life. It is fair to say, however, that most research to date has focused most specifically on either the video games themselves, or the direct engagement of gamers with a specific piece of game technology.

In contrast, *Video Gamers* is the first book to explicitly and comprehensively address how digital games are experienced and engaged with in the everyday lives, social networks and consumer patterns of those who play them. In doing so, the book provides a key introduction to the study of video gamers and the games they play, whilst also reflecting on the current debates and literatures surrounding the gaming practice.

Garry Crawford is a Senior Lecturer in Cultural Sociology at the University of Salford. He is the author or editor of a number of books, including *Consuming Sport* (2004), *Dictionary of Leisure Studies* (2009, with T. Blackshaw) and *Online Gaming in Context* (2011, edited with V.K. Gosling and B. Light).

Video Gamers

Garry Crawford

Routledge
Taylor & Francis Group

LONDON AND NEW YORK

First published 2012 by Routledge
2 Park Square, Milton Park, Abingdon, Oxon, OX14 4RN

Simultaneously published in the USA and Canada
by Routledge
711 Third Avenue, New York, NY 10017

*Routledge is an imprint of the Taylor & Francis Group, an informa
business*

British Library Cataloguing in Publication Data
A catalogue record for this book is available from the British Library

Library of Congress Cataloging in Publication Data
Crawford, Garry.
Video gamers / Garry Crawford.
  p. cm.
  1. Video games. 2. Video games--Social aspects. I. Title.
  GV1469.3.C647 2011   794.8--dc22
  2011009302

ISBN: 978-0-415-56368-0 (hbk)
ISBN: 978-0-415-67441-6 (pbk)
ISBN: 978-0-203-86337-4 (ebk)

Typeset in Times New Roman
by Bookcraft Ltd, Stroud, Gloucestershire

For Victoria

Contents

List of figures and table

Figures

Table

Preface and acknowledgements

Video games have been part of my life since my early childhood, ever since I first played on my older brother's *Pong* console in the late 1970s. However, I cannot claim to have ever been either a particularly talented or dedicated gamer, especially as it becomes increasingly difficult to find the time to dedicate to playing video games. But as a sociologist what has always interested me is people – what people do, why they do it and what their actions mean to themselves and others. For me, people's passions and interests, whether in film, sport, video games or another cultural area, are what makes us all interesting and significant in our own specific ways. Hence, this book is less about video games, and certainly less about my particular gaming history and preferences, and more about people who play video games, their lives and their culture, and also the theoretical tools we might employ to better understand this.

This book draws and builds upon my developing thoughts and work on video games and video gamers. It therefore incorporates ideas developed in previous published work, both sole-authored and written with Ben Light, Jason Rutter and, in particular, Victoria K. Gosling. So I owe Ben, Jason and Victoria a big thank you, as well as an acknowledgement of their contributions to many of the ideas and work utilized in this book.

I would also like to thank those who have shared in my video gaming over the years, and sometimes still do so, and in particular Ian Groom, Toby Hill, Stephen Lees, Eamon Mason, Mark Mundy, Ian Peek, Daniel Seddon and Jason Storr, without whom my video gaming would have been a much poorer, and lonelier, experience. I would like to thank Paul Joyce for being Paul. I would like to thank Frans Mäyrä for permission to use, and also for supplying, the diagram in Chapter 5 (Figure 5.1); similarly, Russell Fenton for Figure 5.2. I thank also the organizers of, and contributors to, the annual 'Under the Mask' conference at the University of Bedfordshire, and in particular Steve Conway and Gavin Stewart, where over the last few years I have listened to many significant papers that have greatly advanced my understanding of video game culture.

As always, I would like to thank my (other, not already mentioned) family and friends for their continued support. Finally, Victoria Gosling deserves a second mention, not only for contributing ideas and comments throughout the entire process, but also for putting up with me. Thank you to you all.

1   Studying video games

Introduction

This is a book about video gamers. That is to say, it focuses specifically on those who play video games, their practices and their culture, as well as the theoretical tools that can be used to understand associated social patterns. Though it is probably fair to say that video games were once a relatively under-researched area, certainly in comparison to other entertainment industries and forms, such as cinema and music, since the early to mid-2000s, interest in and research on video games and gamers have risen significantly. This is a welcome development, as it is evident that video games do matter, and not just to those who play them.

Though the origins of video gaming can be traced back to the 1950s, it was in the late 1970s and 1980s that it began to develop as a common leisure activity, largely as a result of the rapid rise in popularity of arcade-based games such as *Space Invaders* and home-based consoles and computers such as the Nintendo NES and Commodore 64. Today, video gaming is a major cultural industry whose economic worth rivals that of the film, music and book publishing industries, if not frequently out-performing all of these sectors. Major video game and console releases have become important consumer and cultural events, as witnessed by the release of *Call of Duty: Black Ops*, which in November 2010 sold over 1.4 million copies on its first day of sales in the UK alone (Dring 2010). Research by the Entertainment Software Association (ESA 2010) suggests that 'more than two-thirds' (67 per cent) of all American households now 'play computer or video games' (see also Chapter 4).

However, the significance of video gaming cannot be captured in sales statistics and participation rates alone, as video games also matter in many other ways – educationally, socially, culturally and theoretically. For example, video games are proving an extremely useful way of engaging and educating children (see for example the Quest to Learn School in New York), provide a source of identity, conversation and friendship networks (discussed further in Chapter 8) and have also had a significant impact on other cultural forms, such as films (such as *eXistenZ* and *Scott Pilgrim vs. the World* – see Chapter 8). Books, too (such as *The Beach* by Alex Garland), have begun to draw on the culture and even styles of video games (see du Sautoy 2010). Furthermore, video games provide patterns and models of use and engagement which can significantly advance our understanding of contemporary consumer patterns.

Video games are therefore an important and very contemporary area of study; however, it is fair to say that most research, to date, has focused specifically either on the video games themselves, such as their content or systems, or the direct engagement of a player, or players, with a specific piece of game technology. They are of course important areas of study, and are discussed in this book, but there has been significantly less focus on the importance of video gaming and its culture away from the actual video game machine and screen. There are, of course, some very good books that pay attention to the culture of video games in the course of their wider consideration of the genre, such as Dovey and Kennedy (2006) and Mäyrä (2008), to name but two, as well as a small number that look at video game culture more specifically, such as Newman (2008). However, this book aims to provide a more general overview and theoretical introduction to the study of video gamers. Though the book covers and draws on a wide range of theoretical tools and approaches, the main theoretical thrust is a sociological analysis of video game culture.

Though there are sociologists who have provided significant insight into video games and gamers, such as Mary Chayko (1993), Graeme Kirkpatrick (see, for example, 2004), Jason Rutter (see, for example, Rutter and Bryce 2006), T.L. Taylor (see, for example, 2003, 2006, 2007) and Holin Lin (see, for example, Lin and Sun 2008, 2011), to name but a few, the potential contribution of sociology to video game studies is still a significantly underdeveloped area. Also, the willingness of sociology, as a wider discipline, to engage with this developing area of study has been somewhat underwhelming. In particular, Albrechtslund (2008) sums up what appears to be a more general attitude towards the contribution of sociology to video game analysis, when she suggests that game studies as a discipline (a subject I turn to shortly) has been dominated by three key approaches: the theoretical/aesthetical, technological/design-oriented and the sociological/ethnographic. Her assumption appears to be that sociology is at least closely related to, if not interchangeable with, ethnography and distinct from a 'theoretical' approach to game analysis. That is to say, while sociology can, and does, provide some insight into the patterns and intricacies of video game culture, researchers tend most commonly to look elsewhere for their theoretical tools. Even when sociological theories and scholars are drawn on in game analysis, their disciplinary origins are often overlooked or confused. Salen and Zimmerman (2004: 454), for instance, who cite the work of Gary Alan Fine and Erving Goffman, describe both of these professors of sociology as 'psychologists'. Therefore, a second, related aim, and one which connects with my own disciplinary background, is to argue that sociology can offer important insights and theoretical tools for the study of video games and gamers. This is not necessarily to argue for a specific and distinct 'sociology of video games' as a separate subdiscipline, but rather to recognize more fully that sociology has a number of theoretical tools and research parallels which can prove useful in the analysis of video games, video gamers and video gamer cultures.

However, before we can begin to address further important and relevant questions, such as 'who plays video games?' and 'what do video gamers do?', a much more fundamental question must be 'what is a video game?' The answer is far from simple, as before we even begin to consider how to define a video game, we must first agree as to whether this is in fact the most suitable term.

Terminology

Perron and Wolf (2009) argue that an inconsistency in terminology is one of the key challenges to the study of video games. Certainly, for what is now a fairly common and widespread leisure activity, there is surprisingly little agreement as to what term, or terms, should be used to describe games played on electronic game consoles, arcade machines, computers, mobile (cell) telephones and similar technologies. Probably the most commonly used term, both outside and within academia, is 'video games'. It is the term used by Nielsen *et al.* in their book *Understanding Video Games* (2008), by Newman in *Videogames* (2004) and *Playing with Videogames* (2008) and by Perron and Wolf in their two edited collections, *The Video Game Theory Reader* (2003) and *The Video Game Theory Reader 2* (2009), to name but a few. It is primarily for this reason that this book adopts the term 'video games'; not necessarily because it is the most useful or best suited, but simply because it is probably the most recognizable and widely used term currently on offer.

However, it is important to recognize that this is by no means the only term available. For instance, 'computer games' is sometimes used instead of, or inter-changeably, with 'video games'. For instance, Carr *et al.*'s 2006 book is entitled *Computer Games: text, narrative and play*. Though Carr *et al.*, and others, use the term 'computer games' to refer to all games played on consoles and computers, and in arcades and so forth, this term is sometimes used by others more specifically to refer only to games played on personal computers. Similarly, the term 'video games' is sometimes used just to refer to games played on game consoles or in game arcades. Some academics drop all prefixes, preferring just to use the solitary word 'games'; one such is Mäyrä in *An Introduction to Game Studies* (2008). This, as discussed below, is inspired by a 'ludic'- (play-) focused perspective, which suggests that video games can and should be considered as sharing fundamental features with other games.

To complicate matters more, the game industry tends to use its own terms and phrases, but, again, with no universal definition or term dominating. For instance, the USA's main video game trade organization is called the Entertainment Software Association (ESA), but before this (between 1998 and 2003) it was known as the Interactive Digital Software Association (IDSA).

In recent years, the term 'digital games' has been offered by some in academia as an alternative to the somewhat confusing and interchangeable use of terms such as computer and video games. This is the term adopted by the Digital Games Research Association (DiGRA), the leading academic organization in this field, which was founded in Finland in 2003, and, similarly, it is the term preferred by several authors, such as Jason Rutter and Jo Bryce in their edited collection, *Understanding Digital Games* (2006). However, this is just as problematic as any other term, since many non-computational games could equally be described as digital. 'Digital' simply refers to the delivery of information in binary; hence, a game of peek-a-boo could be seen as digital, as it has at its core a binary code (the person can be seen or not seen). Furthermore, as the case of Esperanto has proved, it is very difficult to convince everybody to speak the same language, especially when there already exist more common and popular terms. So, at least for now, I am adopting the term 'video games' in this book. Now that we have a term, the next question is, how do we define it?

What is a video game?

Addressing the question of 'what is a video game?' is not as straightforward as many may first assume, and attempting to answer it has provided considerable debate and disagreement. As with most words and terms in common usage, the majority of people will at least have a basic understanding of what the term 'video games' means, and a universal dictionary can provide a rudimentary definition. For instance, the *Compact Oxford English Dictionary* defines a video game as 'a game played by electronically manipulating images produced by a computer program'. However, this becomes *necessarily* more complex when we consider video games as an area of academic study. This is not merely a case of semantics, but rather the fact that how we define and categorize video games provides an important indication and direction as to how we study and understand them and also what falls within this particular domain of analysis (Nielsen *et al.* 2008).

Though authors have offered a sizeable list of ways of conceptualizing video games, for instance Jenkins (2005) suggests that video games could be understood as works of art, by far the two most dominant readings of video games are either as 'media texts' or 'games'.

Video games as media

The consideration of video games as media texts has sometimes been characterized as a narrative or narratological approach. In many respects, this is a somewhat misleading label. At its simplest, a narrative can be understood as comprising a 'discourse' and a 'story' where the story provides resources for the narrative but the form that each particular narrative takes will be shaped by discourses (Carr 2006a). However, many authors (such as Juul 2001) question whether video games possess the same kinds of narrative structures and elements as other media forms, such as those evident in many films and novels. The presence of narratives in video games, and therefore the relevance of narrative analyses to video game studies, is considered in more detail in Chapter 5. However, narratives are only one of the many forms of representational systems or elements present in media texts. These include, but are not limited to, ideologies, discourses, representations of gender, race, sexuality, and much more. The influential work of Janet H. Murray, and in particular *Hamlet on the Holodeck: the future of narrative in cyberspace* (1997), provides many of the sources for the labeling of an approach to video games informed by media and literary studies as 'narratological'. In this important book, Murray considers computers as a medium of representation and links this to discussions of other media, such as films, literature and television, and in doing so, suggests that computer technologies expand the possibilities of storytelling. Murray's, and others', focus on narratives has resulted in many studies of video games that draw on literary, cultural or media theories being, somewhat inaccurately, labelled and critiqued as a 'narratological approach'. As we shall see in Chapter 5, narrative analysis is but one of many forms of content analysis, and content analysis is but one approach among many employed by literary, cultural or media scholars, many of which could be useful and applicable to the study of video games.

In particular, Nieborg and Hermes (2008) suggest that several of the questions that video game studies has wrestled with, and continues to do so, are similar to those also encountered in disciplines such as cultural, literary, or media studies. For instance, questions of interactivity, interpretation and representation are central to the analysis of both video games and other media forms. Nieborg and Hermes (2008), and others, therefore suggest that other disciplines may provide important parallels and tools in the analysis of video games, while, similarly, video games may cast new light on existing debates.

However, the assertion that video games are media, and hence that parallels can be drawn between these respective literatures, is challenged by some. In particular, this is illustrated by the provocative arguments of the game designer and writer Frank Lantz (2009). Lantz presents four key arguments. First, he suggests, 'media' refers specifically to contemporary electronic forms of communication, particularly those from the twentieth century onwards, while games are thousands of years old, and hence predate media. This is very closely linked to his second argument, which suggests that games are frequently seen as media, as they are associated with computers, but he argues that computers are merely the contemporary means by which a game is played. Third, Lantz argues that video games are not content that is *consumed*, but rather, like other games, such as soccer (football), video games are *played*. Fourth, Lantz suggests that video games are not primarily message carriers. That is not to say that video games do not have meaning, but Lantz argues that unlike forms of media, games are not a process of communication between a sender and receiver, but rather meaning in video games is created though the active participation of the gamer.

There are, however, a number of fundamental weaknesses to these arguments. First, turning to Lantz's (2009) argument that 'media' refers specifically to contemporary electronic forms of communication. The word 'media' is simply the plural of 'medium', and hence means midway, linking or communicative points. Most people would accept that newspapers are media whose origins can be found in 'popular prints' that became fashionable in Europe from the fifteenth century onwards (Blackshaw and Crawford 2009), but all forms of language, whether written, spoken or pictorial, are media, all of which significantly predate the twentieth century (Long 2009).

This relates also to Lantz's second argument, which suggests that computers are merely a contemporary form of a much more ancient practice of gaming. This argument I find less contentious, as it is evident that video games do share many continuities and similarities with non-computational games. However, as discussed in the following section of this chapter (see below), this does not mean that video and non-computational games are necessarily the same, and it is important to look for differences as well as continuities here.

Third, Lantz argues that video games are games that are played and not media that are consumed. However, this presents a very limited understanding of what consumption is. The act of consumption has frequently, and long before Lantz wrote, been dismissed as a passive, even destructive and hence largely an uninteresting endpoint to processes of production. Raymond Williams (1976) alerts us to the etymology of the words 'consume', 'consumption' and 'consumer', which refer to processes of destruction and wasting away, such as something being consumed by fire or a person suffering from a consuming disease, like tuberculosis. Hence, while production is understood as the process of creation, consumption is perceived simply as an endpoint, reception or destruction. It is also the case that 'consumption' is not a term usually associated with new technological forms, such as the Internet and video games. Consumption is frequently seen as a passive act that 'belongs to the "bad" pre-digital media' (Lister *et al.* 2009: 248), while new technology users are seen as engaging in participatory acts, such as surfing, browsing and gaming.

However, the sociology of consumption teaches us that consumer practices need to be seen as creative processes and part of a cyclical relationship. In particular, Lury (1996: 1) argues that consumption needs to be understood as part of a wider 'material culture'. 'Material culture' is the term given to the study of 'person–thing' relationships; such as the relations between a person and a video game console or piece of software. That is to say, the study of material culture is the study of objects and how they are used. Lury, following Warde (1990, 1992), suggests that consumption, rather than being the outcome and antithesis of production, needs to be understood as a constituent part of a continuing process and cycle of various forms of both production and consumption. As Lury (1996: 3) writes:

> The identification of consumer culture as a specific form of material culture helps ensure that it is studied in relation to interlinking *cycles* of production and consumption or reappropriation. The consumption that is referenced via consumer culture can, through the lens of material culture, be seen as conversion, or, more precisely, 'the manner in which people convert things to ends of their own' (Strathern 1994: p. x).

Lury (1996) suggests that consumer objects should be seen to have a social life of their own. In this view, consumer goods will have changing and different meanings throughout their lifespan, depending on who is viewing or using them and in what context they are located. People will use consumer goods in different ways and they will have different meanings invested in them by different people. It is the consumer who gives a product meaning and use, and therefore this needs to be understood as a process of production. However, Lantz, as well as numerous others, such as Frasca (2003), would argue that there are still fundamental differences between the activities of players of a video game and the consumers of a television show or book. The main line of argument here is that video gamers engage with a dynamic and interactive game system, while media audiences consume static texts. The question of interactivity is discussed in more detail in Chapter 5; however, it is my assertion that the interactive potential of video games is often greatly overestimated, while audiences of media forms such as films and literature are too readily dismissed as passive. This is not to say that playing a video game and reading a book are necessarily the same, as of course they are not, but merely that the differences here have been somewhat exaggerated in an attempt to distance video game scholarship from disciplines such as cultural, literary and media studies.

Fourth is Lantz's (2009) argument that video games are not necessarily conveyors of messages. This argument is particularly weak, for semiotics teaches us that all 'signs', such as a word or image, carry with them meaning, whether it is intended or not – see Chapter 5 for a consideration of semiotics. All games, video or otherwise, convey varying levels of discourse, meaning and message. As Long (2009) clearly argues:

> Philosophically speaking, all it takes to disprove Lantz's implied argument that 'Games are not media because games do not subscribe to the message model of meaning' is trotting out *one* game that *does* subscribe to the message model of meaning, and as counter-evidence I'd like to introduce as exhibit A every *Final Fantasy, Dragon Quest* and other delightfully story-centric role-playing game ever released. As long as *one* game *does* subscribe to the message model, then it disproves Lantz's argument – and you'd better believe that at least one game out there most certainly does.

Video games do carry messages. They can be quite simple: in *Tetris* the gamer is shown that if they do not stack the falling shapes quickly enough into a tessellation then they will lose the game – this is a message. However, messages can be far more complex and multilayered. For example, 'success' in *The Sims* is normally seen in the player acquiring more and better household items, this therefore carries a simple (denotative) meaning of the need to acquire items, but possibly a deeper (connotative) meaning about the importance of capitalist accumulation (see Chapter 5).

Authors such as Lantz (2009) and Frasca (2003), as well as numerous others including Aarseth (1997), Salen and Zimmerman (2004) and Juul (2005), to name but a few, suggest that the most profitable way of understanding and analysing video games is to consider them first and foremost as games. However, for most writers, unlike Lantz, this does not necessarily preclude also discussing video games as media. For instance, Jesper Juul (2005), one of the key advocates of a game-focused (or ludological) approach to video game analysis, seems comfortable referring to video games as media, and, as discussed in Chapter 5, most contemporary writers, such as Mäyrä (2008), seek to define video games as involving play and representational, as well as social, elements. However, most ludologists argue, what fundamentally distinguishes video games from other media texts, like books, films and television, is that video games are game systems that are played, and it is this which renders their study particularly significant.

Video games as games

A play-focused, or ludological, approach argues that video games are fundamentally similar to, if not the same as, any other game. As game designer and Carnegie Mellon University professor Jesse Schell stated in interview, 'a game is a game is a game' (Schwartz 2003). Furthermore, Salen and Zimmerman (2004: 86) argue, 'computer hardware and software are merely the materials of which the game is composed', and, they add, 'digital games are systems, just like every other game'. Following such lines of argument, ludologists have often been less concerned with specifically defining what a video game is, but rather seeking to incorporate them into a wider definition and discussion of games more generally. This is particularly evident in the work of Salen and Zimmerman (2004) and Juul (2005).

Juul (2005: 23) seeks to define and understand games, including video games, through his development of what he terms the 'classic game model'. That is to say: 'the model is *classic* in the sense that it is the way games have *traditionally* been constructed ... a model that applies to at least a 5,000-year history of games' (Juul 2005: 23, original emphasis). In seeking to understand and define this classic game model, Juul draws on and interrogates seven definitions of games and play (the section on theories of play in Chapter 2, below), ranging from the work of Huizinga ([1938] 1949) to Caillois (1962), to more contemporary definitions of games, which were specifically created to incorporate video games within their parameters, such as Chris Crawford (1984) and Salen and Zimmerman (2004). Juul analyses these definitions, and concludes that 'classic' games can be understood to share six common features. These he categorizes as:

1 *Rules*: games are rule-bound.
2 *Variable, quantifiable outcomes*: games have variable, quantified outcomes.
3 *Valorization of outcomes*: the different potential outcomes of the game are assigned different values, some positive and some negative.
4 *Player effort*: The player exerts effort in order to influence the outcomes (games are challenging).
5 *Player attached to outcomes*: the player is emotionally attached to the outcome of the game in the sense that a player will be a winner and 'happy' in case of a positive outcome, but a loser and 'unhappy' in case of a negative outcome.
6 *Negotiable consequences*: the same game (set of rules) can be played with or without real-life consequences.

Juul 2005: 36

These six features Juul summarizes into a general definition of games: 'a game is a rule-based system with a variable and quantifiable outcome, where different outcomes are assigned different values, the player exerts effort in order to influence the outcome, the player feels emotionally attached to the outcome, and the consequences of the activity are negotiable' (Juul 2005: 36).

This is generally a well-thought-through and potentially useful definition of some of the key characteristics of a game. But it is not without its weaknesses and limitations. For instance, Juul asserts that the 'player exerts effort' and 'feels emotionally attached to ... outcomes', but as Nielsen *et al.* (2008: 35) highlight, not all game players 'exert much effort ... nor feel particularly attached to the outcome'. This may also be particularly evident in terms of more 'mundane' gaming, such as playing a mini or puzzle game on a mobile telephone, an area explored further in Chapter 8.

Furthermore, Juul himself starts to encounter, and readily recognizes, difficulties with his definition when dealing with what he refers to as 'borderline cases' of games. This includes open-ended simulations like *SimCity* which Juul suggests do not conform to his model because they have no explicit goals. 'Pen and paper' (sometimes referred to as 'tabletop') role-playing games (RPGs), such as *Dungeons & Dragons* and *Call of Cthulhu*, are again not seen as 'classic games', in Juul's terms: 'having a human game master' their 'rules are not fixed beyond discussion' (2005: 43). Beyond borderline games, Juul also suggests that many aspects of life have gamelike qualities, but his classic game model allows us to distinguish them from actual (classic) games. For instance, he highlights how traffic could be viewed as gamelike, as it has many gamelike qualities, such as rules, variable outcomes, 'player' effort, attachment to outcomes and so forth. But for Juul, what makes traffic not a game is that the consequences of this are not optional (as they would be in a 'classic' game) – 'moving in traffic always has real-life consequences' (p. 43).

It is actually this question of 'consequences' that I have most issue with in Juul's definition of classic games. For Juul, following Huizinga, the consequences of games for 'real life' are 'optional' (p. 41). For instance, Juul argues that association football (soccer) can be played professionally and generate income and profit and hence has 'real-life' consequences, but this is optional; football can be played without any income or profit occurring. But this all seems based upon a highly subjective idea of what are 'real' or 'important' consequences and what can or cannot be negotiated. Both playing a game of football and driving in traffic can have 'real-life' consequences, which we only have a certain degree of control over. For instance, a game of friendly non-professional football could result in a broken leg, a falling out, an appointment missed or any number of 'real-life' consequences. In contrast, and unlike Juul's assertion, taking a leisurely Sunday afternoon drive may result in no significant consequences at all.

I wholly agree with Juul's argument that not all of life is a game, and in most circumstances we can distinguish between what is a game and what is not. This is also illustrated well by Erving Goffman (1961) when he counters the argument that 'game theory' can help us understand all aspects of life. Goffman (1961: 37) suggests that, for instance, kissing and 'love-making' do not conform to a game model, as 'once started, time out cannot easily be declared, kibitzers are usually lethal, and substitutes ordinarily cannot be brought in'. However, any clear boundary between what is and what is not a game is always going to be problematic and ultimately subjective. For instance, Juul suggests that *SimCity* is not a classic game because it does not have explicit goals, and pen-and-paper RPGs are also 'borderline' because they do not have fixed rules (2005: 43). But Gary Alan Fine (1983) argues that games do not necessarily need set goals. For Fine, what makes a game is 'engrossment', and anything can be brought into a game if it increases the player's engrossment in it. Moreover, for Fine (1983: 185), pen-and-paper RPGs, rather than being a borderline game, are a clear example of a 'pure game' because they tend to involve high levels of engrossment.

However, Fine's assertion that what defines a game is engrossment could be challenged by the work of Graeme Kirkpatrick (2004). For Kirkpatrick argues that video gamers are often not immersed in the fantasy of the game that they are playing, particularly when faced with difficult or repetitive game tasks which may see them having to monotonously repeat actions, sometimes over and over again, to progress within a game. Kirkpatrick refers to this as the 'cynicism' of the gamer, who recognizes games as consisting of a series of tasks and seeks to complete them in a pragmatic way.

Fine would probably suggest that in these 'cynical' instances, the gamer temporarily shifts out of a gaming 'frame' (that is, their mindset or understanding of what they are doing, which is discussed in more detail later in this book) into a more mundane everyday, or even worklike, frame. But this does raise problems for the argument that gaming is about engrossment, because even though the non-engrossed cynical video gamer may not be in a pure game frame, few would deny that they are still playing a game.

What Fine highlights, however, is that how a game is defined will depend on the people playing it, and this can change almost in an instant, as people move in and out of a game frame. This is something that Juul (2005: 42) himself recognizes when he writes that 'we associate a game with the *context* in which it *usually* appears; that is, we tend not to think of something as a game if we have only seen it performed with serious consequences' (emphasis added). Hence what Juul recognizes here is that what is defined as a game depends wholly on its context and how those who are playing it, and those who are viewing it, see it. This is rather subjective, and people's perceptions of what a game is can rapidly change, as when a cynical video gamer playing *Super Mario Bros.* loses their engrossment with a game and begins to view their progression to the next game level as more 'work-like'. In any one case the views of different participants and onlookers can differ as to whether something is a game or not. Returning to the issue of consequences highlighted earlier, Goffman (1961) is again useful here, as he illustrates that what defines a situation as 'serious' or 'non-serious' is not whether it conforms to some objective category of what a game is, but rather the social situation – its context and frame. It is, therefore, how a social encounter between participants plays out which defines its seriousness and whether it is a game or not.

It is thus evident that there are many difficulties defining explicitly what a game is; moreover, there are also questions about whether a game model is a useful mechanism for understanding video games at all. Juul himself suggests that video games challenge and therefore do not wholly conform to the 'classic' game model, and suggests that all six attributes of the classic game model need to be modified to some degree to incorporate video games. Furthermore, Randall (2011), in his consideration of online boardgames, argues that boardgames, both online and off, are fundamentally different from video games, and hence cannot be analysed in the same way. This, he argues, is because video games and boardgames are not played in the same way, have different patterns and experiences of immersion, narrative, simulation and interaction, and involve different player norms and cultures. Randall argues too that the nature of rules is quite different in video games and boardgames, much more clearly regimented and maintained by the video game itself in the former, while in the latter, boardgamers play a much more participatory role in developing, agreeing and maintaining game rules during play.

This is a point also made by Liebe (2008), who argues that though all games can, and often do, have rules or guidelines that predate a particular instance of play, with non-computational games there is always some room for negotiation between players and the opportunity to change and adapt the rules during play. However, beyond hacking the program code, this is usually not possible within video games. The key difference here, Liebe argues, is that traditional non-computational games provide the boundaries and *restrict* what is possible, while video games dictate much more limited options of only what is *possible*.

Liebe (2008) probably stretches this argument a little too far. As Nielsen *et al.* (2008: 28) write: 'while it is true that we cannot negotiate with our computers, we are often not competing solely against a program'. As argued throughout this book, and as others have argued before, playing a video game is a social activity which involves a lot more than the simple interaction between a person and a video game machine. For instance, players will frequently play with others and determine codes of practice and patterns of play which extend beyond the systematic structures and rules found within the video game program. Liebe does, however, make an important point in illustrating that video games are not, as Salen and Zimmerman (2004: 86) argue, 'just like every other game'.

It is therefore important to recognize that the meanings of all games are subjective and socially created. As Jones (2008: 3) rightly asserts:

> The meaning(s) of video games are constructed and they are collaborative. They are *made* by social interactions of various kinds rather than *found* in the software and hardware objects themselves. The meanings of games are not essential or inherent in their form (though form is a crucial determinant), even if we define form as a set of rules and constraints for gameplay, and certainly not in their extractable 'stories' (though the fictive storyworld matters in most games), but are functions of the larger grid of possibilities built by groups of developers, players, reviewers, critics, and fans in particular times and places and through specific acts of gameplay or discourses about games.

Jones (2008) effectively argues that what constitutes a video game is not just the software on a disk or even a gamer's use of it, but, rather, the meaning of a video game is determined by a complex web of media, understandings, interpretations and interactions. He argues that it is evident that any 'text' also involves 'paratext'. For instance, when we communicate with another person we do this not just through language, such as the words that we speak, but also through paralanguage, such as our tone, deportment, mannerisms and gestures. Similarly, the meaning of a video game comes not just from the game itself, but also reviews and comments written about it, opinions offered by friends and family, advertising and promotional material and a whole myriad of other sources and texts. Hence the meaning of a video game will always be a complex social construction. It is therefore my assertion here that focus on the question 'what is a video game?' frequently detracts from the more important questions of what a video game means and how it is used, consumed and utilized by gamers.

(Video) game studies

As outlined above, many contemporary scholars see video games as first and foremost an example and subcategory of games. Therefore, so this argument goes, the study of video games needs to be understood as part of, and located within, a wider study of games more generally. Hence, in recent years and inspired by the rise in interest in video game analysis, many scholars, such as Mäyrä (2008), have argued for the development of a discipline of 'Game Studies'. This discipline, then, incorporates the study of video games, but also other game forms, like boardgames, and draws and builds upon classic theories of play and gaming, such as the work of Johan Huizinga and Roger Caillois (see Chapter 2), and prioritizes the action of, and culture of, play.

However, there are at least three fundamental, and interlinked, difficulties with the way that game studies, as a discipline, has been set out. First, as already argued (see above), it is problematic to assume that all games are similar, and particularly problematic to argue that they are all fundamentally the same. This, in itself, is not *necessarily* an insurmountable problem for the discipline of game studies, as most academic disciplines cover a wide range of diverse subject matter with little similarity or overlap. However, it is problematic to underplay differences here, which many game studies scholars frequently do. A second, related problem, highlighted by Perron and Wolf (2009), among others, is that though game studies claims to incorporate the analysis of all forms of gaming, it most commonly considers only video games. Most game studies work focuses on the analysis of video games, but there is often an inherent, but unsupported, assumption that the case under consideration could apply to all games. This is shown by how many authors use the term 'games' interchangeably, and with little clarification or justification, to refer to either video games alone or all games more generally.

A third problem with game studies is how this discipline tends to prioritize the importance of play in video game analysis, a subject discussed further in Chapter 2. For example, Perron and Wolf (2009: 11) argue that 'before exercising analytical or interpretive skills, one has to draw on one's ability to play a game (or know someone with the ability)'. This is a point also made by Espen Aarseth (2003: 3), who argues:

> For any kind of game, there are three main ways of acquiring knowledge about it. Firstly, we can study the design, rules and mechanics of the game, insofar as these are available to us, e.g. by talking to the developers of the game. Secondly, we can observe others play, or read their reports and reviews, and hope that their knowledge is representative and their play competent. Thirdly, we can play the game ourselves. While all methods are valid, the

third way is clearly the best, especially if combined or reinforced by the other two. If we have not experienced the game personally, we are liable to commit severe misunderstandings, even if we study the mechanics and try our best to guess at their workings.

Though games and play should be taken seriously, elsewhere (Crawford *et al.* 2011b) I have argued that other aspects of video games are equally important and other approaches to research can be adopted. For example, studies such as Aphra Kerr's (2011) analysis of the democratization and innovation processes within the video game industry do not require her to play any video games, it may be suggested. Here Kerr (2011) is considering video games as products and discussing their developmental trajectory in much the same way that scholars in science and technology studies (STS) have been doing for many decades when they study the historical development of artefacts such as the bicycle (Pinch and Bijker 1987) and fluorescent lighting (Bijker 1994). We suggest, that within this academic tradition, although ethnography is sometimes deployed, no one demands that a lived experience is the gold standard, especially as it is sometimes neither possible nor desirable. Alison Adam (2005), for example, discusses the Internet with respect to cyber-stalking, but she has not been criticized for not undertaking this herself (Crawford *et al.* 2011). As Pearson (1993: xvii) suggests, 'the ethnographer does not have to be a competent burglar, or prostitute, or policeman, or miner in order to deliver competent ethnographies of life, work, and crime … It is an old adage of social research that you do not need to be Caesar in order to understand Caesar; indeed, it might even be a handicap.'

Hence I remain unconvinced of the usefulness of game studies as a discipline which incorporates the study of all games and prioritizes play. Furthermore, there still seems little agreement as to whether a coherent discipline of game studies is even desirable. In this book, therefore, I use the term 'game studies' (without capitalization) to refer simply to the study of games, rather than a specific discipline. It is important to be clear from the outset that this book is a consideration of *video games*, and, more specifically, those who play them and their culture. Inevitably, and rightly, this will at times draw on literature on games more generally, as well as other literatures, but it is crucial to note that the arguments and conclusions made in this book are not intended to be unproblematically applied to all games. This is a book about *video gamers*.

Chapter summary

- Video games are an important and contemporary area of study, and it is evident that their influence extends into many diverse areas of social and cultural life.
- This book provides an overview and introduction to the study of video gamers and video gamer culture. In doing so, it considers and draws on theoretical tools from a range of academic disciplines, but, most notably, argues that certain key sociological theories can significantly contribute to the analysis of video games.

- There is little agreement over the use of terminology in this field, with authors using a variety of terms, such as 'computer games', 'digital games' or similar to describe the subject under consideration. But the term adopted by most authors, and used in this book, is 'video games'.
- Defining what a video game is proves rather problematic. Generally, this debate sees video games often categorized as a form of 'media' or 'game'.
- Considering video games as media is often (but problematically) called a 'narratological' approach; as it tends to draw on cultural, literary and media studies approaches, such as narrative analysis.
- The application of cultural, literary and media studies approaches is useful, as they deal with many of the same debates also considered by video game analysis, such as those relating to interactivity and interpretation. Also, in turn, the analysis of video games can provide new insights for older disciplines.
- However, several authors, such as Lantz (2009), argue that video games are not media. Lantz suggests that media are a twentieth-century invention, while games are much older; unlike media, games are played and not consumed; and games do not convey messages.
- This can be challenged on a number of fronts, as it is evident that media are as old as the first word or picture, and video games do involve representational systems, which are consumed and convey meaning.
- The argument that video games can be analysed as a form of play is often termed 'ludology'. This perspective argues that video games are fundamentally similar to, if not the same as, other game forms.
- This approach tends to draw on classic theories of play and gaming, and frequently attempts to define and conceptualize games, such as Juul's (2005) 'classic game model'.
- Analysing games and play is useful as it recognizes the particularities of play and gaming. However, a potential problem is that this frequently identifies play as separate from ordinary life and a wider social context.
- This emphasis on games and play has led some scholars to advocate the development of a discipline of 'game studies', which covers the study of all game forms. However, this is potentially problematic, as too often, too much is made of the similarities, and too little of the differences, between video games and other game forms.
- This approach also tends to prioritize the act of play and assumes its prominence in video games analysis. However, this fails to recognize that the importance of video games does not begin and end with the instance of play.

Book structure

This book sits as a happy medium somewhere between a monograph and a textbook. Its aim is to provide an accessible introduction to the study of video gamers, gameplay and its culture, by summarizing and reviewing a number of key theories and approaches to their study. Consequently, each chapter features a 'Chapter summary' at the end, to provide the reader with a simple overview of the key arguments discussed, and a short 'Further reading' list which suggests a few places the reader might like to go next, if they want to learn more about the debates covered. However, unlike most textbooks, this book also makes particular arguments, suggests new literatures not commonly associated with video games analysis and points to new ways forward for this area of research.

The following chapter considers and reviews a number of key theories that have been applied to the study of video gameplay. It begins by considering key theories of play, and then considers two theoretical approaches that have been applied to the study of gameplay: those of the magic circle and frame analysis.

Chapter 3 argues that video gamers can be understood and theorized as an audience. Of course, video gamers are not the same as other media audiences, but similarly, other audiences are not necessarily the same as each other; for instance, reading a book is quite different in nature from watching a film in a cinema. However, there are certain similarities, as well as differences, here, and an analysis of video gamers is helped by locating it within a more historical consideration of the changing nature of audiences and consumer patterns.

Chapter 4 looks at various approaches to understanding who plays video games. It considers how video gamers are frequently stereotyped, recorded in large-scale surveys, defined by patterns of exclusion or conceptually located within typologies. This chapter concludes by offering an alternative way forward and suggests that a model of career progression may be a more profitable way of theorizing the nature of video gamers.

Chapter 5 is the longest chapter in the book, as it covers a number of key aspects, or elements, of video gameplay that have been identified in existing literatures and studies. These are, specifically, rules, effects, interactivity, immersion, engagement and flow, performance, identity, roles and embodiment, intertextuality and transmedia, narrative and geography. Here, a number of key approaches and literatures are covered, but specific arguments are made in relation to each, and, in particular, a recurrent theme is the need to extend analysis beyond the instance of play.

Chapter 6 considers various concepts that have been utilized to understand video game culture, and in particular those of subcultures, neo-tribes, fans, knowledge community, players, Otaku, gamers, scenes and habitus. The argument made here is that though each concept casts its own, often useful, light on video game culture, Bourdieu's theory of habitus, a rather under-utilized concept in video game analysis, may offer a useful way forward, particularly as it retains an awareness of structural social forces.

Chapter 7 focuses on video gamer productivity. It considers first textual forms of production, such as game mods, walkthroughs, fan fiction and art. The chapter then discusses the creation and maintenance of community and narrative identities as other forms of gamer production.

The final chapter is a culmination of many of the arguments set out in the book and specifically argues for greater attention to be paid to the location of video gaming within patterns of everyday life. Here it is argued that far too often video gaming is seen as a spectacular and out-of-the-ordinary leisure activity, rather than a more everyday and mundane practice, located and often concurrently undertaken with many other ordinary practices.

Further reading

Kirkpatrick, G. (2004) *Critical Technology: a social theory of personal computing*, Aldershot: Ashgate.

Mäyrä, F. (2008) *An Introduction to Game Studies: games in culture*, London: Sage.

Nieborg, D.B. and Hermes, J. (2008) 'What is Game Studies Anyway?', *European Journal of Cultural Studies*, 11 (2), 131–46.

Perron, B. and Wolf, M.J.P. (2009) 'Introduction', in B. Perron and M.J.P. Wolf (eds) *The Video Game Theory Reader 2*, London: Routledge, 1–22.

2 Understanding video gameplay

Introduction

As argued in Chapter 1, it is evident that the act of play is central to many considerations of the use and patterns of interaction with, and surrounding, video games. Hence, this chapter focuses specifically on key theories that have commonly been used to analyse gameplay and, more specifically, video gameplay. It begins with a brief general introduction to theories of play before specifically considering two key theoretical frameworks that have proved dominant in contemporary video gameplay analysis: the magic circle and frame analysis.

Theories of play

Having determined in Chapter 1 that the question 'what is a video game?' is extremely complex, this chapter turns to the equally troublesome question of what it means to play a video game. This is difficult because the concept of 'play' is equally contested and debated, if not more so. The problem starts with the very relationship between the terms 'play' and 'game'. As Salen and Zimmerman (2004) highlight, there is no agreement as to whether games should be seen as a subset of play, or whether it should be the other way around, with play understood as part of games. For instance, individuals can play at a wide variety of activities, such as children throwing a ball back and forth or skipping with a rope or an author playing with a pen while trying to conjure up the words for the next sentence. This view is consistent with the argument that play is a fundamental expression of either our biological nature (Sutton-Smith 1997) or an expression of human culture (Huizinga [1938] 1949). Play is something that we all do. From this perspective, then, games are, typically, seen as more formalized or organized forms of play. For instance, as highlighted in the previous chapter, Juul (2005) suggests that rules are one of the key defining characteristics of a game, and I would probably agree that for most people, most of the time games usually involve rules, which other forms of play may not. Hence, this argument would suggest that throwing a ball is a form of play, but baseball and basketball are a particular form of play: they are games.

However, we could equally well see play as *part of* a game. For instance, in sport people will often talk about 'playing a ball', or 'making a play', similarly in a card game, participants may discuss 'playing a hand'. And certainly for Erving Goffman (1961) (following Neumann and Morgenstern 1944) play is best understood as a particular instance within a game.

This relationship between 'play' and 'games' is confused even further when we move beyond the English language. For, as Juul (2005) highlights, some languages, such as French, Spanish and German, make no distinction between (what in English are referred to as) 'play' and 'games', which is particularly problematic when translating and comprehending the work of authors in this field who write in these languages such as Ludwig Wittgenstein and Roger Caillois, whose original work is in German and French, respectively.

However, it is not necessarily important that we agree upon a definitive definition of the relationship between play and games, as in much of the academic literature, as in everyday conversation, people frequently flip between referring to play as part of a game and games as a form of play. These ideas are not mutually exclusive. But what this highlights is the difficulties of trying to conceptualize and theorize terms like 'play', which, for many authors, for better or for worse, are at the very core of game studies.

The difficulty of separating play from games leads Juul (2005) to draw on theories of both play and games when developing his own definition of games, as outlined in the previous chapter. Consequently his 2005 book *Half-Real* provides a good introduction to key theories and definitions of play and games. Similarly, several other writers on video games, such as Kirkpatrick (2004), Dovey and Kennedy (2006), Nielsen *et al.* (2008) and Mäyrä (2008), as well as numerous others, provide good introductions to theories, categories and definitions of play and (video) games. The key theorists invoked here, and those whom writers have frequently found most useful in game analysis, usually include Johan Huizinga ([1938] 1949), Roger Caillois (1962) and Brian Sutton-Smith (both alone and in his work with E.M. Avedon, such as Avedon and Sutton-Smith 1971).

For Huizinga play is seen as a voluntary activity, which takes place outside of 'ordinary' life. It is absorbing, but it is also essentially 'unproductive'; for instance, he suggests, no profit is usually gained from play. What many theorists writing on video games have found most useful in the work of Huizinga is the idea that play takes place outside of ordinary life. Certainly, most people, most of the time, seem to be able to distinguish when they are playing at something (like play fighting) and when they are not (like fighting to inflict harm). Furthermore, there are certain distinct and identified places, or arenas, where play commonly takes place, such as a sports field. What Huizinga then provides us with is a 'divide' between play and ordinary life, and in doing so sets up the opportunity for analysing what takes place in these arenas of play and how this may differ, or share similarities and links to, the world outside of play.

One such arena of play Huizinga ([1938] 1949: 10) refers to as the 'magic circle', and though he makes no clear indication of what he means by this term, it is one that has been taken up (sometimes quite enthusiastically) by several video game scholars (such as Salen and Zimmerman 2004) as a useful metaphor for conceptualizing and understanding the spaces, places and times where games are played. However, the usefulness of this term in understanding video gameplay, and the level of distinction this suggests between realms of play and ordinary life, has become a major battleground and area of great debate within video game studies, and, consequently, this is a debate considered in more detail in the following section of this chapter.

Huizinga was also a major influence on Roger Caillois (1962), who sought to critique, as well as develop, the writings of Huizinga. Caillois largely agrees with Huizinga's definition of play, but further refines this by identifying and classifying different forms of play. These he labels competition (*agōn*), chance (*alea*), imitation (*mimicry*) and vertigo (*ilinx*). Furthermore, he suggests that forms of play can be located along a continuum ranging from unregulated play (*paidia*) to more rule-based games (*ludus*). Some authors, such as Eskelinen (2001), have found these categories useful in understanding types of video games or video gameplay. Of course, play, including video gameplay, can involve more than one, if not all, of these elements. For instance Nielsen *et al.* (2008: 26) use the illustration of the video game series *Super Monkey Ball*, which involves elements of mimicry (as the player controls a monkey), agōn (in competition against other players or the computer) and ilinx (in the abyss that surrounds the paths the monkey rolls along, and frequently falls into). However, it is this fluidity of play that some authors, such as Juul (2003), argue makes this model unhelpful. In particular, Juul (2003: 11) suggests that the selection and demarcation of 'types' of games is somewhat arbitrary and hard to justify in any concrete way.

The work of Sutton-Smith emphasizes a more biological and evolutionary view of play. Sutton-Smith (1997) suggests that play is usually understood through seven key rhetorics, some of which are ancient, while others are quite modern. These are: play as progress (such as play as a form of social or skill development), play as fate (such as play associated with gambling), play as identity (such as can be seen in community celebrations), play as power (where play represents conflict, or is used as a display of power), play as imaginary (such as the imaginative and creative nature of play), play as an expression of 'self' (such as performing our or others' identities through play) and play as frivolous (hence, unproductive, if not dangerous). Sutton-Smith suggests that these rhetorics, or ways of understanding play, rightly highlight the ambiguous nature of what play is and what it means. For Sutton-Smith, play is a fundamental characteristic of humans, and many other animals, based in our biological make-up; in humans we can certainly see how play has evolved in line with our continuing biological, and in particular neurological, evolution. Again, these ideas have found some application in video game studies, for example David Myers's (2009) discussion of video gameplay forms, looking at how video games involve learned locomotive play, such as the control of a gamepad.

As discussed in the previous chapter, several writers on video games, such as Salen and Zimmerman (2004) and Juul (2005), take these and other theories of play and apply (and sometimes adapt and expand them) in considering video games and their gameplay. As with defining what a (video) game is, there seems to be a similar concern with defining play in a way that can be operationalized and isolated from what is not play. Much of this is largely influenced by Caillois's structuralist approach to defining and categorizing the formal elements of play and games (Dovey and Kennedy 2006).

However, as we have similarly seen with the term 'video game', defining what 'play' is, is a largely arbitrary and highly subjective endeavour, and unfortunately (as with definitions of video games) most of these categorizations of play overlook the players themselves. As Genvo (2009) rightly points out, most structures are 'playable'. Of course, some things are more playable than others. For instance, *Doom* is more playable than Microsoft Word; but there is no reason why Word could not be used in a playful way, or for that matter *Doom* used for 'serious' purposes, such as military training (Genvo 2009). Similarly, some places are more conducive to play, like a playground, rather than an office. But again, an office does not preclude the possibility of play. To fully understand what play is, therefore, we need to understand the social situation, those involved and their (and others') perceptions of what is going on. We also need to recognize that all of these are extremely fluid and liable to change at any moment. For instance, many authors, such as Fine (1983) and Arsenault and Perron (2009), highlight how individuals engaged in play can, and often do, frequently flip between play and non-play states, sometimes even in an instant. Examples of this would be a 'play' fight which gets 'serious' before both participants feel embarrassed and go back to playing, or players of *World of Warcraft* who shift between conversations about drinking in-game with drinking out-of-game. As Jones (2008: 9) again points out, rightly: 'it's important to remember that … playing is always in the social world, always a complicated, highly mediated experience'.

Therefore, rather than developing universal models of play, what is needed is a more situated approach to understanding video gameplay. One of the most popular attempts to provide this in game studies in recent years has been the application of the concept of the 'magic circle', as coined by Huizinga but popularized in contemporary game studies most notably by Salen and Zimmerman (2004). However, this chapter highlights several key weaknesses with this model, most particularly how it lacks the tools to adequately locate video gameplay within a wider social framework. It is suggested here, therefore, that Erving Goffman's frame analysis might prove a more useful way of theorizing the social nature of play and games, and the way gamers change between interpretations of what they and others are doing. However, similarly, I argue that this theorization is not without its weaknesses.

The magic circle

The concept of the 'magic circle' has over recent years become one of the most widely debated and contested ideas within contemporary video game research. For some, such as Salen and Zimmerman (2004), Juul (2005) and Adams (2010), it has proved a useful tool for framing and understanding patterns of play and gamer interactions; others, such as Nieborg and Hermes (2008: 135), suggest that it has become an 'unproductive orthodoxy' which tells us little about the social and cultural location and importance of video gaming.

The origins of this concept lie in the work of the Dutch historian Johan Huizinga, and in particular his 1938 book *Homo Ludens* (first published in English in 1949), whose title roughly translates into English as 'human player'. For Huizinga, the magic circle is one example, within a list of others, of places where play takes place. Huizinga outlines these in this, now extensively quoted, passage:

> More striking even than the limitations as to time is the limitation as to space. All play moves and has its being within a play-ground marked off beforehand either materially or ideally, deliberately or as a matter of course. Just as there is no formal difference between play and ritual, so the 'consecrated spot' cannot be formally distinguished from the play-ground. The arena, the card-table, the magic circle, the temple, the stage, the screen, the tennis court, the court of justice etc., are all in form and function playgrounds i.e. forbidden spots, isolated, hedged round, hallowed, within which special rules obtain. All are temporary worlds within the ordinary world, dedicated to the performance of an act apart.
>
> Huizinga [1938] 1949: 10

What is significant here is that Huizinga does not explicitly state what he actually means by the term 'magic circle', nor how this is different from, or similar, to the arena, the card-table, the temple, the stage, the tennis-court or any other arena of play. This passage does tell us certain features of this place of play, and others, such as being 'isolated' spots with 'special rules'. However, the meaning and significance of Huizinga to game studies is not necessarily to be found in the original work of Huizinga himself, but most notably in how this has been applied within contemporary game research, and in particular by Salen and Zimmerman (2004).

Though the application of Huizinga's conceptualization to game studies predates the work of Salen and Zimmerman (2004), such as its use by Eskelinen and Tronstad (2003), it is Salen and Zimmerman who are most notably associated with the contemporary popularization of this theory in game studies and in particular the application of the magic circle. For Salen and Zimmerman (2004) the magic circle is a useful metaphor for understanding the space where gameplay takes place. It is a temporary place and time where the players of games establish, negotiate and maintain the rules of play specific to that particular time, place and game, rules that do not necessarily apply outside of the circle. A good, though non-computational, illustration of this is boxing. Once the opponents step into the boxing ring they agree to abide by certain rules that govern the sport, which would not apply to, say, another sport or a street fight. The rules and patterns of behaviour under which the boxing match takes place are specific to that one location and time, and wholly dependent upon the two opponents agreeing to conform to these rules. As Salen and Zimmerman (2004: 98) indicate, playing a game involves an act of 'faith'; that is to say, an investment by participants in the rules of that particular play space and time.

Eskelinen and Tronstad (2003) suggest that this 'difference' between 'play' and 'ordinary life' can be understood in three key ways. First, that during play individuals are, by free choice, subjected to rules and goals that do not apply to their lives outside of the game; second, that play is fixed and limited to a specific location and time; and third, that this is connected to 'make-believe, transforming the real time and place of play to an imagined time and place' (Rodriguez 2006). As Rodriguez (2006) writes: 'According to Huizinga, the consciousness of play as a separate and self-contained sphere is often reinforced by the pervasive tendency to enclose the players within a spatiotemporal frame, the so-called "magic circle", which isolates their game from the more serious tasks of daily living.'

Salen and Zimmerman (2004: 94) suggest that the boundaries between play and wider social life can at times be quite clear-cut and at others quite 'fuzzy and permeable'. The examples they give are of playing with a doll, which can be done in a very mundane, everyday way, such as 'idly kneading its [the doll's] head while watching television' (p. 94), or playing tic-tac-toe (known as 'noughts and crosses' in the UK), where participants are much more clearly playing a game with set rules and objectives. This, they suggest, is also applicable to video games, where, for example, toylike interactive screensavers, like the once popular PC applications *Dogz* and *Catz* (which found a second lease of life on the Nintendo DS), do not involve the same level of concentration and separation from other more ordinary tasks and life rules as playing a video game like *Quake*. For Salen and Zimmerman (2004: 94) this appears to be one of the key features that distinguish 'games' from ordinary 'play' (see previous section), in that games involve greater engagement and clearer boundaries between the game and wider social life: it takes place within a 'magic circle'. As they write: 'the fact that the magic circle is just that – a circle – is an important feature of his concept. As a closed circle, the space it circumscribes is *enclosed and separate* from the real world' (p. 95, emphasis added). However, elsewhere they are keen to indicate that this is always a negotiated and fragile boundary, established and maintained by participants. In particular, Salen and Zimmerman (2004: 98) suggest that it is this that makes the circle 'magical'; that games are created 'out of thin air' by their participants.

It is evident that many scholars have found useful the application of the magic circle concept to the study of video games, including Juul (2008: 60), who argues: 'playing a game not only means following or observing the rules of that game, but there are also special social conventions about how one can act towards other people when playing games. The concept of the magic circle is useful to describe the boundary at which these rules and norms of game-playing are activated.' For instance, Edward Castronova (2005) uses what he refers to as an 'almost-magic circle' to describe the membrane that encloses what he terms the 'synthetic worlds' of video games. For Castronova, this membrane is like a shield 'protecting the fantasy [game] world from the outside world' (p. 147). It is within this circle, membrane or shield that gamers play out a fantasy world, with its own rule system and logic, which can be quite different from the world outside of the game and gameplay environment. However, Castronova is careful to point out that this is a porous membrane, as, of course, a game cannot be completely sealed off from the outside world. People will frequently move back and forth and will bring with them into the game attributes from the outside world, and, to some degree, vice versa. In particular, Castronova finds this metaphor particularly useful for understanding how economic, political and legal issues cross over, but also change, between the 'synthetic' game world and the world beyond. For instance, Castronova uses the example of how in-game items and currency in massively multiplayer online role-playing games (MMORPGs) such as *EverQuest* could frequently be found for sale on Internet auction sites. Hence, in-game economics cross over but are transformed into out-of-game economics, and back again.

The usefulness of the magic circle concept for these and other scholars, therefore, lies in understanding how game players create and maintain social norms and practices, which may not apply in the same way in wider social interactions. However, for each author who utilizes and supports the use of the magic circle, or similar theories of play, there seem to be an equal number who are keen to challenge its assumptions and, in particular, its applicability to the study of video games.

Challenging the magic circle

One of the key criticisms levelled at the magic circle hypothesis concerns the divide between play and the wider social world. One of the most fervent criticisms of this has been offered by Pargman and Jakobsson (2008: 227), who suggest that the magic circle can be understood as a 'strong-boundary hypothesis'; that is to say, it represents a clear boundary between gameplay and the world outside of it. As Taylor (2007: 113) writes of the magic circle theory: 'this rhetoric often evokes a sense that the player steps through a kind of looking glass and enters a pure game space'. There certainly is some evidence to suggest that this concept is used, at least by some writers, in this way. For instance, on page five of the second edition of his *Fundamentals of Game Design* Ernest Adams (2010) depicts a circle, labelled 'the magic circle', next to, but clearly separate from, a box he labels 'the real world'.

However, writers such as Copier (2005) argue that rather than being bounded and outside of the ordinary social world, play is in itself a *social* activity and hence needs to be understood as located within ordinary life. However, in countering these criticisms Juul (2008) suggests that most of these arguments are based upon a misreading of Salen and Zimmerman (and Huizinga), as it is clear that these and other advocates of the magic circle recognize, if not emphasize, the social nature of this boundary, as well as its temporary and often permeable nature. It can hardly be seen, therefore, as a strong-boundary or anti-social hypothesis. In particular, the heart of Huizinga's original argument is the centrality of play to modern social life. In an attempt to counter the derisive attitude towards play held by many of his contemporaries, Huizinga argued that play was key in understanding the nature of language, civilization, law, war, knowledge, poetry, mythologies, philosophy and art (Blackshaw and Crawford 2009). For Huizinga, it was play that shaped these and other aspects of human culture.

Many of those who have employed the work of Huizinga in contemporary game studies also recognize that gaming is not, and never could be, totally isolated from the world outside. Eskelinen and Tronstad (2003: 205), for instance, acknowledge that games may have 'intended and unintended consequences that do affect the player's "ordinary life" too'. In addition, Adams (2010: 6) suggests that sometimes 'the distinction between the real world and the pretend reality is not always clear', and on page six of his book depicts an alternative diagram showing 'the magic circle' within 'the real world'.

It is likely, then, that critics such as Copier (2005) and Pargman and Jakobsson (2008) may have been a little too disparaging of the magic circle, and in particular how it has been applied by authors such as Salen and Zimmerman. However, it must be said that many of these authors do themselves no favours in their use of language, often referring to the magic circle as 'a distinct place' 'separate' from 'the *real* world' (Salen and Zimmerman 2004: 97, emphasis added). What they are certainly guilty of is providing, at times, a rather vague and ambiguous definition of this term and its application to game studies.

However, there are three other real problems with how Huizinga's and other classic theories of play have been applied to video game studies. First, Huizinga seems an odd, and probably ill-equipped, choice of theoretician to apply to contemporary game studies, since he was not specifically interested in setting out a theoretical framework for analysing games. Rather, Huizinga, and later Caillois, provide more philosophically based discussions of the general location and role of play within human history, culture and the development of modern civilizations (Liebe 2008: 326). As Jones (2008) rightly highlights, a 'romantic idealism' runs through Huizinga's work. Moreover, this is a philosophical argument that few in contemporary game studies even acknowledge, let alone attempt to adequately engage with. It seems as if the idea of the 'magic circle', and a few choice quotations, have simply been lifted from this body of work and imported into contemporary game studies with little recognition of, or interest in, where they come from, save for the imported kudos they bring with them.

This approach to game studies also needs to be understood as a clear, and often concerted, effort to distinguish this subject from cultural, literary, media and similar studies, and their focus on novels, television, radio, cinema and so forth. It is also possible to offer a rather cynical interpretation of this approach to game studies, which Pargman and Jakobsson (2008) at least allude to. It could be argued that ludology (see previous chapter), in its attempt to distance itself from fields such as media studies and establish itself as a distinct and emerging discipline, runs the risk of having no theoretical foundations or traditions on which to establish its academic credibility. The philosophical writings of authors such as Huizinga and Caillois, therefore, provide game studies with a respectable prehistory and a certain gravitas. Furthermore, Pargman and Jakobsson (2008) argue that it is understandable how a concept like the magic circle would be so appealing to game studies writers, as playing a game can sometimes feel as if the gamer is living in an imaginary, fantasy game world, separate from the real world outside. However, Pargman and Jakobsson are perhaps being a little too critical in their reading of ludology here, and certainly many writers, like Salen and Zimmerman (2004: 455), challenge what they see as the 'immersive fallacy' and the idea that gamers become lost in another world.

In addition, for Salen and Zimmerman (2004) one of the distinguishing features between 'games' and 'play', as we saw earlier, is that games involve greater engagement and clearer boundaries between the game and wider social life; the game thus takes place within a metaphorical magic circle. However, the argument that people step into a magic circle and out of 'normal' social activities and relations is difficult to sustain when one considers that gameplay can often, and may increasingly, be a relatively mundane act. Salen and Zimmerman (2004) do recognize that 'play' can be undertaken with only limited attention, and that the boundaries between games and other activities are often hard to identify. However, as already highlighted and discussed in more detail in the following section, definitions of what is taking place at any particular time and place can change in an instant, or people may have different perceptions of this. It is problematic to see play as occurring within an identifiable circle, when participants' and observers' perceptions are constantly changing, multilayered and at times even conflictual.

Furthermore, it could be argued that changes in technology make video gaming much more pervasive. For over two decades now we have had mobile game machines, such as the Nintendo Game Boy, the popularity of which has only grown over time, with the Nintendo DS constituting the best-selling video game console ever (Nintendo 2009). Advances in mobile telephone technologies and video gaming, however, and in particular the launch of the Apple iPhone in 2007, mean that many more people are carrying relatively powerful video game machines with them, and playing video games in a much more common and mundane way, such as on the bus, while watching television or (as we know from experience) in lectures. Gameplay, and in particular video gameplay, is becoming a relatively mundane and everyday activity, which seriously undermines the idea that we can understand it as somehow separate from the world outside (the everyday nature of video gameplay is discussed in more detail in Chapter 8).

A third key weakness in the magic circle, and what I feel is its most fundamental flaw, is that it does not provide us with the theoretical tools for understanding what is outside of the circle. As Pargman and Jakobsson (2008) argue, a real problem with game studies is that many scholars tend to consider gaming in (relative) social isolation. Though several authors are keen to emphasize the magic circle as permeable, and a social construct, most studies still focus on what happens within this perceived circle. The fundamental reason for this is that what occurs within this circle is seen to be different from the social world outside. There is sometimes a cursory recognition that 'the social' has an impact upon gaming, and similarly that gaming patterns can have wider social 'consequences'. However, there is rarely much consideration of what this actually means, beyond possibly listing a few examples, and this also provides authors with an excuse to largely ignore all that is deemed to be outside of the circle.

Though gaming does involve particular social norms and rules, which include those imposed upon the players (such as the rules of a video game) and those devised and maintained by the participants, so do most, if not all, aspects of social life, from playing sport to getting married, attending a class or simply having a conversation with a friend (Nielsen *et al.* 2008; Gosling and Crawford 2011). As Nielsen *et al.* (2008: 24) write:

> Games are special contexts where particular rules apply, but we can apply this definition to a wide array of utterly different activities: work, family life, university classes, weddings, the nightlife of a big city. All of these situations are governed by special rules and norms that do not always … apply to other contexts.

Gameplay might be different and special, but so is every social situation. To fully understand gaming we need to reflect upon its relationship to, and location within, other social patterns. We need theoretical tools that can appreciate this and help us to understand the social world beyond play, and the magic circle cannot do this.

Even advocates of the magic circle, such as Jesper Juul, have started to look elsewhere for less contested concepts. For instance, Juul in 2008 proposed the replacement of the magic circle with the metaphor of the 'puzzle piece'. This metaphor, he suggests, more clearly sees gaming as fitting, like a jigsaw puzzle piece, into a wider social setting and context. Similarly, Arsenault and Perron (2009) offer their own development of the magic circle, proposing instead that this be reformulated as a 'magic cycle'. Here they suggest that gameplay needs to be understood as three layered spirals of interaction between the gamer and the video game. At the core is the 'gameplay' spiral, which is the gamer's interaction with the game aesthetics, such as moving through game platform levels or exploring an alien landscape. This leads on to the second level, the spiral of 'narrative', where the gamer interacts with the story or setting of the game. Finally, narratives feed into a 'hermeneutic' spiral, which incorporates the player's interpretation of the game and its narrative and context.

For Falcão and Ribeiro (2011) the magic circle needs to be reconceived using the metaphor of Lewis Carroll's Alice stepping 'Through the Looking Glass'. What they mean by this, is that the magic circle, rather than being a divider of worlds, is rather a mediator between them and a point of intersection. What determines the relative separation of the game world from the world outside is the degree to which the gamer is immersed in the gaming environment, and this immersion can be strengthened by game narratives, spatial navigation within games, as well as interactions with other players. Hence, virtual worlds are the product of game objects, such as technologies, structures and narratives, but are also shaped by the gamers themselves, while in turn, the game world plays a role in shaping gamer identities and interactions.

Though these theoretical developments might be preferable to the magic circle (as originally conceived), we do not necessarily have to look outside the existing literature and language of game studies, or start to invent new concepts, to counter many of the weaknesses of the magic circle and similar concepts. Though the magic circle would appear to be the most popular idea taken up from their work, it is not the only theoretical framework for understanding gameplay utilized by Salen and Zimmerman (2004). A body of work they also consider is Gary Alan Fine's (1983) application of Erving Goffman's concept of 'frame analysis'. In particular, Salen and Zimmerman (2004) frequently refer to the magic circle as a 'frame', and, understood as one example of a 'frame', the magic circle does make more sense. Frame analysis may prove more useful than the magic circle, or similar theorizations, as it more fully locates patterns of play within a wider social context, and provides theoretical tools that can be used and applied beyond the study of play.

Frame analysis

Frame analysis is a theoretical and methodological tool of analysis first introduced by the Chicago sociologist Erving Goffman, and developed most clearly in his book *Frame Analysis* (1974). However, the use of frames as a tool and unit of analysis is, significantly for our purposes, first introduced by Goffman in 1961 in his essay 'Fun in Games'.

The focus of this essay and its companion essay on 'Role Distance', which were published together in the book *Encounters* (1961), is what Goffman refers to as 'focused' interactions. Goffman suggests that 'unfocused' interactions occur all of the time, such as when two people, being in the same room at the same time, may 'check up on each other's clothing, posture, and general manner, while each modifies his own demeanour because he himself is under observation' (1961: 7). However, what interested Goffman was what occurs when individuals actively choose to 'sustain for a time a single focus of cognitive and visual attention', for example, in a conversation or a game.

Put simply, a frame is what allows the participants, or 'actors', in any particular situation to understand 'what is going on here'; it is the rules, the norms, the expectations, the possible roles and so forth, which are available to the actors to make sense of any given situation or encounter. Though one may assume that anything is possible within a given social encounter, Goffman argues that this is not the case. Social interaction works on the basis of shared expectations, accepted roles, patterns of behaviour, codes of interaction and so forth; they are quite struc- tured. Social actors, to use one of Goffman's own metaphors, are like players of a card game, drawing from an already set and ordered deck (Goffman 1961: 25). Even by actively choosing not to follow expected social conventions, individuals are simply choosing a different course of action, a different card from the deck (to continue the metaphor), and observers may well react to this in expected ways.

Unlike the magic circle, or the work of one of Goffman's key inspirations, Alfred Schutz (1973), play is not seen as specifically different from other aspects of social life (Chayko 1993). It is merely one frame within a social order that is saturated with other, often multilayered frames. Gameplay, then, is just one of many, though as Goffman argues finite, frames that govern social behaviour.

Goffman (1961) describes the boundaries of each frame as a 'membrane' or a 'screen', while Gary Alan Fine (1983) finds it useful to describe a frame as 'bracketed off'. Goffman considers how patterns of interaction and behaviour within a specific frame, such as in playing a particular game, are notably different from that seen in other frames, and social patterns evident in other frames are 'transformed' as they pass through the 'metaphorical membrane' of the frame. Frames are subject to 'rules of irrelevance', where characteristics deemed rele- vant in other situations and times are deemed as insignificant or of differing importance within another frame. For example, Goffman highlights how the objects used to play a game of backgammon, be they valuable counters or simply bottle tops, become of less significance once a game is in play. This is because people become engrossed, what Goffman calls 'spontaneously involved', in the activities and frame at hand.

This language is similar to that used by many game scholars to describe the magic circle, but the key here is that Goffman is always emphasizing, and never missing out, other frames and the interplays between them. A key difference between frame analysis and game-specific concepts, such as the magic circle, is precisely the interplay between frames evident in the work of Goffman. For instance, Fine (1983: 183), in his application of frame analysis to pen-and-paper role-playing games, indicates that though the fantasy world of gaming may be 'bracketed off', 'all events are grounded in the physical world'. As Goffman wrote: 'fanciful words can speak about make-believe places, but these words can only be spoken *in* the real world (1974: 247, emphasis in original, cited in Fine 1983: 183).

The fact that frames are everywhere highlights the particular usefulness of Goffman to video game studies, as it locates gameplay within a wider social context, and understands it as just one form of social encounter. Hence, the bracket, or however you wish to label it, around gaming becomes truly permeable, as we understand what is outside of it, and we can therefore look for similarities, differences and influences relating to other social frames which we have the theoretical tools to similarly understand. It is not possible to do this with a theoretical tool like the magic circle, which has been specifically developed to understand gaming alone. It is not possible to take the magic circle and simply see how this fits to other social situations, for, as Goffman argues, everyday life is not a game (see previous section).

In the book *Frame Analysis* (1974) Goffman develops more clearly the way that frames are layered, or what he refers to as levels of 'lamination'. Goffman suggests that when an individual encounters a particular situation, they apply a 'primary framework' to make sense of it and determine their own and others' appropriate behaviour. Primary frameworks include both 'natural' and 'social' frameworks. Natural frameworks are those that are 'purely physical' and unchangeable, such as the weather, while social frameworks provide a 'background understanding', which includes the 'will, aim and controlling effort of an intelligent … agency, the chief one being the human being' (Goffman 1974: 22). But beyond the primary framework there is often the need for more detailed explanation and guidance. These Goffman refers to as 'keying' and 'fabrications' (or 'design'). Keying is where all the actors are aware of the nature of the situation. For instance, a primary framework may define a situation as a 'fight', while a more nuanced level of description (keying) means that all the actors understand this as a 'play fight' (Smith 2006). However, a fabrication or a design is where a deception (either benign or exploitative) takes place; for instance, where one person is playing a practical joke on another, and hence not all of the actors are fully aware of what is 'really' going on.

Though Goffman's frame analysis provides useful theoretical and methodological tools for understanding patterns of human behaviour, Fine (1983) argues that, beyond illustrative examples, Goffman does not apply this to any one social world in a detailed and sustained way. Fine (1983) seeks, therefore, to address this by applying frame analysis to the study of pen-and-paper (or tabletop), role-playing games and their players, and it is through the work of Fine that Goffman has found most application in contemporary game studies, such as in the work of Chayko (1993), Salen and Zimmerman (2004), Pargman and Jakobsson (2008) and Rossi *et al.* (2011).

Fine (1983) makes the work of Goffman more accessible, as well as developing his ideas, through their application to a specific case. In particular, Fine clearly demonstrates how pen-and-paper fantasy gamers employ (at least) three frameworks. These are a primary ('common-sense') understanding of themselves and their situation in a wider social context; a secondary frame, which identifies them as players of a game, with its own specific rule and patterns; and a third frame, which locates them as fantasy characters within a game world, which is again governed by further rules and appropriate patterns of behaviour. Hence, for Fine, though the game world may, to some degree, be bracketed from wider social frameworks, it is not separate but rather *embedded* within them. For example, Fine highlights that it is impossible to escape the fact that the fantasy world of role-playing games is one structured and understood through the gamers' contemporary Western knowledge, understanding, morals, language and so forth. It is a bracket world, but one constructed from the building blocks of the social and natural world in which it is located.

Furthermore, what Fine clearly shows here is how players are quite skilled at both bracketing off aspects of their lives, to fit in with a particular frame, and quite easily slipping between frames, sometimes within the same conversation or even sentence. For instance, fantasy role-players must often deny their game characters information that they know themselves, in order to retain the integrity of the game. However, in conversations players will readily flip between using the pronouns 'I' or 'me' to refer to either themselves or their game characters, and between 'in-character' and 'out-of-character' subjects. This may be seen in conversations about characters eating, which can easily turn into conversations about the players themselves eating, and back again. Hence, Fine highlights how social actors are often very skilled at juggling worlds; engrossment in a game therefore does not mean that the influence and interplay of other frames is excluded.

Also of relevance here, and predating the work of authors such as Salen and Zimmerman (2004), Pargman and Jakobsson (2008) and Rossi *et al.* (2011), is Mary Chayko (1993), who seeks to develop and update Goffman's work for a 'digital age', and in particular seeks to consider how new technologies, such as the Internet and video games, may change the nature of social interactions and frames. Chayko (1993) is rightly cautious not to fall into a technologically deterministic tradition of reifying distinctions between the 'real' and the 'virtual'. What is 'real' is a largely discursive construction, and there have always been competing and multiple interpretations of what 'reality' is (see Chapter 5). However, many new technologies, such as the Internet and video games, do further complicate Goffman's question 'what is going on here?' For instance, when playing a video game like Microsoft's *Flight Simulator*, the player is not flying a 'real' aeroplane; however, they are still engaging in a very 'real' activity, which can have real implications, such as when flight simulators are used to train pilots. In particular, Chayko argues that contemporary social frames may be less clearly bounded than they once were, and suggests that rather than understanding frames as either being present or not, we need to understand their influence as operating along a continuum of relevance.

Of course, frame analysis is not without its weaknesses and limitations. For instance, Goffman does not see frames as the creation of specific social actors, but rather as pre-existing schema that they simply employ. Furthermore, Goffman is not particularly interested in where frames come from. This is largely to the result of Goffman's interest in more micro-level social phenomena such as interactions, encounters or strips. Goffman's research was not directed towards areas where one might look to find the origins of frames, such as in macro-social structures or the individual psychologies and motivations of social actors. These were simply not areas that interested Goffman. For this reason, Goffman needs to be considered and applied in context, and with an understanding of what his focus and aims were. Frame analysis can be used to locate gaming within a wider social context and it is certainly a *more* social theory than that of the magic circle. However, a 'fully social theory' (Taylor *et al.* 1973) and a comprehensive analysis of the culture of video gaming would probably need to apply other tools and ideas which would allow us to understand the many intricacies of this phenomenon, rather than being tied into any one orthodoxy. This therefore reflects the aim of this book, to provide an introduction and overview to video gaming practices, while outlining a number of theoretical tools and perspectives, which, when put together, provide a fuller understanding of the role and importance of video gaming within contemporary culture and the practices of everyday life.

Chapter summary

- 'Play' is a difficult and complex term. It is sometimes understood as a subset of gaming, while games are sometimes seen as a more complex and rule-bound form of play.
- Contemporary game research tends to draw on classic theories of play, such as Caillois, Sutton-Smith and most notably the work of Johan Huizinga.
- For Huizinga play is seen as a voluntary and unproductive act, which takes place outside of ordinary life. One example of a time and place of play Huizinga lists is the 'magic circle'.
- The concept of the magic circle, as adopted from Huizinga, has been widely used within contemporary game studies to understand instances of play.
- The magic circle is used to signify that, through free choices, participants are subject to rules and norms that do not necessarily apply outside of the game. Play is fixed to that specific time and place, and transforms this into an imagined time and place.
- The boundaries of the magic circle are sometimes quite clear, while at others can be 'fuzzy and permeable' (Salen and Zimmerman 2004: 94).
- However, Huizinga does not provide a clear definition of what he means by the 'magic circle', and does not provide coherent and easily applicable theoretical tools for the analysis of play.
- Critics suggest that the way the concept of the magic circle has been used

often draws a false and strong boundary between play and the world beyond, or at best fails to fully locate play within, and consider the importance of, wider social patterns.

- Though the magic circle may be subject to specific rules and norms, so are all areas of social life.
- Distinctions between play and non-play are easily and quickly transgressed and are largely arbitrary. What defines a situation as play, or not, is how it is defined by participants, as well as observers.
- Advances in technologies, such as mobile game machines, make the distinction between times and places of play and ordinary life even more difficult to maintain.
- These weaknesses are, to some degree, countered by 'frame analysis', which recognizes that all areas of social life are governed by specific social norms, rules and roles which Goffman terms a 'frame'.
- For Goffman, frames can be multilayered, so that at each more detailed level, there is a more specific set of rules, roles and understandings of the social situation. Hence, here, play is understood as a nuanced level or understanding within a wider series of social frames. It is not separate, but rather built of, and built within, the social world.
- Frame analysis is not without its weaknesses, and in particular Goffman does not consider the origins of frames.
- Though frame analysis is a more useful theory than that of the magic circle, it does not alone provide a full and comprehensive understanding of the culture of video gaming.

Further reading

Chayko, M. (1993) 'What is Real in the Age of Virtual Reality? "Reframing" Frame Analysis for a Technological World', *Symbolic Interaction*, 16 (2), 171–81.

Pargman, D. and Jakobsson, P. (2008) 'Do You Believe in Magic? Computer Games in Everyday Life', *European Journal of Cultural Studies*, 11 (2), 225–43.

Salen, K. and Zimmerman, E. (2004) *Rules of Play: game design fundamentals*, London: MIT Press.

Smith, G.W.H. (2006) *Erving Goffman*, London: Routledge.

3 Video gamers as audience

Introduction

In this chapter, as elsewhere (see for example Crawford 2005b; Crawford and Rutter 2007; Crawford and Gosling 2008; Gosling and Crawford 2011), I make the argument for considering video gamers as a *media audience*. Admittedly, it is quite clear that video gamers are different from other media audiences, but so too are other audiences significantly different from each other; for instance, the audience for a contemporary television documentary programme is quite different from the audience at a gladiatorial event in a Roman amphitheatre. However, there are similarities and continuities, as well as differences, here.

Furthermore, the assertion that video gamers can be considered as an audience does not necessarily prohibit the recognition that video games are games, or that the literature on play and gaming can provide important insights into video game-play. As argued in Chapter 1, considering video games as media and considering them as games do not need to be mutually exclusive. Therefore this chapter's central aim is to add audience research to the mix, and use this to cast greater light on how video gamers are both similar to and different from television, cinema, radio or sport audiences, among others.

In particular, this chapter utilizes Abercrombie and Longhurst's (1998) three-stage model to contextualize developments in audience research. Following this model, the chapter begins with a consideration of audience research within what Abercrombie and Longhurst refer to as a 'behavioural paradigm' model, which sees audiences as passive recipients of media messages. The chapter next deals with debates located within an 'incorporation/resistance paradigm', which recognizes the active engagement of audiences with media texts, before considering the 'spectacle/performance paradigm', which advocates the consideration of how media consumption becomes diffused into everyday life and acts as a resource for social performance. The chapter concludes by considering the continued applicability of audience research in light of changing audience patterns and the advent of new technologies, such as video games.

Video games as 'audienceless'

Some writers on video games, such as Kline *et al.* (2003), Crawford (2005b) and Jenkins (2006a, 2006b), highlight the similarities between video gamers and other media audiences, and indicate the potential benefits of taking a more long-term and contextual approach, which locates video games within a history of media texts and audiences. However, as Chapter 1 showed, there is a continued and fervent denial by a significant number of game scholars that video gamers can be understood using theoretical tools developed in the study of television, cinema or literature texts and their audiences. One justification for this, as illustrated by the arguments of Lantz (2009) and others (see Chapter 1), is that video games are not media. In the arguments of many, particularly early, video game scholars, such as Chris Crawford (1984), media such as television, literature and cinema, and in turn their audiences, are cast as 'passive', which is contrasted with the perceived 'interactivity' and 'participation' of video gamers. For example, Loftus and Loftus (1983: 41) argue that 'when we watch a movie or read a book, we passively observe the fantasies. When we play a computer game, we actively participate in the fantasy world created by the game' (cited in Newman 2004: 94). The perceived 'interactivity' of video gamers, compared with the 'passivity' of media, such as television, audiences is explored further in Chapter 5, but the assertion is often made that video gamers are *players* of a game rather than an *audience* of media. As Eskelinen and Tronstad (2003: 200) categorically and simply put it: 'games are audienceless'.

Eskelinen and Tronstad (2003), and Lantz (2009) some years later, draw comparisons between video games and other games, and in particular soccer (football), which they argue do not *require* an audience to be present. Hence, in a similar way to how a group of youths can play football in a park without anyone (that is to say, anyone apart from the participants themselves) watching, they suggest that an individual or group can play a video game, and most frequently do, without an 'audience' present. Eskelinen and Tronstad's argument is that a book, television show or a film is created primarily for the consumption of an audience, while video games are made to be played by a player. They further support this argument by asserting that video games, like sport, do not necessarily have narratives, which tend to be a fundamental structure of most media forms, for example books and films. The absence of narratives from video games is a very contentious point, and many (such as Genvo 2009) would argue that video games do contain narrative forms. However, the question of video game narratives is explored further in Chapter 5 so I wish to put it aside for now. The issue I wish to raise here is that Eskelinen and Tronstad fail to recognize that an individual or group can occupy the dual positions of participant and audience at the same time. As Eskelinen and Tronstad (2003) themselves acknowledge, video gameplay can involve significant elements of performativity, which will frequently involve participants taking on and acting out specific roles. Hence, through their gaming performances, video gamers create spectacles which they are also an audience to (Rehak 2003). As Long (2009) argues:

> Many players *are* audiences, and in fact are *willing* audiences – I myself prefer the linear, 'on rails' type of RPGs [role-playing games] over non-linear 'Western' RPGs because of the value I place on a really wonderful story. I *willingly and happily* concede a good degree of my agency because I want

> to experience the story the storyteller is constructing for me, and I want to
> experience it in a video game as opposed to a novel or a film because of the
> greater degree of immersion afforded by video games. (emphasis in original)

Though Long is referring here to specific types of video gaming experience,
such as the 'on rails'-style play evident in video games such as the *House of the
Dead* series, all video games involve the gamer watching or listening to a video
game spectacle. This includes not just 'on rail' games and cut-scenes, but also the
visual- and audio-scapes present in standard video gameplay, such as observing
the bloody spectacle of the player-controlled character Kratos in the *God of War*
games as he slashes his way through numerous adversaries. Video gamers can in
addition be understood as an audience in a much more traditional sense; that is to
say, watching others perform. As Newman (2004: 95) writes: 'it is essential to note
that videogame experiences are frequently shared by groups, perhaps crowded
around a television set in a domestic setting, or as Saxe (1994) has observed,
around coin-op machines in arcades'. This can be seen in Figure 3.1, where at a
particular Xbox event, the gamers had a clear audience of onlookers.

However, the real usefulness of an audience-focused approach, as set out below,
is that it locates video gameplay within a wider socio-political framework, as well
as recognizing that the importance and influence of video games often extend far
beyond a single moment of play. That is to say, while play-focused approaches
may shed light on how video gamers play and interact with a video game, they
cannot tell us about the role video gaming plays in people's everyday lives away
from the screen, such as in their conversations, social network interactions and
identity formations, or how social forces such as capitalism and patriarchy shape
the nature of play. However, as Jenkins (2004) argues, it would be ill-thought-out
of any author to presume that theories and concepts can be lifted wholesale from
one area and easily and unproblematically applied to another; but this equally
applies to literature developed to understand non-computational forms of games
and play as well as audience research. The key is to apply a different lens to the
study of video games and through this consider what they reveal, as well as what
this new case may add to existing models.

Audience research

The literature on audiences is now quite extensive. Though it was certainly the
case that the greater part of early media and textual scholarship focused almost
exclusively upon processes of production, over recent decades more and more
interest has been taken in reception, audiences, fans, consumers and users. The
assumption in social science fields dominated by positivistic perspectives was that
audiences and consumers were a direct, inevitable, and therefore largely uninteresting, end point of processes of production.

This is certainly the perspective that dominated early telecommunication
studies. In particular, one of the earliest studies of telecommunications was
conducted by Claude Elwood Shannon, who worked for the Bell Telephone
Corporation in America in the 1940s. Shannon developed a mathematical model

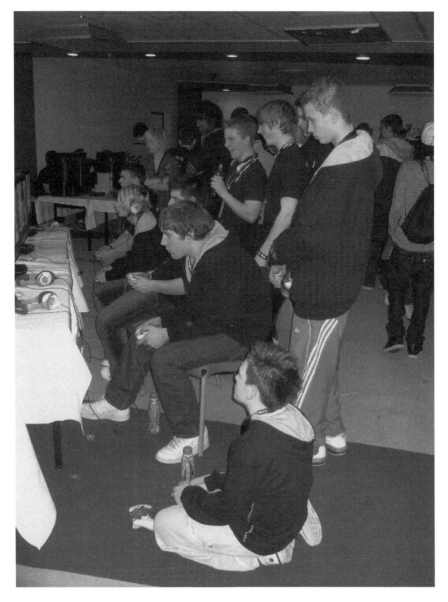

Figure 3.1 Video gamers and onlookers (photo: G. Crawford)

of communication that was concerned with the most effective way of transmitting information and attempted to eliminate any disruption of the original message. This disruption in the transfer of a message Shannon referred to as 'noise' (Longhurst *et al.* 2008). Hence, for Shannon, the receiver of a message is understood as an empty vessel, passively receiving a message. If the message received was not exactly that which was intended, then Shannon assumed there must be something (some 'noise') interfering with the process of communication, which needed to be overcome. In this model, therefore, there is no room for, or consideration of, audience interpretation or activity, they are cast as merely the recipients of a message.

Of course, people have been writing about audiences since antiquity. Guttman (1986) in his history of sport spectators, for instance, uses historical accounts to consider audience behaviour at ancient Grecian and Roman games. However, contemporary audience research developed most significantly when academics began to pay more, and specific, attention to the recipients of processes of communication, and in particular mass media. To understand early and subsequent audience research, Abercrombie and Longhurst in their book *Audiences* (1998) provide a useful categorization of three significant historical stages, or paradigms, through which this research field has developed. These stages they refer to as the 'behavioural paradigm', the 'incorporation/resistance paradigm' and the 'spectacle/performance paradigm'. This categorization, or model, of theories of audience research, can be plotted along the development paths of two parallel, and interlinked, theorizations: patterns of reception and social power. In this, first, the movement from the behavioural to the incorporation/resistance to the spectacle/performance paradigm signifies a greater awareness of audience activity, use and engagement with texts and meanings, and, second, a shift to understanding social power relations as fluid and operating through, rather than on, individuals.

The behavioural paradigm

The first paradigm in Abercrombie and Longhurst's model, the behavioural paradigm, covers many psychological theories of audiences and some of the early thinking of sociologists in this area, which includes the work of Katz *et al.* (1974). This perspective is heavily influenced by early thinking on processes of communication (such as Shannon's work, cited above), and is sometimes referred to as a 'syringe' model, where the medium is seen as a stimulus from which audiences passively absorb messages. In this paradigm, audiences are seen as a response to the mass media and are often portrayed as inactive 'passive dopes' (Garfinkel 1967). It is within this paradigm that Abercrombie and Longhurst (1998) locate 'media effects' research, such as the work of Anderson (1977), who considers the 'effect' television violence has on young children. Though Abercrombie and Longhurst suggest that each paradigm is subsequently followed by new perspectives on audience research, crucially, early paradigms do not die, and in particular, media effects debates have continued to thrive, often moving on to new media and audiences, such as video games.

The question of the effects of video game violence on players is considered in more detail in Chapter 5; however, it is worth noting here that this is a deeply problematic area of research. Video game violence effects literature tends to draw on, and build upon, earlier research on other forms of media, such as television and film, which proposed a link between violent media and increased levels of audience aggression. However, authors such as Dill and Dill (1998) suggest that violence in video games could potentially be more damaging than that seen in television and film because of the 'interactive' nature of gaming. As Emes (1997) argues, video games often require that players actively direct the in-game aggression, and hence the violence in video games is more 'participatory'. However, as discussed in Chapter 5, there are a number of fundamental difficulties with most research on media effects, most notably its often inconsistent methodologies and small and unrepresentative sample groups. This research has also been criticized for overestimating the ability of video games to influence the specific attitudes and behaviour of individuals or groups, and for seeing video gamers as passive and vulnerable to representations of violence within games (Bryce and Rutter 2006).

It is therefore possible to identify a number of limitations, if not fundamental flaws, in a behaviour paradigm approach, such as the media effects thesis. But the most crucial is probably that this model sees audiences as passive, unquestioning, unintelligent recipients of media messages. As Jenkins (2006a: 211) argues, most video games effects arguments attribute 'almost no conscious cognitive activity on the part of the gamers, who [are perceived to] have all the self-consciousness of Pavlov's dogs'. It is for this and other reasons that Abercrombie and Longhurst suggest that, particularly from the late 1970s onwards, a significant proportion of audience research began to move in a new direction, one that sought to recognize, understand and in some quarters celebrate the active role of the audience.

The incorporation/resistance paradigm

From the 1970s and 80s onwards media and cultural studies debates became increasingly sensitive to the active role of media audiences, and for the most part focus began to move away from the idea that audiences uncritically and passively absorbed messages conveyed to them in the mass media.

Though Abercrombie and Longhurst's model is one of historical progress, it must be noted that this is a rather 'loose' linear progression. The idea that audiences actively engage with texts can be found, for example, in the work of Walter Benjamin in the 1930s, where he argued that being witness to art and culture in a state of 'distraction', that is to say, paying only partial, or even a subconscious, attention to the piece, could suggest high levels of appreciation and knowledge. Here, the original 'aura' (privileged status) of the piece recedes and the audience is able to appreciate it from the perspective of a true critic (Benjamin 1931). Similarly, the rise in popularity of the 'active audience' model in cultural theory in the 1970s and 80s did not mean the end of behavioural paradigm arguments, as can clearly be seen in the contemporary media effects literature on video games (see Chapter 5). However, it was an increasing awareness of the contradictions and limitations of the behaviour paradigm which (for many) led to this being supplanted by the incorporation/resistance paradigm, which sees audiences as, potentially, active consumers.

Audience activity is commonly seen, as highlighted by Fiske (1992), to take three key forms: semiotic, enunciative and textual. Semiotic activity refers to how audiences actively interpret and reinterpret media themes, stories and messages. Enunciativity relates to social and interactive activities, such as talking about television shows or imitating one's favourite film or pop stars. Textual activities refer to the creation of new texts, such the new stories, art, poetry and songs based upon their favourite television shows produced by *Star Trek* and *Doctor Who* fans (Jenkins 1992). Drawing on de Certeau (1984) Jenkins refers to this as 'textual poaching'. In particular, these three forms of audience activity are used to categorize video gamers' production in Chapter 7.

A significant contribution to the shift towards an active audience model was provided by a group of scholars working at the Centre for Contemporary Cultural Studies at the University of Birmingham. This work began in the late 1960s, but it was in the 1970s and early 1980s that it became most prominent under the directorship of Stuart Hall. Though the work of the Birmingham School (as it came to be known) was diverse, it is evident that much of their work, particularly through the 1970s and early 80s, was influenced by the ideas of the Sardinian neo-Marxist writer Antonio Gramsci (1971) on hegemony, which they combined with semiotic studies of the mass media. In particular, Stuart Hall and other authors at Birmingham argue that the mass media provide ideological messages that portray a false ideology, which is created by, and benefits, the state and the bourgeoisie.

However, a crucial dimension of hegemony is that this is a form of negotiated domination, and hence it is never complete or wholly fulfilled, as the weak struggle to empower themselves and others. This focus on class-based domination and resistance took the form of a number of ethnographic studies throughout this period by Birmingham scholars, such as Dick Hebdige's (1979) work on youth subcultures (see Chapter 6 on subcultures) and Paul Willis's (1977) study of working-class schoolboys, but it is Stuart Hall's (1980) paper on encoding and decoding that had the most impact on media studies.

In 'Encoding/Decoding' Hall (1980) argues that television programmes, and by implication all other forms of text, should be understood as 'meaningful discourses' which are 'encoded' by those involved in their production, and in turn capable of being decoded by the audiences who watch them. Hall argues that television texts are very complex and hence can be decoded in different ways by the audience. Hall identifies three positions from which televisual discourses may be decoded. These he calls the 'dominant-hegemonic', the 'negotiated' and the 'oppositional' (1980: 136–8). In the dominant-hegemonic position the logic and discourse of the television programme is accepted. The negotiated code may also operate within this framework, but allows for some disagreements within it. Thus, on the basis of personal experience or class-based position, for example, there may be specific challenges to aspects of the dominant discourse. In the oppositional position, the dominant framework is directly resisted, in a 'globally contrary way' (Hall 1980: 137–8).

Where previously audiences were understood as the end point of a linear process, consumers of products and empty vessels into which the media poured their messages, Hall sees this as a cyclical process, where the messages created by the media are processed, interpreted and given meaning by the audience; hence, the audience themselves similarly engage in a process of production. Crucially, this is a cyclical process of production and consumption understood and located within a wider social and political framework. So whereas for earlier scholars, everyday conditions were an annoying set of variables that needed to be controlled in laboratory experiments, here the social world provides a context for and an understanding of audience processes.

This shift in audience research also led to a greater interest in the activities and patterns of reception and consumption of audiences. In particular, through the late 1980s into the early 1990s some authors, most notably John Fiske (1987, 1998a, 1989b and 1992) and Henry Jenkins (1992), among others, sought to focus upon the creativity, resistance and subversion of audiences, and in particular fans. For Fiske, fandom is by its very nature subversive, with fans taking pleasure in creating their own meanings and rejecting encoded dominant ideologies (see Chapter 6 for a further discussion of fans). The theoretical inspiration for both Fiske and Jenkins is the work of Michel de Certeau (1984) and his focus on how individuals 'make do', get by, find their own space and undertake small, but significant, acts of resistance in their everyday lives (see Chapter 8). The work of these authors, and in particular Fiske, has often been dismissed as being overly celebratory of popular culture as a means of social resistance, but their work is still important as it recognizes that audiences are far from passive.

The idea of audiences actively engaging with media texts has proved an appealing concept and metaphor for some writers on video games (such as Kline *et al.* 2003; Crawford 2005b; Crawford and Rutter 2006) as a way of understanding what video gamers do. For instance, Kline *et al.* (2003), in their discussion of the legacy of the Birmingham School, highlight the usefulness of an active audience model in considering how some female video gamers may challenge and reinterpret the dominant masculine themes within some video games, or the way some video gamers subvert the preferred readings of strategy games such as *Civilization* and *SimCity*.

However, there are some limitations to this model. In particular, the conclusion drawn by many is that this model suggests active engagement with media texts by only *some* audience members. Hall's (1980) three audience positions model (put simply as incorporation, negotiation and opposition) has been used by many to suggest three levels of audience engagement, ranging from an active challenging of media ideologies, to a part-active negotiation, to a passive acceptance. Similarly, the focus of other Birmingham scholars like Hebdige and Willis on deviant and resistant subcultures leads many to assume that outside of these subcultures the rest of the population are an uninteresting and passive acquiescent mass. This then leaves a legacy in media and cultural studies which sees many authors and researchers searching for evidence and conclaves of the active and resistant audience or subculture, while ignoring wider patterns of consumption. This distinction between resistant (active) and incorporative (passive) audiences, and by extension assumptions about 'good' and 'bad' audiences, is particularly apparent in many studies on both media and sport fans (see Crawford 2004).

However, many recent studies have shifted focus towards the consumption of more 'ordinary' and everyday users (such as Longhurst 2007) and suggest that audience activity is not restricted to a small subversive minority of consumers. In particular, Abercrombie and Longhurst (1998) argue that limitations with the incorporation/resistance paradigm, as well as the changing nature of audience patterns (see below), have led to a shift, for many audience research writers, towards what they term the spectacle/performance paradigm.

The spectacle/performance paradigm

Abercrombie and Longhurst argue that key to the theoretical shift to the spectacle/ performance paradigm is a wider reconceptualization of societal power relations. Abercrombie and Longhurst argue that the incorporation/resistance paradigm works from the structuralist perspective that there exists a finite and unequal distribution of power in society. This, they suggest, can be contested in two key ways. First, drawing on the poststructuralist work of Michel Foucault (1979), it can be argued that power, rather than being stationary, is in constant flux. Power relations can therefore never be resolved. Second, the incorporation/resistance paradigm revolves primarily around relations of power based upon social class strata. However, in contemporary society power relations are increasingly complex and multiplicit, and hence it proves increasingly difficult to talk of a central power axis around which the incorporation/resistance paradigm revolves.

Concurrent with this shift in theoretical position, Abercrombie and Longhurst suggest, there have been significant developments in the nature of contemporary audiences. In particular, they argue that the mass media are becoming increasingly omnipresent in our everyday lives. Drawing on the work of Appadurai (1990), they suggest that we are surrounded by a mediascape, which like the landscape, often goes unnoticed, but plays a fundamental role in shaping the nature of our world and our place within it. This mediascape is characterized by the convergence and personalization of media, such as mobile telephones, which allow users to watch films, listen to music, surf the Internet, as well as communicate with others via a range of means, all with a simple-to-operate device (this is explored further in Chapter 8). Media become increasingly globalized and participatory, and narratives and themes become increasingly transmedia-based, crosscutting multiple formats and technologies (see the section in Chapter 5 on intertextuality).

Abercrombie and Longhurst (1998) suggest, therefore, that it is possible to see a development of audience behaviour, from what they refer to as the 'simple', to the 'mass', to the 'diffused' audience. All three forms of audience have their origins in different historical periods, but continue to exist within contemporary society. The simple audience was the dominant form in the premodern period, and would, for example, include a theatre or a live sport audience. Here, there is direct communication between sender and receiver within a localized, often public, space. Significantly, this is 'not … the stuff of everyday life' (1998: 44); the audience has a high level of concentration and the event and their behaviour often involve elements of ceremony.

The mass audience has its origins in the development of mass media in the early to mid-modern period. It is evident that watching television or listening to music at home are markedly different from attending a football match or going to the theatre, as

> mass audience events do not involve spatial localization, the communication is not so direct, the experience is more of an everyday one and is not invested in quite the same way with ceremony, less attention is paid to the performance,

which is typically received in private rather than public, and there is even greater social and public distance between the performers and audience.

Abercrombie and Longhurst 1998: 58

They argue that, crucially, both simple and mass audiences depend upon performance, a factor that becomes even more important in their third form of audience, the diffused audience. Here the essential feature of the diffused audience is that in 'contemporary society everyone becomes an audience all the time. Being a member of an audience is no longer an exceptional event, nor an everyday event. Rather it is constitutive of everyday life' (1998: 68–9). That is to say, we live in an increasingly 'performative society' (see also Tulloch 1999) where individuals will draw on and utilize the mass media as a resource to construct their identities and social performances, and 'play' to an audience in their everyday lives (performance is explored further in Chapter 5).

Abercrombie and Longhurst (1998) submit that all three forms of audience can be found in contemporary society, and the spectacle/performance paradigm presents an attempt to understand the relationship that exists between them. But the diffused audience is a particular phenomenon of a media-saturated late modern period, which has come into existence thanks to several key, interrelated factors. First, they point out that people spend a lot of time in the consumption of media, both privately and publicly. Second, the mass media and everyday life have become so closely interwoven that they are increasingly inseparable. Third, we are increasingly living in a narcissistic society where everyday, mundane events become increasingly performative. Fourth, they maintain that so ingrained are performances in everyday life that they become almost invisible and the distance between performer and audience becomes almost entirely removed. As they argue: 'Life is a constant performance; we are audience and performer at the same time; everybody is an audience all the time. Performance is not a discrete event' (1998: 73). Finally, they argue, we also live in an increasingly spectacular society. Just as Foucault (1979) argued that we live in a society of surveillance and observation, where the few watch the many, Mathiesen (1997) suggests that society has equally become about the many watching the few. A key example of this would be our contemporary fascination with celebrity (see Rojek 2001), but it is also easy to see how media, including video games, are increasingly about intense audio-visual experiences; the louder, brighter, more spectacular, the better (see Debord 1967). Here, then, the mass media become a resource for identity construction, social networks and performances. Examples of this include celebrities informing how people act and talk; football team, pop band, film or video game preferences displayed on T-shirts or in conversation; television make-over shows, newspapers and magazines telling people how to dress themselves or their homes and what the latest trends, fashions, crazes, dances, games are. These are the tools and consequences of a media-saturated performative society, a society of which video game culture is very much part. In particular, it has been argued by many, such as Wright *et al.* (2002), Kerr *et al.* (2004) and Crawford and Rutter (2007), that video games are particularly performative, and this is an argument taken up in Chapter 5. Video gamers perform in-game actions, which they then became an audience to. Video games also allow players to perform to others they are playing with, both in-game and out-of-game. Furthermore, video games can be, and frequently are, the subject and source of conversations and social perform-ances away from the game screen (see Chapters 7 and 8).

Video gamers, performers, users and the continued importance of audiences

All video game research may not necessarily fit neatly into Abercrombie and Longhurst's model of audience research. This is because video game research is diverse in its focus and multidisciplinary in its influences. Few models are ever perfect, but this does provide a useful means of understanding, contextual-izing and highlighting ways forward for the study of video games and gamers. For example, this model is helpful in locating and understanding the origins and critiques of the video game violence effects debate – a subject covered in more detail in Chapter 5. The video game violence effects literature builds upon earlier behavioural paradigm research, and continues to fall into many of its pitfalls, by seeing audiences as passive recipients of media messages. Furthermore, many studies of video game representations, such as the work of Leonard (2004, 2006, 2009) on depictions of 'race' within sport-themed video games, could be under-stood as (at least sharing similarities with) an incorporation/resistance paradigm approach. What is more, key features of the spectacle/performance paradigm are themes central to contemporary video game debates, such as the increasing fluidity of identity (see for example Filiciak 2003) and the importance of social performance (see for example Wright *et al.* 2002).

Video game research is a new and rapidly developing area which has fought hard, and is still fighting, to establish its own identity, separate from other fields and disci-plines such as cultural and media studies (see Mäyrä 2008, 2009). This is both an advantage and disadvantage for this fledgling area of research. Nieborg and Hermes (2008) argue that game studies is in many respects ahead of similar disciplines such as cultural studies, and is pushing at the boundaries of academic knowledge and debate. In particular, they suggest, while older fields often carry the baggage of founding debates, such as the 'old Marxist legacy' that cultural studies continues to be shaped by, video game research circumnavigates many of these, beginning a trajectory of debate informed by what Foucault (1984) would refer to as 'govern-mentality'. That is to say, areas of research like cultural and media studies were largely built upon structuralist foundations, such as neo-Marxist approaches, critical theory and linguistic structuralism (Longhurst *et al.* 2008). These theories operate with an assumption that power exists within the hands of select and elite social groups. Hence, the search here is often for structural patterns, such as evidence of dominant, most commonly class-based, ideology and responses to this. Abercrombie and Longhurst's (1998) spectacle/performance paradigm quite clearly reflects an attempt to break free from this debate informed by the 'dominant ideology thesis' (Abercrombie *et al.* 1980) and look towards a theorization more informed by post-structuralist, and in particular Foucauldian, approaches, which understand social power as more fluid and dynamic, operating through, rather than on, individuals.

For many writers, poststructuralism swept away the focus on rigid societal structures, replacing it with a recognition of the fluidity of social categories and identities. Old social categories such as social class, race and gender become what Ulrich Beck (2002) terms 'zombie categories', which have been stripped of any real meaning or substance within contemporary debates. Attention shifts away from ascribed status, moving towards how individuals construct and perform social identities from the resources society, the mass media and consumer culture provide.

It was into this poststructuralist-informed era of social research that (video) game studies was born. Though some writers (rightly) continue to draw on more structuralist debates, and most notably in video game studies this can be seen in discussions around the representation of gender and marginalization of women within video game culture, many writers look towards a more poststructuralist- (and at times postmodern-) informed approach. This approach focuses less on who people are and more on what they do, and is also less about social categories and more about individual action; this is certainly a key theme witnessed in much of the literature on video gameplay, as well as the use of new media more generally.

The discourses surrounding new media use are rarely those of collectivity, but more commonly of individual users, individual choice and the personalization of media. The language of new media is not directed towards a collective, but towards the individual user, whose viewing and listening no longer has to be the same as everyone else's, or what the controllers of broadcast media tell them to consume. They are the Internet surfer who goes wherever they want to, or the video gamer who actively participates in the creation of the games that they play. Hence, 'audience' has been replaced, in new media discourse, with the figure of the gamer, the surfer, the user or other similarly active, but individualized descriptors. The term audience has been consigned to a previous era, one of unidirection broadcast media and passivity. The concept of, and focus upon, the user, gamer or similar terms removes, or at least marginalizes, processes of communication, authored texts, corporate and institutional power, and ideas of collectivity and social position. For example, this can be seen in Lantz's (2009) argument that video games are not conveyors of messages (see Chapter 1). As Livingstone (2005: 45) argues: '"user" does not necessarily relate to communication at all, for it applies just as well to users of the washing machine or toaster'. But social structures, inequality, collectivity and patterns of mass communication do still matter, and continue to significantly shape social patterns, including gameplay.

As argued in more detail in Chapter 5, the interactivity and user-control of new media technologies, such as video games, is often greatly exaggerated. So too is the idea that new media users are necessarily any more participatory than other media consumers. One example, and a point made in Chapter 7, is that though Jenkins (2006b) highlights Wikipedia as a key illustration of the participatory new media culture, it is evident that its content is generated by only a very small percentage of users; for most, it is used like any offline, hardcopy encyclopaedia. Patterns of participation and democracy built upon new technology and new patterns of consumption will inevitably be open only to some, possibly a small minority, as a result of the limitations imposed by economics, location, gender and so forth, a point Jenkins (2006b) does briefly acknowledge.

Kline *et al.* (2003: 44) highlight how the active audience accentuated by writers such as Stuart Hall (1980) has in recent years become replaced by the somewhat toothless idea of the 'sovereign consumer', which is taken to simply mean that audiences have the power to choose what they consume and how they consume it. Kline *et al.* suggest that this is problematic in three key ways. First, it tends to celebrate audience activity irrespective of the qualities of the media with which they are engaging. Second, this perspective often underplays the commercial structuring and dominance of the culture industry (see Adorno 1991). Third, focusing on the activity and creativity of users runs the risk of ignoring how audiences are themselves (at least to some extent) created by the culture industry. That is to say, audiences are the product or commodity that the culture industry, such as television networks, websites and increasingly video game producers, sell to advertisers.

Though a focus on audience activity, performance, identities, interactions and consumer patterns remains important, it is equally important not to lose sight of continuities and persistent power structures. For instance, it is apparent that media corporations still hold a great deal of power, much more than a typical audience member (Couldry 2005). As Bottomore argues in his introduction to *The Dominant Ideology Thesis* (Abercrombie *et al.* 1980), the baby often gets thrown out with the dominant ideology bathwater. That is to say, in our search to move beyond what are perceived to be outdated concepts of social power, structures and patterns of engagement, we cease to look for the continuity and the presence of structural processes and forces. Hence, research focus shifts towards the micro, and studying individuals or group behaviour, at the expense of old certitudes such as class, race, ethnicity and gender, and structural power relations, which continue to be important influences on consumer and media use patterns and industries, including video games.

Abercrombie and Longhurst's spectacle/performance paradigm is useful, as it recognizes that though being an audience can still involve consumption in specific and meaningful locations, such as in a theatre or in front of a television set or video game console, the importance and influence of the event and text extend far beyond a specific place and time. In an increasingly media-saturated society, consumption and performance are not necessarily tied to discrete and isolated events, and, hence, being a performer and audience member becomes an integral and diffused part of our everyday lives, social networks, identity formations, social interactions and culture. This argument thus alerts us to the fact that though playing a video game may often take place at a specific time and location, it is not isolated from the world outside (in a magic circle) but rather located within, and increasingly diffused into, our everyday lives. However, it is equally important not to forget or overlook continuities. It is therefore essential that we do not leave behind all of the arguments of the incorporation/resistance paradigm, as it is evident that our consumer practices, including our video game purchases and patterns of play, are still shaped by structural forces, such as social class, gender and sexuality, as well as industry, state and economic forces. In particular, these are factors far too often ignored in many discussions of video games and those who make and play them.

Chapter summary

- Many game scholars deny that video gamers are an audience, arguing that whereas films, books and other media forms are made to be consumed by an audience, games are made to be played by players.
- This ignores that players are also observers. Video gamers are frequently an audience to game content, such as cut-scenes, to their own play and that of others.
- This chapter utilizes Abercrombie and Longhurst's (1998) model of audience research as a tool for categorizing key arguments within this field.
- The first paradigm within Abercrombie and Longhurst's (1998) model is the behavioural paradigm, which covers early sociological and psychological research and casts the audience as passive recipients of media messages.
- Key examples of behavioural paradigm research include work on media effects, such as that on the effects of video game violence on players.
- Abercrombie and Longhurst suggest that the behavioural paradigm was subsequently superseded by the incorporation/resistance paradigm, which recognizes the more active role of audiences.
- The incorporation/resistance paradigm suggests that audiences do not necessarily passively accept media messages, but can actively negotiate or even resist dominant ideologies.
- The incorporation/resistance paradigm suggests that only some audience members are active and tends to largely ignore the consumer patterns of a wider audience.
- Abercrombie and Longhurst suggest that changes in audience patterns and theoretical frameworks have led to the incorporation/resistance paradigm being replaced by a spectacle/performance paradigm.
- Whereas the incorporation/resistance paradigm operates with a structuralist understanding of power relations, where power and social structures are seen as largely static, the spectacle/performance paradigm recognizes them as increasingly fluid.
- The spectacle/performance paradigm suggests that audiences have developed from a simple, through a mass, to a diffused form of audience, where patterns of consumption shift from isolated public spots, to the home, to being diffused into our everyday lives and social performances.
- The spectacle/performance paradigm reflects the fact that we live in a world where media consumption becomes increasingly omnipresent and intertwined with our everyday lives and identities. It is a society that is increasingly narcissistic, performative and spectacular, where media are drawn on as a resource in fuelling identity constructions and social performances.
- Abercrombie and Longhurst's model of audience research is useful as it helps contextualize many key debates within video game research. However, it is important that the arguments within the spectacle/performance paradigm do not dominate audience and video game research, as it is crucial to recognize that structural power relations continue to persist in contemporary society and play a key role in shaping video games, the industry and patterns of play.

Further reading

Couldry, N. (2005) 'The Extended Audience: scanning the horizon', in M. Gillespie (ed.) *Media Audiences*, Maidenhead: Open University Press/McGraw-Hill, 184–222.

Crawford, G. and Rutter, J. (2007) 'Playing the Game: performance in digital game audiences' in J. Gray, C. Sandvoss and C.L. Harrington (eds) *Fandom: identities and communities in a mediated world*, New York: New York University Press, 271–84.

Kline, S., Dyver-Witherford, N. and De Peuter, G. (2003), *Digital Play: the interaction of technology, culture, and marketing*, London: McGill-Queen's University Press.

Longhurst, B. (2007) *Cultural Change and Ordinary Life*, Maidenhead: McGraw Hill.

4   Who plays video games?

Introduction

The question 'who plays video games?' may seem a rather simple and straight-forward one. Most of us have, usually common sense-based, ideas of who video gamers are, and it is also an area that has been the focus of extensive research, both academic and industry-based. However, as with most apparently common-sensical questions, once we begin to interrogate this further, it appears that the answer is not as straightforward as one might have first assumed. Furthermore, research findings are often at best partial and sometimes contradictory. The question 'who plays video games?' is, we find, far from straightforward.

There have been four broad approaches to answering the question, each of which will be considered in turn in this chapter. First, a focus on 'types' (or more commonly 'stereotypes') of gamers; in other words, what 'kinds' of people play video games? Second, demographics, which draw on often large-scale quantitative data on the different demographics (such as gender, age, ethnicity and so forth) of video gamers, as well as other statistical information about frequency, who plays what and so on. Third is the question and debate concerning 'exclusion', that is to say, 'who does not play?' or, more specifically, 'who does not play in numbers proportionate to their population size?' The fourth approach considers who plays more conceptually, and utilizes typologies to categorize and understand video gamer patterns. However, the chapter concludes by suggesting that rather than categorizing gamers into 'types', a more profitable way forward might be to consider video gaming as a social career involving a dynamic process of changing positions and structures.

Of course, these debates and approaches often link and overlap with each other, either implicitly or explicitly, as well as with others outside the scope of this discussion, but conceptualizing these debates in this way helps us understand current knowledge and attitudes towards video gamers and who they are.

(Stereo)typing video gamers

It is evident that there have been several assumptions and stereotypes of who gamers are, and that many continue to persist. These are the stereotypes most commonly perpetuated in the popular press as well as so-called 'public' opinion, but similar themes can also be seen in, and can play a significant role in directing, academic literature and debates. Stereotypes include, most commonly, the view of video gamers as, largely, anti-social, aggressive, addicted, male and white adolescents.

A criticism often levelled at video gaming is that it is an anti-social and isolating activity, producing a generation of passive 'mouse potatoes' (Kline *et al.* 2003). For instance, recent research published by Brigham Young University scholar Laura M. Padilla-Walker and her colleagues based upon a survey of 813 college students (Padilla-Walker *et al.* 2008) received widespread media coverage when it suggested that the amount of time their respondents spent playing video games directly related to 'poorer quality of relationships with peers and parents' (Brigham Young University 2009). Padilla-Walker suggests that she could not be sure whether this was the result of video games taking gamers away from 'normal' social interactions, or whether video games simply attracted those who already had difficulties with interpersonal relationships. Either way, it seems that Padilla-Walker and her colleagues see video gaming as an anti-social activity, and their findings were even more negative for women who played video games, suggesting that those who spent a large amount of time playing video games often had 'low self-esteem' (Brigham Young University 2009). The publication of this study led to international newspaper headlines: *Wall Street Journal*, 'Xbox to Exile? Videogames linked to antisocial behavior' (Silverman 2009), *Telegraph* (UK), 'Computer Game Players "more likely to drink, ignore family and have low self-esteem"' (Devlin 2009).

However, equally there are numerous studies that challenge this wholly negative view of video games and their impact on the social lives of gamers. For instance, Cowell and Payne (2000) in their study of over 200 London schoolchildren found no evidence to suggest that those who regularly played video games had fewer friends. In similar fashion, Fromme (2003) suggests that there is no evidence to support the assertion that playing video games reduces a child's participation in sport. On the contrary, he suggests that his survey had produced some evidence to suggest that 'daily use' of video games was positively associated with increased levels of sport participation. Similarly, my own study (Crawford 2005a) of UK undergraduate students' video gaming and sport participation patterns found no evidence to suggest that playing video games had a negative effect on levels of sport participation, and that sports-themed video games might actually increase interest in, and knowledge of, some sports. As one would expect, the idea of video gaming as anti-social is frequently countered and challenged by the video game industry itself, for example, research undertaken for the Interactive Software Federation of Europe (2010) declares that 58 per cent of all gamers who are parents reported playing video games with their children. Figure 4.1 shows two children playing a video game together, in front of their family.

The view of video gamers as aggressive, or even violent, is another common assumption. One of the clearest illustrations of this can be seen after the Columbine High School shootings of 1999, where no action was taken to control the sale of guns in America, but rather attention was clearly directed towards the tighter control and censorship of violence in the mass media, and in particular video

Figure 4.1 Children playing video games collaboratively in a family setting (photo: G. Crawford)

games. Parent groups of the victims of Columbine filed an (unsuccessful) lawsuit against 25 video game companies, including Acclaim, Activision, Capcom, Eidos, Nintendo, id software, Interplay, Sega, Sony, and the game *Doom* (made by id) was specifically singled out as a key influence on the perpetrators Harris and Klebold (Bryce and Rutter 2006). The question of video game effects is dealt with in Chapter 5 of the present book, but it is important to note here that the academic literature linking increased levels of aggression with patterns of video gameplay is often deeply flawed.

This idea of video games as potentially dangerous, and by extension video gamers as deviants, also extends to the perception of video gamers as 'addicts'. Since the early 1980s, if not before, certain academics have labelled video games as a potentially divisive and addictive pursuit. For instance, writers frequently employ the language of drug addiction when describing the 'need' for video gamers to get a gaming 'fix' (Klein 1984: 396, cited in Newman 2004: 62), or video gamers as 'users' who have games 'pushed' onto them (Grossman 2001, cited in Newman 2004: 63). Though the rather extreme comparisons of video gaming to drug addiction need to be seen as a politicized metaphor rather than truly accurate (Newman 2004), it is evident that the fear of addicted video gamers continues to be a popular, if not a growing, concern and stereotype. Of particular note here is the work Mark Griffiths and his colleagues at Nottingham Trent University (such as Griffiths and Hunt 1997; Griffiths 2002), who continue to pursue research into video game 'addiction'. Though Griffiths is careful to high-light also the possible positive aspects of video games, such as their potential for improving dexterity and that some can teach socially significant skills, the greater part of their work focuses on the dangers of video gaming and how many gamers can demonstrate 'signs of addiction'.

Of course several authors, as well as Griffiths, are keen to highlight the alleged positive aspects of video gaming, which include increased dexterity and hand–eye coordination, social skills, improved motor skills and reaction times (see for example Orosy-Fildes and Allan 1989; Kuhlman and Beitel 1991), while others point to the potential for gaming to be cathartic (for example Kestenbaum and Weinstein 1985). And this is not to mention the fact that video games can be designed in ways that allow them to be used as educational tools or aids. However, being dexterous, learned or calm are not attributes usually associated with video gamers in the popular press or public opinion. However, there are numerous problems with all media effects arguments, be they 'positive' or 'nega-tive', for they cannot account for the numerous ways video games (and other media) are used, experienced, played with, interpreted and reinterpreted by those who consume them, or for how these practices are located within wider social and structural patterns.

The stereotype of video gamers as predominantly white male adolescents is one probably best assessed by turning to video gamer demographics, and more specifically the large number of surveys, both academic and industry-based, that have sought to count, record and measure those who video game.

Counting video gamers

To quote the famous dictum attributed to the former British prime minister Benjamin Disraeli (among others): 'there are lies, damned lies, and statistics'. Statistics are a powerful weapon, because numbers appear to carry the weight of authority and objectivity. Numbers, people frequently assume, do not lie. However, numbers can be presented in a variety of ways: some statistics can be excluded, while others are emphasized, and of course who is asked what ques-tions, as well as numerous other factors, can all radically shape any given statistic. Therefore, when considering any numbers, it is always important to understand not only the origin of the figures, such as how they were collected, who was sampled and so forth, but also the agenda of those presenting them. This is partic-ularly important when considering figures produced by any industry, such as the video game industry, which will invariably use data that present their business, and their customers, in the best possible light.

In the video game industry, the main source of video gamer demographic information is the annual *Essential Facts about the Computer and Video Game Industry* report produced by the main North American video game industry body, the Entertainment and Software Association (ESA). Reading this report it is very clear that the ESA has a particular agenda, which is to counter the commonly held stereotype (see above) of video gamers as exclusively anti-social adolescent boys. The report for 2010 declares that 'more than two-thirds' (67 per cent) of all American households play computer or video games, that the average game player age is 34, and that in fact 26 per cent of Americans over the age of 50 play video games, with women making up 40 per cent of video gamers in the USA (ESA 2010). These statistics are also used to counter the idea of video games as 'dangerous', advocating that over 82 per cent of all video and computer games sold in the USA carried the age restriction rating of 'E' for 'everyone', 'E10+' for everyone over the age of ten, or 'T' for 'teen', and also that 87 per cent believed that video games were 'fun for the entire family', which suggests that most video games are suitable for all age groups.

Similarly, the UK equivalent of the ESA, the UK Interactive Entertainment Association (UKIE, formerly known as the Entertainment and Leisure Software Publishers Association, ELSPA), presents its own statistical evidence, as well as selectively drawing on other, often academic, research to present a particularly positive picture of video gaming. For instance, in March 2009 ELSPA (as it then was) issued a press release based upon research by (unnamed) academics from Nottingham Trent University which suggested that playing 'active' video games (such as Nintendo *Wii Sports* or with the Sony EyeToy) rather than 'traditional' (such as gamepad or mouse-and-keyboard-controlled games) involved, on average, 42 per cent more energy expenditure by video gamers. Citing this research, Michael Rawlinson, director of ELSPA, presented it as evidence of how video games could contribute to 'the recommended daily physical activity for children in the secure environs of their homes' (ELSPA 2009). The assumption here was that young video gamers are not only healthy, but also safe, by carrying out a home-based leisure activity. The idea of the video gamer as 'healthy' is an assertion also advocated in an earlier press release by ELSPA from May 2008, which cited research that suggests that 42 per cent of respondents stated that video games kept them 'mentally healthy' (ELSPA 2008).

It is not to say that these kinds of findings and assertions should be simply mistrusted; they have their value. However, very little information is usually provided on how the data sets are collected and analysed and in the case of secondary data, the original sources are often poorly referenced, making following up this research difficult. It is also important to recognize that organizations representing an industry that is prone to bad press and negative stereotypes issue their own press releases and use the findings of positive reports to convey a very particular image of video gaming as a normal, social and healthy pursuit.

Surveys of this kind, and their presentation, also tend to focus most notably on headline-grabbing statistics, and therefore tend to lack detail on specific aspects of video gaming, such as breaking video gamers down by platform type or genre of video game and so forth. It is evident that different video games, types of video games and game platforms have different player profiles, and here we usually have to look at more specific, and most often academic, studies.

For instance, in 2005 it was proposed (Crawford and Gosling 2005) that female undergraduate respondents to the survey in question were significantly less likely to play sports-themed video games than their male counterparts, the explanation being the propensity for sports-themed video games to feature male participation sports and male-only protagonists. However, this survey also suggested that the female respondents were more likely than their male peers to play video games on their mobile telephones, as the female respondents appeared more interested in simple and quick 'casual' games, frequently found on mobile devices. Furthermore, Griffiths *et al.* (2003) suggest that the MMORPG *EverQuest* does not reflect a typical gender divide of video gamers, with men making up 85 per cent of gamers in the secondary surveys they draw on. However, the survey data that Griffiths *et al.* (2003) utilize in this and other papers (such as Griffiths *et al.* 2004) are taken from respondents to polls posted on two *EverQuest* fan sites (www.everlore.com and everquest.allakhazam.com), so all this actually tells us is that 85 per cent of respondents to this particular survey, on this particular website, stated that they were male, which may or may not bear some relation to the actual demographics of *EverQuest* players.

This raises questions, not just about the findings of this one survey, and its legitimacy as a source for academic papers, but also the validity of all 'gray literatures'. 'Gray literature' refers to non-academic, non-peer-reviewed publications, such as those that can frequently be found on the Internet (Griffiths *et al.* 2004). This is not just academic snobbery, and academic peer-review is not without its problems, but the Internet has opened up a floodgate for self-publication with little or no quality control.

One of the most interesting recent surveys of video gamers and their demographics was commissioned and published by the BBC in the UK in 2005. The BBC, still primarily a broadcast-focused, non-profit, publicly owned institution, may have less invested interest in advocating a particular image of the video gamer. However, the BBC's government-funded position means that it always has to justify its remit, market share and viability, so in some respects this report could be seen as the BBC's attempt to understand a newly developing media market, as well as stake its interest, and possible future active role, within this sector – which we have started to see with its production of online games such as *Doctor Who: The Adventure Game*.

This BBC report suggests that 59 per cent of 6- to 65-year-olds in the UK (their sample group) are 'gamers' (defined by the fact that they indicated that they had played a game on a console, PC, the Internet, mobile, handheld device or interactive TV in the last six months), and 48 per cent of 6- to 65-year-olds stated that they played at least once per week (Pratchett 2005). The average age of these gamers was 28, and their gender divide was fairly balanced, averaging out at 45 per cent female and 55 per cent male (Pratchett 2005). What is particularly useful about this report is that it does provide at least some level of information about its methodology and sample, in addition to providing specific information about the video gaming habits of different age groups, as well as where people play video games, on what, what technologies they own, preferred gaming genres and so forth. This means that, to date, this is probably one of the most comprehensive and useful profiles (at least in the UK) of who plays video games.

However, given the present author's geographical location and limited language capability, the data highlighted above are inevitably Anglophone-centric, and it is evident that video gamer profiles vary across Europe, and certainly across the world. For instance, Martin *et al.* (2006) suggests that only 20 per cent of the population in Spain play video games, some way below the European average, though women do appear to make up a respectable proportion of this, constituting just under 40 per cent of Spanish video gamers, while Krotoski (2004) suggests that in Korea women make up to close on 70 per cent of all video gamers. However, leaving aside my cultural naiveties, it is certainly the case that a lot less is known about the demographics of video gamers outside of the Anglophone world, and certainly more cross-national and cross-cultural research is necessary. Furthermore, information of this kind usually tells us only something about those who do game, and very little, if anything, about those who do not, or why?

Gender and excluded gamers

One way in which video gamers are often defined is in relation to who they are not; in other words, who is excluded from, or marginalized within, video game culture. Here, most frequently, and most notably, the literature focuses upon the marginalization and exclusion of women as video gamers.

As already suggested, video gaming has often been seen as an almost exclusively male activity, with research in the 1980s and 90s consistently suggesting that video gaming was dominated by male participation (see Colwell *et al.* 1995 and Buchanan and Funk 1996). In particular, Bryce and Rutter (2003b) offer some possible explanations as to why women have been traditionally marginalized as video gamers. First, women continue to be much more restricted in their leisure choices and opportunities than men. This is due to numerous social factors, such as restrictions placed upon women's presence in many public places, economic constraints, domestic and caring responsibilities, the limited leisure time of many women and social expectations of women's location and roles within society (see also Enevold and Hagström 2008, 2009, 2010). Second, women often lack equal access to technology. For instance, it is evident that boys tend to dominate computer technology at school, and, hence, computers frequently prove 'unpopular' with many girls (Green 2001). Third, it is argued that the themes and goals of video games often do not reflect the interests of many women. Kinder (1991) suggests that video games are primarily designed for male audiences, and most commonly feature 'male' themes, such as violence and sport, and tend to lack female protagonists. Moreover, when female characters are featured within video games, they are usually portrayed in sexualized or passive roles (Greenfield 1996; Kafai 1996; Dietz 1998; Bryce and Rutter 2002). Women often fulfil a peripheral and marginalized role within video game culture: they are the parent who buys video games for their children, or, as Bryce and Rutter (2002) observe, the mothers or girlfriends who accompany their sons or boyfriends to LAN events and competitions (see Figure 4.2).

However, over the last decade or so many have suggested that the number of female video gamers has started to increase, as women begin to make inroads into this (once) male-dominated domain (Cassell and Jenkins 2000). As both a consequence of and contributing factor to these changes, Bryce and Rutter (2003a) suggest that the themes and content of many video games have become less gendered, with more featuring female characters and fewer 'male'-dominated

Figure 4.2 An 'uninterested'-looking 'girlfriend' at a LAN event (photo: G. Crawford)

themes and narratives. Nonetheless, it is notable that most studies on female video game participation rates have focused on school-age girls, and surveys of older participants tend to be less optimistic in their findings. Our (Crawford and Gosling 2005) survey of undergraduate students suggests that adult (18–55-year-old) female respondents were still considerably less likely to play video games, and those that did tended to play them a lot less frequently than their male peers.

It still appears that the majority of video gamers, in most countries (with the odd few exceptions), are still men, and the most popular video games still feature male-centric themes such as sport and violence. However, this does not necessarily mean things cannot change, or even that they are not currently changing. It is certainly apparent that the kinds of video games available are expanding to include more 'active' and 'casual' games, such as music games like *Guitar*

Hero, Rock Band, Singstar and *Lips*, dance games like *Dance Central*, and quiz- or puzzle-type games like *Buzz* or *Dr Kawashima's Brain Training*. Video game hardware innovations, such as the Nintendo Wiimote controller, the Sony EyeToy and Move, and Microsoft's Xbox Kinect, as well as advances in mobile telephone technologies, such as the Apple iPhone, and the popularity of mobile telephone gaming, such as *Mafia Wars* and *Farmville*, are all changing the way many people play and view video games (see Chapter 8). And significantly, the kinds of games that are being made possible, and increasingly common, are those that have often proved popular with many female gamers (Crawford and Gosling 2005).

The kinds of video games listed above, such as party and music games like *Singstar* and *Dance Dance Revolution* and those played on mobile telephones such as *Mafia Wars*, are often referred to as 'casual games' and the players of these as 'casual players'. This subject is considered in more detail in Chapter 8, but it is important to note that several authors, and most notably Juul (2008, 2009), have questioned the clear distinction between 'casual' and 'hardcore' games and gamers. For example, our previous research (Crawford and Gosling 2005) suggests that some women who play video games on their mobile telephones may invest a considerable amount of time and effort in it, and hence, at least for some, their patterns of play are far from 'casual'. It would also be wrong to assume that women play only casual games. In particular, research such as Taylor (2003, 2006) and Enevold and Hagström (2008), to offer but two examples, suggests that MMORPGs such as *EverQuest* and *World of Warcraft* are popular with many female gamers. Taylor (2003) suggests this is because MMORPGs provide women with freedom and opportunities frequently denied to them away from the in-game environment. For instance, MMORPGs allow women the freedom to explore online worlds and in-game 'public' spaces and compete with men on a more equal footing, something which is often denied to women.

It is important that academic literature does not just acknowledge women as a minority or excluded from video game culture, but also seeks to understand their participation and role within it. This is a point made by Shaw (2010: 409), who argues that 'what is necessary is a critical reexamination of the place of women and girls in spaces of gaming culture that have been traditionally defined as male', and growing and important work in this area includes that of Enevold and Hagström (2008, 2009, 2010) (discussed further in Chapter 8). Furthermore, it is important to recognize that women are not a monolithic market and not all women enjoy the same kinds of video games, and, in particular, not all female gamers want video games specifically designed for women, particularly those based upon often sexist gender stereotypes. In this respect, Bryce and Rutter (2003a) high- light the literature on 'oppositional reading', such as the work of Hall (1980) (see Chapter 3), which suggests that audiences can often reinterpret and 'play' with cultural texts. They point to Yates and Littleton's (2001) consideration of female gamers, who they suggest often 'reinterpret' games such as *Tomb Raider*. In particular, Yates and Littleton (2001: 113) argue that though 'Tomb Raider sets up a classic male ... position for the player ... in which the female (in this case Lara Croft) is passively watched', it also offers, particularly female video gamers, the opportunity to take the position of an active female character. Cassell and

Jenkins (2000) also highlight the popularity of so-called 'male' genres of video gaming, such as first-person-shooters, like *Quake* and *Doom*, with certain female (or 'grrl') gamers. This is supported in our earlier research (Crawford and Gosling 2005), which included female gamers who suggested that they enjoyed playing traditional 'male' genres of games, such as sport-themed games. For instance, 'Cathy' (female, aged 20) indicated that playing *FIFA* was a regular social event in her student household, and, moreover, conversations about this football-themed video game would often continue away from the game and household.

> We [her student household] got *FIFA* on the *PSOne* [PlayStation] and we talk about that all the time, like who beat who, and how we're gonna get 'em back so bad next time … it's such a laugh really.
>
> Crawford and Gosling 2005: 416

However, there is still too little written on how women game, and how video games are located within the social networks, everyday lives and identity formations of female video gamers. Moreover, discussions of the exclusion, as well as participation, of video gamers in relation to other lines of social stratification, such as ethnicity, disability, sexuality and social class, are still extremely rare.

There does exist a growing literature on video games, race and ethnicity, which includes Chan (2005), Byrne (2008), Everett and Watkins (2008), Higgin (2009), Leonard (2004, 2006, 2009) and Massie (2011). This remains a significantly under-researched area, however, particularly when compared with the sizeable amount of work done on gender and video gaming. In addition, most of this research has focused almost exclusively on textual analysis and the representation of race and ethnicity in video games. For instance, Massie (2011) considers the representation of race, as well as gender, in the MMORPG *EverQuest* and notes how characters with black skin are deemed in-game to be a completely different race, with different attributes, from 'Human' characters, who are invariably white.

Leonard (2004) discusses how the majority of protagonists in many sport-themed games are white, and when black and minority ethnic characters do appear they are often racially stereotyped and placed in stereotypical locations, such as urban ghettoes. In particular, Leonard highlights how sport-themed games such as *NFL Street* (Leonard 2004) and urban gangster-themed games like *Grand Theft Auto: San Andreas* (Leonard 2009) perpetuate stereotypes of the urban ghetto and 'common-sense' ideas of black people as 'naturally' gifted but aggressive, spending most of their time playing or fighting, rather than working. Leonard suggests that many video games are specifically designed by, and targeted towards, young white men, and that these video games give white players the opportunity to play with race and put on (in Leonard's terms) 'blackface'. However, Leonard argues, this is not done in a way that transgresses or challenges racial boundaries, but rather reinforces traditional racial stereotypes.

Textual analysis of video games can provide an important and potentially fruitful area for further analysis, and authors such as Leonard (2006) and Massie (2011) offer useful examples of this. However, there exists very little research on black and minority ethnic video gamers. Research on video games and social class is even rarer. Some does exist, but it is rather hard to find. For instance, some studies consider the social class of video gamers, but this is usually discussed in relation to other forms of social stratifications (such as gender and ethnicity), hence there is rarely any detailed consideration of how class affects and shapes patterns of play and video game cultures. For instance, Greenfield and Cocking (1996) highlight how social class affects, in a rather straightforward way, what video games and technologies can be purchased, and also how class can shape video game choices, suggesting that middle-class parents are more likely to encourage their children to play, and buy for them, video games that involve puzzle-solving or odyssey-like exploration, as opposed to the more working-class choices, which tend to favour military or urban-themed video games. Greenfield and Cocking's (1996) consideration of video gaming and social class, and this area of research generally, is, however, rather limited and desperately in need of further examination.

In terms of disability, there is some academic work on video game accessibility and also on how video games can be used in physical and mental rehabilitation, such as the work of Green and Bavelier (2006), who discuss the utilization of video games for improving visual processing, or Armiger and Vogelstein's (2008) work on the use of a modified game controller used with the game *Guitar Hero III* as a way for training amputees. Of particular note here is the work of Fern Delamere (2011), who considers *Second Life* as a place that allows those with disabilities to learn new communication and technical skills, to grow in confidence and develop social capital (discussed further in Chapter 6). However, there is still not currently enough research like this, which focuses on the video gameplay of individuals with disabilities.

Similarly, there is very little research on video gaming and sexuality. Notable exceptions include Mia Consalvo's (2003), and Jenny Sundén's (2009) developing ethnographic work on *World of Warcraft*. For instance, Sundén explores the heteronormativity of video game texts, and also, through participation observations and interviews, how gay video gamers negotiate and reinterpret game spaces, characters and interactions. However, this is certainly another area that demands greater academic attention.

Video gamer types

The fourth area I wish to consider is how video gamers are categorized and conceptualized into 'types' of gamers. Probably the most widely used categorization (or typology or taxonomy) of video gamers is that offered by Richard A. Bartle (1996, 2003). Richard Bartle is an academic and video game designer who most famously, along with his fellow University of Essex student Roy Trubshaw, created the video game *MUD* (also know as *MUD1*) in the late 1970s, the game that would give its name to a whole genre, the multi-user dungeon (or domain). Bartle was not the first, and is certainly not the only, author to have noted that people play video games in different ways, but his categorization of play (and player) types has become the starting point for many subsequent writers. Bartle informs us that his typology developed out of discussions with experienced players of the video game *MUD2* in 1989 and 1990 about 'what do players want out of a MUD?' (Bartle 1996). In particular, he noted four key types of in-game activity that players highlighted as important. These were:

- 'Achievement within the game context' – this describes video gamers who are primarily interested in achieving certain game-related goals, such as amassing large quantities of game treasure or a certain number of kills.
- 'Exploration of the game' – Bartle identifies the pleasure a video gamer receives from finding out about the 'virtual world', such as mapping its geography or experimenting with its physics.
- 'Socializing with others' – this refers to the enjoyment video gamers get from utilizing the game's communicative facilities, to connect with fellow gamers, and also the pleasures derived from role-playing within video games.
- 'Imposition upon others' – this refers to video gamers who, in the game, impose themselves on others, most commonly aggressively, by for example attacking or 'griefing' (causing deliberate annoyance) another player, but Bartle suggests that this can also refer to non-aggressive forms of imposition, such as helping other gamers.

From these four types of in-game action, Bartle proposes what he refers to as a 'simple taxonomy' of four player types, each relating to a particular style of play. These he terms 'achievers', 'explorers', 'socializers' and 'killers', or drawing on the metaphor of playing cards, 'diamonds', 'spades', 'hearts' and 'clubs'; diamonds referring to achievers, as they seek treasure, spades to explorers, as they dig for information, hearts are socializers as they empathize with others, and clubs are killers, as they hit other players with objects, such as clubs.

Significantly, Bartle (1996) asserts that this is not a rigid and inflexible taxonomy, as 'players will often drift between all four [types/styles of play], depending on their mood or current playing style'. However, he suggests that 'many (if not most) players do have a primary style, and will only switch to other styles as a (deliberate or subconscious) means to advance their main interest'.

Several other authors have, either independently (such as Farmer 1992; Rosewater 2002, 2006, 2007) or building upon Bartle's work (such as Aarseth 2003; Yee 2006; Jackson *et al.* 2008), offered alternative or expanded typologies of player types or styles. For instance, Mark Rosewater (2002, 2006) develops a categorization of players of the collectable card game *Magic: The Gathering*, which shares many similarities to Bartle's player types. (Though *Magic: The Gathering* is originally, and still primarily, a card-based game, several video game versions have also been released.) Rosewater proposes the player types of 'Timmy', to refer to 'power gamers' who like big and impressive cards, 'Johnny', who are more sociable gamers, and 'Spike', who are tournament players who want to win at any cost. Finally, Rosewater later (2007) adds to this 'Melvin' and 'Vorthos' to refer to gamers who are more interested in the mechanism of the game or its 'mood' and 'tone', respectively. Alternatively, Aarseth (2003) offers an expansion of Bartle's original categorization, suggesting the addition of a fifth category, that of 'cheater', to describe those who either implicitly or explicitly break the rules of play as set out by the video game. This category could also be expanded to include what has been termed by authors such as Salen and Zimmerman (2004) and Newman (2008) 'emergent play', where video gamers exploit bugs and glitches in the video game, to engage in acts of play not envisaged by the game designers.

Another significant development of Bartle's model is offered by Jackson *et al.* (2008), who develop their model based upon research on children playing the Children's BBC (CBBC) online game *Adventure Rock*. In their subsequent report, Jackson *et al.* suggest that Bartle's original model does not fully account for the styles of play they encountered in *Adventure Rock*, and therefore propose an expanded list of eight what they term 'orientations' to this game world. The orientations are as follows (Jackson *et al.* 2008: 19–20):

- Explorer-investigator
  Interested in: following a quest, solving a mystery, going on a journey, being 'outdoors'.
  Likely to be: the more confident children, no age or gender difference.
  Characteristics: examines the detail, curious and communicative, imaginative engagement with the mystery.

- Self-stampers
  Interested in: presenting themselves in the world.
  Likely to be: both genders, possibly more older children.
  Characteristics: boys and girls wanted to 'make their mark' on their avatar, and perhaps have their own face there; older girls wanted to dress her up and have a make-up studio in *Adventure Rock*. Both boys and girls wanted to express themselves through the creation of a home/base.

- Social climbers
  Interested in: ranking, social position within the environment.
  Likely to be: both younger and older children; only some gender bias (boys slightly more than girls).
  Characteristics: competitive; concerned with ranking and exhibiting that rank to others.

- Fighters
  Interested in: death and destruction, violence and superpowers.
  Likely to be: male, slightly biased towards older boys.
  Characteristics: in *Adventure Rock*, frustrated that they did not have a means to express themselves, with the exception of beating crocodiles.

- Collector-consumers
  Interested in: accumulating anything of perceived value within the system.
  Likely to be: older boys and girls.
  Characteristics: collects pages and coins. Wanted *Adventure Rock* to have shops, enabling *gift-giving*, establish an economic system, and have somewhere to put things.

- Power-users
  Interested in: giving everyone the benefit of their knowledge and experience.
  Likely to be: expert in the games, the geography of the environment, the systems.
  Characteristics: spent more than three hours at a time playing/exploring. *Adventure Rock*. An interest in how the game works.

- Life-system builders
  Interested in: creating new lands, new elements to the environment, populating the environment.
  Likely to be: younger children (imagined world without rules), and older children (imagined world with rules and systems – houses, schools, shops, transport, economy).
  Characteristics: in *Adventure Rock* frustrated that they did not have a means to express themselves.

- Nurturers
  Interested in: looking after their avatar.
  Likely to be: younger boys and girls, and older girls.
  Characteristics: wanted to meet and play with others. Wanted to teach their avatar to swim, and somewhere for the avatar to sleep. Wanted pets to look after.

Though Jackson *et al.* develop their model to account for the styles of play of children playing one specific video game, this model is useful as it expands and considers styles of play not specifically addressed by Bartle. Significantly, it also aligns styles of play with particular genders and ages of players, suggesting that boys and girls of different ages will tend towards certain styles of play more than others. This is also suggested in the research of Nick Yee.

Nick Yee's model of video game player types and motivations (such as 2006) again uses Bartle's work as its starting point. Yee's work, based upon an online questionnaire of players of a number of different MMORPGs, suggests three key motivations for players, which he terms 'achievement', 'social' and 'immersion'. Yee suggests that each of the motivations involves a number of sub-elements (see Table 4.1). For instance, 'immersion' involves elements of 'discovery', 'role-playing', 'customization' and 'escapism', and different players will emphasize, and be more keenly motivated by, different aspects of the game.

Yee (2008) suggests that there were some difference in types of motivation in relation to gender, such as women being more likely to emphasize 'socializing', 'relationship' and 'customization' as key motivations for play, with men tending to be more driven by 'advancement', 'mechanics' and 'competition' motivations. However, Yee argues that these differences were not particularly striking, and there appears significant overlap in men's and women's motivations for play. In particular, Yee suggests that key differences in motivations were more likely to be explained by age than gender. For instance, he indicates that older players were less likely to be achievement-orientated, and since women in his survey were

Table 4.1 Factor analysis framework for MMO play motivations

Achievement	Social	Immersion
Advancement progress, power, accumulation, status	Socializing casual chat, helping others, making friends	Discovery exploration, lore, finding hidden things
Mechanics numbers, optimization, templating, analysis	Relationship personal, self-disclosure, find and give support	Role-playing story line, character history, roles, fantasy
Competition challenging others, provocation, domination	Teamwork collaboration, groups, group achievements	Customization appearances, accessories, style, colour schemes
		Escapism relax, escape from real life, avoid real-life problems

Source: Yee 2006: 773.

more likely to be older than his average male respondent, it is their age, and not necessarily their gender, that accounts for fewer women indicating that they were motivated by game achievements.

What can be confusing is that these typologies, as well as the numerous others that exist but are not covered here, often seek to categorize different aspects of gameplay. For instance, Jackson *et al.* set out a model of 'orientations' to play, while Yee is concerned with 'motivations' and Bartle with both 'styles' of play and 'types' of players. That is to say, these models seek to explain either who plays video games, how they play or why they play. In most typologies these three aspects are often conflated, and most notably by Bartle. There seems to be an inherent assumption that there are certain types of gamers, who have specific motivations to play video games, which shape their style of play. For example, in Bartle's model there are 'achievers', who play video games because they seek to achieve certain goals, and in their gameplay will undertake actions that enable them to achieve what they set out to do. However, there is often little consideration of what comes first, and whether there is always an irreversible correlation between types of players, their motivations and styles of play. For instance, is there some pre-existing social or psychological desire to be an 'achiever' which makes someone want to play a particular video game and how they play it? Though Bartle suggests that video gamers can move between types and styles, there is still, in how these categories are articulated and used, a sense of (at least semi-) permanency and some rigidity. Furthermore, most research-developed typologies (such as Yee's model) are based upon respondents' self-categorization. That is to say, how *they* see their style of play. However, it does not necessarily hold true that this is how others would see or label them. For example, an individual may declare that they enjoy playing a particular video game as it allows them to be brave and assertive, but others may deem the gamer's style of play as cowardly. There are always multiple ways of reading actors and actions.

Therefore, the majority of categorizations of video gamers give the impression that there are set types of video gamers who are motivated by certain aspects of the video game and play in certain ways, and though there may be some degree of flexibility, these types still largely hold true and stable. What is lacking from most video gamer categorizations is a sense of progress, change and subjectivity; video gamers seem to be cast as a type, which they largely adhere to and remain, and which others would similarly use to describe them.

It is again here that the literature on audience and fan research might prove useful. Though the audience and fan literature similarly contains many examples of rigid taxonomies of types of individuals, an alternative body of work considers audience and fan 'careers'.

Video gamer careers

The idea of a social or 'moral' career develops out of the work of the French ethnographer Arnold van Gennep's (1908) concept of 'status passage'. Van Gennep uses this idea to describe the passage of an individual through various stages in a life course, such as shifting from being unmarried to married. This has been expanded greatly within sociology, most notably by successive generations of academics associated with the University of Chicago, to incorporate the study of processes of career progression and socialization (Glaser 1968).

Goffman (1968) suggests that 'career' is usually linked to ideas of progression within formal organizations, but can also constitute any form of everyday social development. For example, Goffman (1968) presents a consideration of the 'moral' career of 'mental patients'. For Goffman (1968: 119) the career of the 'mental patient' is a moral one as it involves the development of an individual's identity and 'entails [changes] in the person's self and his framework of imagery for judging himself and others'. The concept of career allows for a two-sided view of progress, where 'one side is linked to internal matters ... such as self and felt identity; the other side concerns official position, jural relations, and style of life' (Goffman 1968: 119). Hence, the concept of a career is based upon both ascribed and achieved status or, as Goffman argues (1968: 119), 'allows one to move back and forth between the personal and the public, between the self and its significant society'.

The idea of a social or moral career has been applied by a number of academics to fan and audience studies, for example in the work of Moorhouse (1991) on hot-rod enthusiasts, Marsh (1982) on 'football hooligans' and my own work (Crawford 2004) on sport fans more generally. Similarly, it has been suggested by several writers on video game culture that gamers could be considered as following a career path involving aspects of socialization, tuition and social progression. T.L. Taylor's (2006) work on players of *EverQuest*, for instance, offers a good overview of processes of video gamer induction, tuition and social progression. Taylor (2006: 35) writes: 'new players are acculturated into the game and essentially taught not only how to play, but how to *be*' (emphasis in original). Furthermore, Taylor's discussion of the more sociable aspects of playing *EverQuest*, such as the development of in-game responsibilities and reputations, can be conceived as socialization along a video gamer career path.

Lin and Sun (2008) in their consideration of players and observers of the arcade-based video game *Dance Dance Revolution* suggest a three-stage career development path, from 'newbie' to 'apprentice' to 'expert'. Each of these steps is associated with, and defined by, certain patterns of behaviour. Lin and Sun suggest, for example, that 'newbies' are less likely to perform in front of others, and are less knowledgeable about the social intricacies and etiquettes of play. Importantly, Lin and Sun assert that these labels are the result of both individual and group definition, are subject to change and that individuals, through observation and tuition, can learn and progress to a new career step. Lin and Sun also highlight the fact that most typologies and considerations of video gamers overlook the important role of onlookers, who not only have an influence on the nature of play, but also themselves have specific social roles and norms that are learned.

Similarly, Steve Conway (2010) proposes that my (Crawford 2003, 2004) model of sport fan career progression (Figure 4.3) could be applied to understanding video gamers. In those papers (Crawford 2003, 2004) I set out a fluid, seven-stage career path, represented in Figure 4.3.

The use of verbs in Figure 4.3 is purposeful, to indicate types of action, rather than types of individuals. Put simply, this suggests that individuals can become interested in a subject, such as video games, and then through a process of practice and tuition become more engaged with this hobby and culture, leading to enthusiasm and possible devotion. For some, it may lead to them becoming 'professionalized', making some profit from their hobby, or even becoming employed full-time in this industry, and hence part of its apparatus. This model could also be used to incorporate onlookers, who could be seen to follow the same career path as video gamers (for instance, onlookers could be seen as 'interested' parties) or similarly onlookers could be seen to follow a different, but intersecting career path. A model of career progression allows much more room for fluidity and complexity, where career progression is not necessarily incremental or unidirectional, as individuals can leap certain stages, advance, as well as retreat, along a career path; multiple career paths can cross-cut; while career paths themselves are also constantly in development and flux.

Conway (2010) suggests that career progression of this nature can be seen with *Pro Evolution Soccer* players, for example, in their game-skill rankings posted online at pesrankings.com, and in the way that certain individuals can go on to become professionalized and play in competitions for prize money, sometimes sizeable. It could be argued that the career path of a video gamer is more complex than that of a sport fan, for which this model (Crawford 2003, 2004) was primarily developed, because the lines between consumers and producers are more blurred in relation to video games than other fan groups. However, this is not an argument

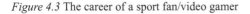

Figure 4.3 The career of a sport fan/video gamer

I would necessarily agree with. There is a long history of, and substantial literature on, the productivity of media fans. Though certain games, such as Sony's *Little Big Planet*, have increased the opportunity for video gamers to produce game elements that others can play, the proportion of video gamers doing so is still relatively small, and they are usually not making any direct economic profit from this. Similarly, the number making game add-ons, mods and so forth (see Chapter 7) is also relatively small, and these activities could easily be located within 'devoted' and 'professional' career points.

Adopting a theorization of career progression does, therefore, have several advantages over using traditional categories or typologies. First, it moves away from restrictive typologies that can caricature patterns of behaviour and force individuals into rigid 'types'. Second, it allows for an understanding of how an individual's position within a career structure can change and develop over time. Third, and relatedly, it also permits a consideration of how the career structure and community itself can change and develop over time. Fourth, since career paths do not categorize individuals as types, it allows for a greater understanding of the fluidity of contemporary identities and social roles, allowing a consideration of how individuals can follow several, often intersecting, career paths, such as following the career paths of being a science teacher, a science fiction fan and a player of *Star Trek Online*.

Chapter summary

- 'Who plays video games?' is a rather complex, but still significant, question for video game studies, as answering this determines important parameters of research. This chapter suggests that most notably there have been four key approaches to answering this question.
- First, many studies focus upon the 'types' of individuals who they see as constituting video gamers; however, these are often based upon simple and common stereotypes.
- Second, survey data are often used to advance specific arguments (such as a more 'positive' view of video gamers), but often lack detailed information on video gamers' behaviour and video game culture.
- Third, a focus on excluded video gamers provides strong evidence to suggest that women remain marginalized as video gamers, but there still exists very little research on other patterns of exclusion, and even less on the participants of marginal groups within video gaming culture.
- The fourth section focuses most notably on typologies of video gamers. It is suggested that the most commonly used and adapted typology of video gamers is that developed by Bartle (1996, 2003), which places video gamers into the categories of 'achiever', 'explorer', 'socializer' and 'killer'; or to use Bartle's playing cards metaphor, 'diamonds', 'spades', 'hearts' and 'clubs'.
- Several authors have expanded or adapted Bartle's original model. Aarseth simply proposes the addition of a 'cheater' category to this model, while others offer a more substantial overhaul, such as Jackson *et al.* (2008), who expand this model to cover eight categories, which also account for differences in play-styles as a result of gender and age.

- However, these typologies often suffer from a number of key weaknesses. They often conflate types of video gamers with motivations and styles of play. They are also usually based upon players' own definitions of their styles of play, and tend to categorize individuals into fairly rigid types.
- It is therefore suggested that a theorization of a 'social career' may offer a more dynamic model. The idea of a social or moral career has been applied by several authors to different audience and fan types (see Crawford 2003), and similarly several writers on video gameplay (see Conway 2010) suggest that video gamers follow a career path of induction, tuition and progression.
- The advantages of a career model is that this avoids categorizing video gamers as types of individuals, it allows for change, both within individual or group patterns as well as within the model itself, and it recognizes that individuals will be engaged with many, often cross-cutting career paths.

Further reading

Bartle, R. (2003) *Designing Virtual Worlds*, Indianapolis: New Riders.

Crawford, G. (2003) 'The Career of the Sport Supporter: the case of the Manchester Storm', *Sociology*, 37 (2), 219–37.

Enevold, J. and Hagström, C. (2008) 'My Momma Shoots Better Than You! Who is the female gamer?', *[Player] Conference Proceedings, Copenhagen: IT University of Copenhagen, 26–29 August 2008*, Copenhagen: IT University of Copenhagen, 144–67.

Goffman, E. (1968) *Asylums*, Harmondsworth: Penguin Books.

5 Key aspects of video gameplay

Introduction

This chapter considers a number of themes that have been indentified in the literature as key components or elements of video games and their gameplay. It is the longest chapter in the book, but it is also inevitably the most incomplete, as each of these areas, such as narrative, interactivity and geography, is in itself an area that has received a significant amount of discussion and is often a key battleground in contemporary video game debates. This chapter therefore aims to provide a brief introduction to key aspects of video gameplay and associated arguments.

As Chapter 1 showed, an early 'schism' within (video) game studies was the debate surrounding the relative importance of play (ludic) and narrative (representational) components of a video game (Dovey and Kennedy 2006). Though it is possible to find examples of rather entrenched advocacy for both sides of this debate, most writers readily admit that video games cannot be wholly reduced to either their play or storytelling elements (Mäyrä 2008: 10). The model that seems to have emerged out of this early debate is an understanding of video games as consisting of both ludic and representational elements, both of which need to be understood in any analysis of video games. However, as the study of video games has matured and expanded, calls to recognize and consider the social context of video games have become increasingly loud. This has subsequently led to the addition of a third, 'social' element or dimension to video game analysis, which has been labelled as, for example, 'the rest of the world' (Juul 2005), the 'communal' (Burn and Carr 2006) or 'context' (Mäyrä 2008).

Juul (2005: 37), for instance, presents a tripartite model of 'the game', 'the player' and 'the rest of the world', which is based upon his definition of 'the classic game' (as discussed in Chapter 1). In this model, 'the game' consists, for example, of elements such as rules and outcomes of play, 'the player' includes values the player attaches to outcomes and 'the rest of the world' relates to the negotiable consequences the game has beyond the instance of play.

Burn and Carr's (2006) tripartite model is developed from their analysis of motivations for playing the MMORPG *Anarchy Online*, which they present as consisting of 'representation', 'ludic' and 'communal' aspects of play; but this is a model that could easily be applied to other video games beyond *Anarchy Online*. Burn and Carr (2006), as well as other authors such as such as Kerr *et al.* (2004), focus on the motivations or pleasures of video gameplay, but in seeking to understand what aspects of a video game individuals find most attractive, simultaneously seek to understand the composite components of a video game's structure and play. For Burn and Carr (2006: 104) representation 'involves visual imagery, characterization, performance and narrative factors'. The ludic 'relate[s] directly to gameplay, to the skills necessarily acquired, the rules, competition, statistics and objective'. Finally, they define the communal as the 'social' and 'shared nature' of the video game. Though Kerr *et al.* (2004) focus primarily on elements of 'play' and 'text', they break these down further to the play components of 'immersion', 'control', 'performance', and the textual elements of 'narrative' and 'intertextuality'.

The model Mäyrä (2008) sets out is similar to those presented above, in that it divides video games into the elements of 'game', 'player' and 'context'. However, the advantage to Mäyrä's model is that context is not simply a third and separate element, but is rather presented as two frameworks in which the game and the player are set, which he depicts in a useful Venn diagram (see Figure 5.1). Mäyrä provides no justification for why he represents the context of the game as largely separate, though intersecting with, the context of the player. However, I presume this is done to signify that the player may decode the game in a different way from how it is encoded.

The models outlined above, as well as the wider literature on video game analysis, suggest a number of key components to a video game. From this we can then construct a list of key video gameplay elements, which include:

* rules
* effects
* interactivity
* immersion, engagement and flow
* performance
* identity, roles and embodiment
* intertextuality and transmedia
* narrative and content analysis
* geography.

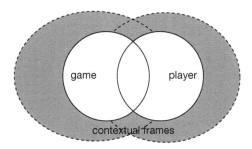

Figure 5.1 The focus of game studies in the interaction between game and player, informed by their various contextual frames (Mäyrä 2008: 2)

This is not a necessarily exhaustive list, and I recognize that setting out a list like this will inevitably invite others to highlight what or who is missing; but I invite this. The aim of this book is not to provide all of the answers to video gamer analysis, but rather to provide steps that might carry this debate forward. For instance, two areas that could, and possibly should, be added to this list are 'production' and 'aesthetics, design and interface'. Of course, they are crucially important areas, which do impact on the video gamer, but my feeling is that a focus on areas such as production and game design begins to move beyond my specific focus on the video gamer *per se*, and so I leave their study to other authors better equipped to do this, such as Aphra Kerr (2006) on the video game industry, Ernest Adams (2010) on game design and Graeme Kirkpatrick (2011) on game aesthetics.

Furthermore, the elements in the list above should not be seen as necessarily separate and coherent, as each will inevitably run into and cross over with many of the other elements. For instance, narratives will often (arguably always) draw on intertextual components, and a good narrative can add to a player's immersion, as do the rule system and a video game's geography. It is tempting to group this list into a meta-list, where rules, interactivity and geography could be understood as elements of 'the game', immersion, performance and identity categorized as 'the player' and intertextuality and narratives as elements of 'representation'. This would then raise the question of whether 'context' or 'the social' needs to be added as a fourth meta-category. However, it is not particularly easy or wise to categorize these elements as being wholly about either the game, representation or the player. For example, geography plays a key role both in the video game (the game world in which the video game is set) and the context in which the video game is played (the physical location of the game machine and its players). Also, I resist adding 'the social' or 'context' as an additional category, as it is my assertion that the social comes into, and defines, all of the elements, and therefore is not external or additional to any of them.

Rules

It is evident that many, particularly ludology-focused, writers consider rules to be one of the most important elements of games. In particular, the presence of rules is a key feature of Juul's (2005: 36) definition of what a classic game is. As he writes: 'games are rule-bound' (see Chapter 1). A similar assertion is made by Salen and Zimmerman (2004: 117), who, in their book *The Rules of Play*, argue that 'to play a game is to follow rules'. Salen and Zimmerman suggest that all games have rules, and, therefore, it is this dimension that unites all games, whether a sport, playground game, boardgame or video game. For writers such as Juul and Salen and Zimmerman, rules are at the very core of a game's identity. Though other elements, such as narrative, history, player demographics and so forth, may contribute to the meaning of a game, they are all seen as secondary to the game's rule system, as it is this that gives the game what Salen and Zimmerman term its 'formal identity'.

Salen and Zimmerman (2004) suggest that all game rules share six general characteristics:

- rules limit action
- rules are explicit and unambiguous
- rules are shared by all players
- rules are fixed
- rules are binding
- rules are repeatable.

However, they then suggest that 'some games question and violate these characteristics' (Salen and Zimmerman 2004: 125), which does question how general these characteristics are. Certainly, Juul (2005) challenges the idea that rules necessarily limit action. Juul suggests, for example, that it is the rules of chess that allow a player to perform a checkmate: without this particular rule, this move would not be possible. Therefore, rules not only limit action, but can also allow and enable it. For Juul, a better way of understanding rules is to consider what they make possible, as well as what they preclude. Here, he draws on Goffman's (1961) notion of 'rules of irrelevance', which suggests that in a game certain things will be deemed relevant, whiles others ignored or precluded (see Chapter 2 for Goffman on play).

Salen and Zimmerman (2004: 130) also identify three different types of rules, which they distinguish as follows:

- Operational rules – these are the 'rules of play', the guidelines that are required for play to take place.
- Constitutive rules – these are the underlying formal structures which exist below the surface of the game, such as the logical and mathematical processes inherent in the game.
- Implicit rules – this refers to the 'unwritten rules of a game', such as rules of etiquette, 'sportsmanship' and other less formal rules.

For example, in the video game *Counter-Strike*, an operational game rule would be that a player cannot carry more than 120 rounds for their Glock pistol. A constitutive rule would be the program behind the game which enables it to operate, such as allowing the gamer to collect Glock pistol ammunition up to a maximum of 120 rounds. An implicit rule would cover rules of etiquette when playing *Counter-Strike*, such as those prohibiting 'camping', that is, remaining in one place for a long time and waiting for opponents to come to you (see Wright *et al.* 2002).

The 'implicit' or social rules governing play can be extremely complex, and in many respects just as important, if not more so, than those embedded in the game system itself. For instance, Myers (2009: 57) discussing online video gameplay suggests that it frequently 'generate[s] strict social hierarchies with strong normative guidelines, often only peripherally related to game goals'. Nielsen *et al.* (2008: 28) provide the example of how players of the strategy game *Age of Empires II* often spend a great amount of time setting out legitimate strategies and tactics in online forums before playing the video game itself.

Chapter 1 showed that there are many writers who assert that the nature of rules in video games can be quite different from those in other games. For example,

Liebe (2008) suggests that with non-computational games, all rules are *potentially* negotiable. However, while video games may sometimes involve complex and extensive player-created and -negotiated social rules, there will always be present a set of non-negotiable rules inherent in the video game's program. Juul (2005) himself recognizes, as suggested in Chapter 1, that many video games do not necessarily fit his classic game model. Therefore, though rules may be an important part of most, if not all, games it does not necessarily hold true that their nature will be the same in all games.

Effects

A major area of debate and concern is the perceived effect video games have on their players, in particular video game depictions of violence. Henry Jenkins (2006a) highlights a common response and attitude towards video game violence when he outlines the arguments of the retired military psychologist David Grossman (2000). For Grossman, video games are a conditioning tool which teaches children the skills and attitudes required of combat soldiers. He argues that: 'every time a child plays an interactive point-and-shoot video game, he is learning the exact conditioned reflex and motor skills [of a soldier]' (cited in Jenkins 2006a: 211). Of course, Grossman is not alone in his indictment of video games, and there now exists a sizeable academic literature that would seem to support his fears that video games can, and do, have a negative effect on their players.

Though I may not necessarily agree with all of their assertions and conclusions, Dill and Dill (1998) provide a useful overview of the then existing literature on video game violence and its perceived effect on gamers. They assert that a large proportion of video games, now and throughout gaming history, have revolved around or included 'violent' themes and content. For instance, they cite, among others, Provenzo's 1991 study, which suggested that 40 out of the 47 most popular games at the time were 'violent' in nature. This is usually the point where video game violence research runs into its first difficulties, as defining 'violent' content and themes proves extremely hard and is highly subjective. This is a lesson that video game research should probably have learned from decades of research on cinema and film violence. For instance, in 2001 the American Academy of Paediatrics suggested that 100 per cent of American-produced animated feature films between 1987 and 1999 (their period of study) contain violent content (Jenkins 2006a). When one considers the large number of 'family-friendly' Disney pictures produced in that period, that is quite an astounding assertion, which instantly leads any critically minded person to ask 'what do they count as violence?' As Jenkins (2006a: 215–16) argues: 'When hunters shoot Bambi's mother [does this] mean the same as the violence that occurs when giant robots smash each other in a Japanese anime movie?' Though Dill and Dill do highlight how problematic operationalizing 'violence' within media texts is, they do not dwell on this point, but rather move on to consider what other lessons can be learned from the television violence literature. Here they provide a succinct, but very uncritical, overview of this literature, highlighting a number of mostly experimental studies that supposedly link the viewing of television violence with increased audience levels of aggression. This includes the work of Leonard Berkowitz (for example 1984, 1990, 1993), which suggests that repeated exposure to violence creates cognitive networks in individuals, who are then more likely to draw on these memories and skills in specific social situations. Hence, looking at these and other studies, Dill and Dill (1998: 411) conclude that 'the television and movie literatures suggest that exposure to video-game violence should increase aggression', before then going on to suggest that this causal relationship between levels of aggression and exposure to violent content may actually be greater with video games.

The main reason they give for this is the 'interactive' and 'participatory' nature of video games. Their argument is that unlike television or film, where the audience vicariously watches the violence, in video games the gamer actively directs and participates in the violent acts. Again, here they provide research findings from a number of both 'experimental' and 'descriptive' (such as questionnaire-based) studies to support their assertion. This includes, for example, the work of Calvert and Tan (1994), who suggest that the video gamer, by actively choosing and carrying out aggressive in-game acts, adds new 'repertoire' to their social behaviour.

Dill and Dill (1998) do highlight that not all studies find a causal relationship, or even correlation, between video game violence and increased levels of aggression or other forms of 'anti-social' behaviour. However, they largely dismiss studies that do not find a relationship, on the grounds of their weak or flawed methodologies. Significantly, however, they are not critical (or even questioning) of the methods employed in studies that do find a perceived relationship between media violence and anti-social behaviour. This is quite surprising, when this is precisely what this literature has been extensively criticized for.

Bryce and Rutter (2006) sum up many of these methodological criticisms, suggesting that the vast majority of studies on video game violence measure only levels of aggression in the very short term, often right after play, and therefore can tell us little, if anything, about potential and significant long-term effects. Most of these studies tend to be conducted on small sample sizes, and the nature of sample groups varies between studies, making comparisons between them difficult. Furthermore, applying research results taken from small and inconsistent sample groups to a wider population is extremely problematic. Most research on video game violence is conducted in experimental conditions which are very different from the settings in which video games are normally played in everyday life, and, once more, it is problematic to suggest that what happens in experimental conditions has any bearing on how video games are played and interpreted outside of a laboratory. When research is undertaken away from the laboratory, in more 'real-world' or 'natural' settings, correlations tend to be less obvious, if present at all. Context is very important in understanding the consumption and meaning attributed to media, as are the individual biographies and social locations of the audience. Audiences are not a mass of empty and separated individuals, but rather part of a society that consists of complex social influences and factors that shape behaviour (Abercrombie and Longhurst 1998).

Significantly, the very same arguments have been used to challenge research on television and film violence for decades. Hence, if the previous research on television and film violence is to teach video game scholarship anything, it is that the methods employed in these kinds of research studies are highly problematic and unlikely to provide convincing results. Kirsten Drotner (1992) suggests that as each new medium is introduced, and as each new generation of academics engages with it and journalists generate new moral panics about its corrupting influences, we seem to undergo a 'historical amnesia', forgetting that they are the same debates that raged about every previous media form, including radio, pulp fiction, cinema, comics, television, the Internet, video games (Livingstone 2005).

Dill and Dill suggested in 1998 that 'the literature on the relationship between video game and virtual reality violence and aggression is still in a fledgling state' (p. 423). This is in many respects an apology for the fact that what was then nearly two decades of research had found very little consistent and coherent evidence of a causal link between video game violence and increased levels of gamer aggression. I would like to say that in the time that has passed since Dill and Dill's overview this literature had moved on, either finding strong and conclusive evidence or finally giving up the search. However, it has not, and the video games and aggression debate continues to plough over the same ground again and again, producing no particularly new or significant breakthroughs or advancements. Media effects research remains firmly located within what Abercrombie and Longhurst (198) describe as the 'behavioural paradigm' of audience research, which views audiences as passive recipients of media messages, but this is a highly problematic and simplistic argument that most within audience studies left behind several decades ago (see Chapter 3).

Ultimately, it seems that research on media violence *does* tend to find, under certain circumstances, a small (though often inconsistent) effect on some segments of the population. This tends, unfortunately, to disappoint both sides involved in the media violence argument, and helps ensure that this debate continues (Livingstone 2005). But what this does show is that causal relationships between media and effects are extremely hard to find, and even harder (I would suggest, impossible) to prove. As Gerbner (1986) convincingly argues, if media do have a direct effect on audiences, then given that we are all surrounded by and engage with the mass media, in an almost endless stream of interactions, introducing one more stimulus in a laboratory is unlikely to have any discernible or measurable effect at all (cited in Livingstone 2005: 23). Furthermore, it is important to note that the images and messages carried by the mass media, including video games, are rarely simple and straightforward, but are often complex, sometimes even contradictory, and open to multiple readings and interpretations by the audience. This does not necessarily mean that we can be complacent, or that images of violence, racism, sexism and homophobia in video games should not be a cause for concern. Simply because we cannot accurately measure or establish a causal relationship between, say, the depiction of violence against women in video games and changes in attitudes or behaviour in gamers, does not mean that we should not question why certain themes continue to be present in many video games.

In addressing the 'problem' of video game, and other media, violence, most research is looking at the wrong side of the equation. As David Trend (2007) argues, it is not the mass media that create violence in society, but rather a violent society that creates the media we consume. As he concludes: 'more restrictions on what is available on TV or the internet won't help the situation very much. But more discussions and more consumer choices will. By discussing the various ways we understand, dislike, enjoy, and use media violence, we move the conversation forward' (Trend 2007: 123).

Of course, there is also a large body of literature that focuses on the possible positive effects of video gameplay. For instance, Kestenbaum and Weinstein (1985) suggest that video game violence may actually have a cathartic effect on children and help them channel their aggression. There are also claims that video gameplay may improve physical skills, such as dexterity, hand–eye coordination or perception. Subrahmanyam and Greenfield (1994) suggest that video games might improve children's spatial skills, while Goldstein *et al.* (1997) suggest that in their research on the elderly, those who had played *Super Tetris* for five hours a week for five weeks had faster reaction times and felt a more positive sense of well-being compared to their non-playing counterparts. Furthermore, there is now a very large literature on the use of video games as an educational tool. As Prensky (2003) argues: 'video games are not the enemy, but the best opportunity we have to engage our kids in real learning'. It is certainly the case that video games can be used for positive social benefit, as Kate E. Taylor (2011) shows when highlighting the role of the video game *Wordslinger* in aiding and empowering women who have experienced domestic abuse.

Unfortunately, however, some of the research evidence presented to support the argument that video games can have positive social, physical and psychological benefits can at times be just as suspect as that which attempts to link increased levels of aggression and violence with video game players. In spite of this, there are cases, such as that of *Wordslinger*, that show how video games can be more than merely a form of entertainment. However, asking 'are video games good or bad?' is probably as futile as asking whether all books, or films, are good or bad.

Interactivity

Chapters 1 and 2 make clear that many, particularly early, writers on video games, such as Chris Crawford (1982) and Loftus and Loftus (1983), sought to distinguish this new entertainment technology from previous forms of media, such as film and literature, by arguing that video games were 'interactive' compared with the 'passivity' of (other) media forms. The interactive nature of video games continues to be seen as one of their key attributes and a defining quality for many contemporary writers, such as Eskelinen and Tronstad (2003), Frasca (2003) and Lantz (2009), to name but a few. For these writers, the video gamer is understood as a key participant, if not co-author, in the video game experience, while audiences of other media forms, such as television and cinema, are seen as consumers of a static text. Douglas Rushkoff (1999), for instance, optimistically writes of video games as a revolution in youth culture; where once audiences simply received media, now gamers can be seen as actively shaping what they see on the screen. For Rushkoff, video gaming is about 'world creation', which subverts traditional hierarchies where knowledge is passed down from above. Of course, this fervent video game and technology evangelism has been challenged by many.

In particular, numerous authors, such as Gansing (2003), Palmer (2003) and Crawford (2006), highlight the overuse of terms such as 'interactivity' and 'user control' when describing video games. Palmer (2003: 160) suggests that new technologies are frequently introduced and sold to the market using the rhetoric of their increased 'user control', as when in the 1970s the Sony VCR promised the ability to 'master time, memory and circumstance' or the multiple possibilities suggested by Microsoft's first global advertising slogan in 1994: 'Where do you want to go today?' However, user control is still restricted by not only the limitations of that particular technology, but also the aims of the designers and manufactures, and the ideologies behind them. In particular, Shaw (2010: 413) argues that a focus on video games as 'highly interactive and audience-dependent texts can lead us to ignore that they are in fact encoded with ideological perspectives just as any other medium'. For instance, most video games tend to be constructed from the perspective of the 'male gaze' and frequently objectify and sexualize women (Yates and Littleton 2001), or revolve around capitalist values, such as economic accumulation (Nutt and Railton 2003). This is illustrated by Carr's (2006b: 51) discussion of the RPG video game *Baldur's Gate*, where she suggests that 'this apparent flexibility has its limits. If the player does attempt to play as a "baddie", for example, it quickly becomes clear that *Baldur's Gate* makes certain traits and acts necessary to scoring and progress, and that the game will veto more extreme behaviour.' Video game designer and journalist Ste Curran (2010) suggests that video game interactivity is an illusion. For instance, he cites the example of *Wii Sports*, where, he suggests, though the video game gives the impression of high levels of interactivity, with the player actually mimicking real actions of playing sports such as tennis, the Nintendo Wii controller (Wiimote) actually detects only a very limited range of movements. Similarly, he discusses other video game examples, such as how *Mario Kart* slows down computer-controlled opponents if the player is currently last in a race, or how in *Pegel*, which may give the impression of requiring great skill, much of the game is down to luck. Curran suggests that the video game industry largely operates on the basis of 'smoke and mirrors', as he puts it. That is to say, video gamers may be given the impression of high levels of control, but what is actually possible within the mechanisms of the video game's design is likely to be much more limited or out of their control.

Of course, a key problem is the lack of clarity and consistency in the use of the term 'interactivity', as authors frequently use this concept to mean many different things and often do not define or operationalize it. Rob Cover (2006) provides a good overview of some of the key debates surrounding conceptualizations of interactivity, and in particular how they relate to new media forms, such as the Internet and video games. One of the more developed definitions of interactivity he considers is the work of Sally McMillan (2002), who divides interactivity into a typology of four intersecting levels. The first she calls 'allocution', where interactivity is minimal (though *crucially* not absent), and this refers to a central broadcaster with a mass audience, as in the case of a lecture or television programme. Second, 'consultation' occurs with the use of a database, where the user actively seeks out information. This does not necessarily involve narrative, and feedback is still minimal. Third, 'registration' records patterns of access and use, such as Internet 'cookies', which track and customize the display of web content for a specific user. Finally, 'conversational' occurs when individuals interact directly with each other, usually in 'real' time.

Cover (2006) suggests that, problematically, some forms of new media, and in particular he cites the example of video games, do not sit comfortably within McMillan's typology. This is a common problem with most typologies, in that many specific examples often do not easily fit within them. However, many video games would seem to best fit into the category of 'registration', as the game program already exists, but the gamer finds their own path through it and the game reacts and sets out a customized path, based upon gamer choices and inputs. What is particularly useful about McMillan's model is that it can be used to challenge the idea of video games as interactive compared to the passivity of other media audiences. Here, video games can be seen as *typically* involving *more* interactivity than that seen with, for example, most television audiences, but similarly video games are not as interactive as a face-to-face conversation. Hence, crucially, interactivity is conceptualized here as *more* or *less*, rather than simply *present* or *absent*.

It is also important to recognize that levels of interactivity are not necessarily set and defined by the medium type, but vary from case to case. Some video games involve very limited levels of user choice or control. Examples would include the 1983 animated video game *Dragon's Lair*, in which the gamer had very limited options, and gameplay largely consisted of pressing a button at the right moment to ensure the continuation of the linear cinematics. This is a model also seen in many 'interactive movie'-style or full motion video (FMV) games, such as *Star Wars: Rebel Assault*, or the numerous cut-scenes that have populated many video games throughout much of their history, where the gamer sits back and watches game narratives progress, with little or no control. Most video games continue to be fairly linear in their design and play, and if the gamer is to play the video game through to completion, their opportunity to deviate from a set course of action is often quite limited, sometimes surprisingly so. In particular, several authors, such as Juul (2005) and Curran (2010), highlight the presence of 'pinch points' in many video games. That is to say, though video games such as *Half-Life 2* may give the impression that they are open and the video gamer can go where they desire, at certain points the game will pull the gamer back to a central, limited and linear narrative.

Furthermore, even many contemporary and complex video games need not necessarily be played in a particularly interactive or engaged way. As will be highlighted in Chapter 8, many gamers may at times pay only very partial attention to playing a video game, or may split their attention between multiple acts, such as reading a book while simply pressing a button on a gamepad to repeat an in-game action. In this case, is pressing a button, the outcome of which the gamer may pay no attention to, necessarily more interactive than the deep engagement they may experience while reading a book?

It is evident that the audiences of older media forms, such as books and films, are participatory and active. For instance, as will be discussed below, Grodal (2003:

131) suggests that narratives are an embodied process, where external information is received, processed and ordered by individuals into 'stories'. Films, books and all media forms present audiences with a series of prompts, signs and elements, which they have to order and attach meanings to, to make sense of. As the journalist James Meek (2010: 29) writes: 'What could be more participatory than a kit made up of nothing but 26 letters of an alphabet? Words are only a sequence of glyphs without the participation of a skilled reader's imagination, memory and wit to dress them with the gift the senses bring.'

However, Frasca (2003: 227) forcefully argues: 'no matter how badly literary theorists remind us of the active role of the reader, that train will hit Anna Karenina and Oedipus will kill his father and sleep with his mother'. However, all texts are open to some degree of reinterpretation, reimagining or even misreading. Even Vladimir E. Alexandrov, in his *Limits to Interpretation: the meanings of Anna Karenina* (2004), undermines his own book title by arguing that 'understanding can be imagined as a net of interpretations and translations of varying degrees of approximation' (cited in Katsell 2005: 497). A reader can also choose not to finish a book, so for them at least Anna Karenina will never die, or Oedipus commit patricide and incest. In addition, both Anna Karenina and Oedipus are characters, particularly in our media-saturated society, that extend and exist far beyond their original textual source, such as in conversations, references in popular culture or metaphors in psychoanalysis; one could easily ask which, or whose, Anna Karenina or Oedipus? However, this, and Frasca's original argument, misses the point somewhat. All media texts, such as films and literature, do provide certain structural, sometimes narratological, parameters, which most readers, most of the time, agree upon and adhere to; however, so do video games.

Umberto Eco (1979) provides an alternative perspective on the idea of interactive texts. Eco distinguishes between what he calls 'open' and 'closed' texts. Open texts deliberately give audiences more than one possible route or way forward; audience participation is required and choice is built into the text. Hence, a contemporary example of this would be video games. Closed texts, which include most televisual or written texts, are designed for unidirectional transmission. However, conversely, Eco argues that 'closed' texts may in fact be more open to audience rereading and reinterpretation than open texts. This is because open texts require audience choice, there is less need to think through interpretations, less need for reflection. The audience, or video gamer, knows there are multiple paths and they choose one of them as their path, and often do not analyse this any further. However, audiences of (supposedly) closed texts can engage in a lot more 'reading between the lines', that is to say, providing their own interpretations and subtexts. Allen (1995) elaborates on Eco's work and suggests that some texts leave more 'gaps' for audience interpretation. For instance, many novels, unlike video games, are less prescriptive in terms of what characters or locations will look and sound like; the reader has to do more work here, use their imagination more, to fill in the gaps.

It is not my aim here to argue that any one particular medium is *necessarily* more or less interactive than another, but rather to highlight the complexity of terms such as 'interactivity' and argue that simple dichotomies between active gamers and passive audiences, based merely upon the type of medium, are extremely problematic. Hence, while it is important to recognize that video games *are* different, in many respects, to traditional media forms such as television, cinema, radio and so forth, it is crucial that we do not seek to overemphasize this distinction. As Kline *et al.* (2003: 19) write:

> There is a real difference, of course, between interactive gaming and the flow of television programming … But the interactive enthusiasts need to take a closer look at the degree and kind of 'active' participation of young audiences in the construction of their 'own' digital culture. Choosing a corridor, character or weapon – a rail gun or a chainsaw in a *Quake* death match – can be very absorbing. But it is hardly a matter of radical openness or deep decision about the content of play.

Immersion, engagement and flow

Diane Carr (2006b) suggests that it is possible to understand a player's 'absorption' in a video game by considering the three interrelated theories of 'immersion', 'engagement' and 'flow'. The first, 'immersion', Carr (2006b: 53) suggests can be defined in a number of ways, depending on whether this is drawn on from the perspective of virtual reality analysis, literature or presence theory. However, both King and Krzywinska (2006) and Carr (2006b), drawing on the work of Lombard and Ditton (1997), suggest that a broad distinction can be made between perceptual and psychological forms of immersion. The first involves a sensory immersion, such as the way in which in a movie theatre the dimmed lights elicit a greater focus on the screen in front of the audience, and the second, psychological immersion, refers to an audience's mental and emotional immersion (Carr 2006b: 53–4). King and Krzywinska (2006: 118) suggest in terms of video games that this can be understood as the difference between immersion in the *game* and the *game world*.

Murray and Jenkins (n.d.: 2) describe immersion as 'the pleasure of being transported to another place, of losing our sense of reality and extending ourselves into a seemingly limitless, enclosing, other realm'. Though this may, to some degree, help us understand some of the pleasures of immersion in a metaphorical sense, it is important that we do not overplay this metaphor. It is highly unlikely that any video gamer would feel that they have actually been 'transported to another place', and as the section on geography below clearly illustrates, the physical location in which video games are played is just as important, if not more so, than the geography of the game.

Kerr *et al.* (2004) suggest that a key element of video gaming immersion is uncertainty, the fear of the unknown and how to resolve this. They clearly highlight how intrigue and suspense are key factors in holding a video gamer's attention and absorbing them in the video game, just as they are in many other media, such as novels and cinema. However, a video game's level of difficulty is also important in maintaining a gamer's continued immersion and attention (Juul 2009). For, as Kirkpatrick (2004) highlights, if a video game is too difficult and a player has to repeat a task over and over again, they can lose their immersion in the game. In contrast, a video game that is too easy can often lead to boredom (Juul 2009).

This relates to Carr's (2006b) second and third concepts, those of engagement and flow. In terms of engagement, Carr underlines how video gamers can be actively engaged in gameplay, but not necessarily immersed. For example, this can occur when attempting a difficult or complex action, where the video gamer may be absorbed in deep concentration, but not necessarily absorbed in the game world. Finally, Carr's third form of game absorption is flow.

The concept of flow was first introduced by the psychologist Mihaly Csikszentmihalyi (1988) to describe a state of heightened awareness and concentration on one's goals, producing greater feelings of enjoyment and connection with the task at hand. Csikszentmihalyi defines flow as having the following fundamental components: a challenging activity that requires skill; clear goals and feedback; a merging of action and awareness; concentration on the task at hand; loss of self-consciousness; the paradox of control; the transformation of time; and 'autotelic experience', which is an event that has within itself the purpose of its existence, such as 'fun' (Conway 2010: 45). Flow is a concept typically associated with the psychological state athletes achieve when they become clearly and specifically focused on achieving a sporting goal, such as during the running of a race, but others, for example, Bryce and Rutter (2001), suggest it could similarly be used to describe the focus and absorption of video gamers. Csikszentmihalyi suggests that the best way to achieve a flow state is to turn an activity into a game, as the establishment of rules, objectives and rewards encourages the individual to become deeply absorbed in the activity at hand (Nielsen *et al.* 2008). However, it is important that this task is neither too difficult or easy. As Juul (2009) suggests, avoiding the anxiety of a too difficult game or the boredom of a too easy game is important in good video game design and in maintaining flow.

Carr (2006b: 57) suggests that the concepts of immersion, engagement and flow may be useful in understanding some of the pleasures of play, but 'in practice it would be difficult to *prove* that these states happen, or that particular aspects of the game generate them'. It is for similar reasons that Erving Goffman avoided considering motives (Smith 2006). Unlike actions, motivations cannot easily be observed, studied or understood.

Performance

Kerr *et al.* (2004) highlight performance as a key element of new media, and in particular video games. As they write:

> New media are seen to possess a performative aspect, insofar as they allow for and foster the users' experimentation with alternative identities (Turkle 1995). This is true for computer games as well as internet chat rooms etc. The pleasure of leaving one's identity behind and taking on someone else's identity is regarded as a key pleasure in digital games.
>
> Kerr *et al.* 2004: 15

Crawford and Rutter (2007) identify four forms of video game performativity: performances to self, performance to others in-game, performances to others present out-of-game, and video-game-related performances away from the game.

First, social performances are sometimes primarily for the individual's own consumption, whether playing a one-player video game, trying on a new outfit or rehearsing answers for a forthcoming job interview (see Sandvoss 2005). Video gameplay involves significant elements of individual performativity, such as enabling gamers to take on and act out specific roles. Video games frequently allow gamers to play with their identities and to imagine themselves in different social or fantastic situations, but even the simplest of games (such as *Solitaire* or *Tetris*) involve the video gamer *performing* in-game actions, such as moving cards or falling blocks.

Second, the presence of others (an additional audience) can greatly influence the nature and intensity of the performance (Lin and Sun 2008). For instance, many multiplayer video games allow gamers to interact with, and perform to, others in-game. This can simply involve competing against another player, such as in a sport-themed video game like *Pro Evolution Soccer* (see Conway 2010), or sending messages to and engaging in synchronous talk with other online players in a first-person-shooter, such as *Counter-Strike* (see Wright *et al.* 2002). More elaborately, this can take the form of performances, such as dressing and adapting characters in video games like MMORPGs, which the player may then use to interact with other human players; sometimes 'in-character'. (Some MMORPGs, such as *World of Warcraft*, have 'role-playing' areas or servers, where the players are discouraged from stepping out of character or discussing 'real-world' subjects.)

For some players, in-game performances with and to other players can constitute a, if not *the*, key focus or object of their gameplay. For example, King and Borland (2003) discuss a group of 15 players of the MMORPG *Ultima Online* who together bought an in-game tavern and set up an acting troupe who performed plays, such as Dickens's *Christmas Carol*, to other players. Other forms of video game performance include what Newman terms types of 'superplay'. Newman (2008: 123) informs the reader that 'Superplay is a generic term to describe a range of gaming practices that are bound together by a common desire to demonstrate mastery of the game through performance.' A key example of superplay is 'speedrunning'. Put simply, speedrunning is the act of completing a video game as quickly as possible. Though speedrunning is most commonly carried out in single-player games, such as first-person-shooters, speedrunning is undertaken to demonstrate skill, not just for the player themselves, but also to a wider video gamer, and specifically speedrunner, community. These and other examples, therefore, show the centrality of performance to video gameplay. Indeed, Wright *et al.* go as far as to argue that the value of gaming may not be found in the video game itself, but the way it is performed within a social context:

> The meaning of playing *Counter-Strike* is not merely embodied in the graphics or even the violent game play, but in the social mediations that go on between players through their talk with each other and by their performance within the game. Participants, then, actively create the meaning of the game

through their virtual talk and behavior borrowing heavily from popular and youth culture representations. Players learn rules of social comportment that reproduce codes of behavior and established standards of conduct, while also safely experimenting with the violation of these codes.

Wright *et al.* 2002, cited in Crawford and Rutter 2007: 279

Third, video gamers' performances and interactions will frequently extend beyond the in-game experience. At the simplest and most obvious level, gamers will often interact and perform to those they game with, and as Schott and Kambouri (2006: 124) argue, this can also be the case even when playing a video game designed to be played by one player:

Games intended to engage a single player were shown to be able to incorporate cooperation with, and the contribution of others. Furthermore, gameplay in groups appeared to constitute quite a natural and consistent component in the life cycle of an individual's progression through such games. We found that participants successfully transformed one-player games into an effective and highly structured *social performance*, in which roles and identities within the group were constantly being negotiated and redefined. (emphasis added)

Fourth, video-game-related social interactions and performances may also extend beyond sight of the game screen. For instance, data collected on players of the *Championship Manager* and *Football Manager* video game series (Crawford 2006) suggest that many gamers would frequently discuss video games and gameplay with family, friends and work-mates away from the gaming screen. As one interviewee ('Ian') indicated:

It [conversation about *Championship Manager*] strengthens the bonds between those who you play it with. Me and a friend who used to play it a lot often make reference to our teams, and it makes me laugh for some reason, I don't know why exactly, something to do with the fact that we have invested so much time in this little world, and that we can share detailed knowledge that only makes sense to us.

Crawford 2006: 502

However, social interactions and performances relating to video gaming do not necessarily have to be face-to-face. Video gamers may exchange tips, gaming solutions or cheats, game add-ons or modifications ('mods'), for example via the Internet, which they have produced themselves, all demonstrating (*performing*) their video game playing or programming abilities to others (see Chapter 7). Furthermore, video gamers can sometimes draw on the video games they play to construct game-related stories and narratives, which they recount to others (again, see Chapter 7).

At the same time, video-game-related conversations, narratives and social performances are not necessarily limited to interactions with fellow gamers. Many sociological considerations of both media audiences (such as Abercrombie and Longhurst 1998) and fan cultures (Hills 2002; Sandvoss 2005) highlight the proliferation and saturation of media forms within contemporary society, which has concurred with, and helped to bring about, a change in contemporary audiences. Abercrombie and Longhurst (1998), in their consideration of the 'spectacle/performance paradigm' of audience research (see Chapter 3), suggest that the mass media increasingly impinge on and saturate contemporary society. This 'mediascape' (Appadurai 1990) provides a resource that individuals draw upon in their social performances. That is to say, we live in an increasingly narcissistic and 'performative society' where individuals will draw on media (including video games) as a 'resource' in constructing their social performances, such as informing the way they dress, speak and act.

In particular, knowledge and information gained from video games can be used to inform conversations or social interactions based around other subject matter, and this is particularly aided by the intertextuality and transmedia nature of many video games – see below. Again, returning to the *Championship Manager* and *Football Manager* research cited earlier (Crawford 2006), it is evident that these video games were frequently drawn on by many of their players as a resource in conversations around football. As indicated by one interviewee ('Shaun'):

> Yes I used to love trying to impress my work mates with my knowledge of relatively unknown foreigners [footballers], never letting on that it was all gained from buying them in *CM* [*Championship Manager*].
>
> Crawford 2006: 509

This example illustrates how the performativity of video gamers is socially located and can be drawn on as a resource in wider, everyday social interactions (this is explored further in Chapter 8). The case also identifies connections between video gaming and football fan interests and interactions, emphasizing the importance of not establishing clear distinctions between types of audiences, as, in this case, video gamers and sports fans may well be the very same people.

Identity, roles and embodiment

Much work on new media has focused on its role in enabling identity play, experimentation or even evolution. Authors such as Stone (1995), Poster (1990) and Turkle (1995) claim that new technologies, such as the Internet, allow for a radical transformation in identity construction and maintenance. For Turkle (1995) the Internet has allowed people to play with their identities and personas, providing a new opportunity to project their fantasies and ideas into this 'virtual reality' or 'cyberspace' and play out an alternative 'life on the screen'. Turkle sees online networks as providing 'identity workshops' where alternative persona can be created and played with. She writes: 'the self is not only decentred but multiplied without limit. There is an unparalleled opportunity to play with one's identity and "try out" new ones' (Turkle 1996: 356, cited in Lister *et al.* 2009: 271).

Such ideas have inevitably been influential in video game research, and Turkle herself frequently uses video games as a key example of new-media-enabled identity play (see for example Turkle 2005). Filiciak (2003), drawing on the work of Turkle, as well as writers on postmodernity such as Jean Baudrillard, argues that MMORPGs allow gamers to develop multiple 'selves'. As Filiciak (2003: 90) writes:

> It is easy to notice the MMORPG user situation is an idealised image of the situation of the postmodern human creature, in which the user can freely shape his own 'self'. On the Internet this freedom reaches a heretofore-unprecedented extent, since we have full control over our image – other people see us in the way we want to be seen. ... On the Internet our appearance is ... a matter of choice.

Here similarities can also be drawn with the concept of cyborgism, and in particular the work of Donna Haraway (1991). The 'cyborg' constitutes the intersection between machines and humans, such as the implanting of mechanical technologies into the human body, but more importantly raises the idea of blurring identities, where the boundaries between humans and machines become less fixed and more malleable.

However, these somewhat utopian (or possibly dystopian, depending on your perspective) views, that individuals can escape their bodies and identities online and create themselves anew, have been widely criticized. For instance, as May (2002: 105–6) writes:

> The notion that we can choose any 'virtual identity' may be a little naive, as many factors mediated by ICT can influence and limit how we are perceived. This may range from speed of typing to the ability to express oneself succinctly or with ready wit. Any new identity may be less freely chosen than we think, as extended social interactions (even across the internet) tend to reveal much more that we might try to conceal.

Unlike their new media predecessors, most writers on video gameplay are much more willing to emphasize the role of the offline or out-of-game in shaping the nature of online and in-game identities and play. For instance, Filiciak (2003) recognizes the role of the offline in shaping online identities when he cites the work of Bechar-Israeli (1995), which suggests that online pseudonyms are most commonly closely related to offline identities, such as the use of actual names or nicknames as screen names. Burn and Carr (2006) consider how players' choices over the appearance and personalities of their avatars in the MMORPG *Anarchy Online* often closely reflect the player's offline identity, and also, in turn, how online experiences can influence how the video gamer feels or views themselves. As they argue: 'for all players, their offline identities will infuse their on-screen activities to some degree, whether they decide to create a fictional identity or not' (Burn and Carr 2006: 107).

However, retreating somewhat from the argument that new media provide users with the opportunity to create multiple identities 'without limit' (Turkle 1996: 356) does not necessarily mean that a consideration of the transformation and presentation of identities in video gameplay is not important. Writers such as Giddens (1991), Bauman (1997, 1998) and Lévy (1997), among others, have commented on the changing nature of identity within late modern societies. Bauman, for instance, suggests that within a consumer society, identities become less stable and fixed, as traditional markers like regional identity, social class and family become less stable and certain (see Chapter 6). In a rapidly changing and liquid world, fixed identities become less useful, and so identities become ever more fluid. It is our consumer and leisure choices and our 'elective belongings', the social groups we choose to be members of, rather than those assigned to us (Savage *et al.* 2005), which define who we are. This includes our use of new media technologies, like the Internet and video games, which can contribute to our sense of self, others' opinions of us and the social groups to which we belong. Chapter 6 considers the culture of video gaming in more depth.

Some authors have made comparisons between in-game and online identities and ethnicity. Pearce (2011), for instance, considers the response of players of the MMORPG *Uru: Ages beyond Myst* after it was closed down. Pearce employs the terminology of ethnicity, describing the players as a 'diaspora' and as 'refugees' from their 'homeland', seeking a new place and home in other virtual worlds, such as *Second Life* and *There.com* (discussed further in Chapter 7). Furthermore, Dovey and Kennedy (2006) borrow the term 'technicity', an amalgamation of the words 'technology' and 'ethnicity', from cyberculture theorist David Tomas (2000) to describe the formation of new identities based upon technology-mediated interactions (Conway 2010). This recognizes how technologies contribute to contemporary social relationships, and Dovey and Kennedy (2006) also use this term to recognize the patterns of hegemony associated with the use of particular technologies. An instance of this is the way in which dominant gender norms are prevalent, but can similarly be challenged, in video game cultures. However, parallels between technologically mediated identities and ethnicity are not particularly useful. Authors' use of the language of ethnicity is employed to emphasize the importance and meaning of computer-mediated identities and group membership, but it is important to recognize that they are still largely elected and temporal, rather than ascribed and largely permanent. Of course, I readily acknowledge that computer-mediated identities do have meaning and importance beyond the online and in-game, and that, similarly, ethnicity and race are social constructs. Computer-mediated identities are not an ethnicity, but this does not necessarily mean that they are not important. Just as football supporter allegiances matter to many, and can at times be a matter of life and death (and more than that, if we are to believe Bill Shankly) and share many similarities, and even connections, with ethnicity, they are not the same. We need to look elsewhere for terms to understand computer-mediated identities and group membership, possibly to concepts such as neo-tribes, scenes or habitus (see Chapter 6).

Moreover, our ability and propensity to play out roles and identities should not be seen as necessarily new, or invariably connected with new media technologies. For instance, in his first book, *The Presentation of Self in Everyday Life*, first published in 1959, Erving Goffman suggests that all social interactions are mediated through 'performance'. This performance occupies a front of stage region, while away from the face-to-face interaction, the back stage region is where actors prepare themselves for performance. Through social performances, individuals engage in a process of 'impression management', where they seek to create and maintain an image of themselves for the consumption of others. However, the performances are not solely created by individual actors, but are rather the result of social competences acquired through socialization, which relate to specific roles and situations, or 'frames' (Smith 2006) (see Chapter 2). Therefore, just as we are socialized into roles, such as what is expected of a student in a classroom environment, players of MMORPGs like *World of Warcraft* learn the dynamics of this video game, its social etiquettes and the roles they must play within it. But further, Goffman, with the introduction of frame analysis, highlights that these identities are not necessarily single-layered. A player of a video game such as *World of Warcraft* will simultaneously operate within a number of roles and frames. They might be fulfilling the role of a 'tank' (there to take the majority of hits from an encounter) within a hunting party, but their role will also be defined by their character being a warrior and their in-game race as an Orc. How the player acts and behaves will be further shaped by their interactions in their current group, possibly also their in-game guild membership, as well as factors outside of the game, such as where they are playing and who they are sitting with, as well as a multitude of other social factors shaping their identity and performances. Video gamers, just like any other social performers, use and rely on multiple pre-existing, in-game and out-of-game frames (see MacCallum-Stewart 2011).

What has further been highlighted as significant in relation to identity and video gameplay is how the gamer's on-screen actions are both part of, and separate from, the gamer. Bob Rehak (2003: 106) argues that the video game avatar is both object and subject: 'appearing on the screen in place of the player, the avatar does double duty as the self and other, symbol and index'. The avatar's actions are linked to those of the gamer, but at the same time they are also a mediated on-screen representation; hence the video gamer is both participant and audience to their actions (see Chapter 3). This distinction between game self and other is explored further by Cogburn and Silcox (2009).

In their discussion of video games and philosophy, Cogburn and Silcox (2009) highlight how gamers will commonly use the first person pronoun 'I', when describing the actions of the in-game character they are controlling. They seek to explain this using Clark and Chalmers's (1998) idea of the 'extended mind'. This suggests that as humans, we are adept at utilizing props within our environment to assist and extend body and brain activities; such as using a pen and paper to assist with calculations. External objects become integrated into our thought processes, and, hence, become extensions of our self. This, they suggest, can be used to explain why people frequently refer to video game characters as 'I' or 'me', because video games fit easily and readily into our patterns of prop utilization and the extension of self. However, conflation of object and subject is not restricted to video games. Cogburn and Silcox (2009) suggest that a similar extension of self can also be seen on social networking websites like Facebook and MySpace. However, as with the playing of roles, these examples need to be understood as merely contemporary instances of the extension of self, which is as ancient as the use of the first word or tool. For instance, when we talk of hitting something with a stick, most commonly we would say 'we hit' rather than 'the stick hit', or when we read a letter, we refer to the words on the page as if they were spoken by the writer, such as 'she said'. Words and language are a mediation and representation; they are similarly both self and object. The relationship, and conflated identity, we have with an on-screen avatar is interesting, but it is far from a particularly new form of self. As Sjöblom (2008: 152) writes: 'there is nothing about gaming that is "virtual". Players are neither outside the game nor inside it, no more than they are "outside" or "inside" other embodied actions, be that writing, drawing or playing soccer.'

Consequently, many authors have emphasized the need to shift focus away from what occurs on-screen, and recognize that the video gamer is a person, with a physical and corporal existence, and that play is an embodied experience. As Sjöblom (2008: 132) continues 'gaming actions (actions performed on or around the screen in the gaming session) can be seen as *embodied* actions. They are actions that occur in real space and time, and are performed through physical manifestations in those dimensions' (original emphasis).

For instance, Emma Westecott (2008: 379) emphasizes the need to 'bring the body back into play'. Westecott argues that video gameplay requires physical input and responses, whether holding and manipulating a gamepad (see Figure 5.2), swinging a Wiimote or PlayStation Move controller or the physical movements of a gamer in front of an Xbox Kinect sensor. Video games often involve touch, such as the use of a game controller, and even new game technologies like the Xbox Kinect, which do away with traditional controllers, do not remove touch altogether from the game experience; for instance, the player still needs to turn on and put a disk in the game machine. It is also the video gamer, through the embodied senses, who watches and listens to the video game, which they need to physically master through learned and repeated actions. In fact, the Kinect and similar technologies make the body more obviously central to play. In turn, video gameplay can have an effect on our bodies, such as causing sweaty palms, aching muscles or eyestrain, from repeated play. Furthermore, as discussed below, Grodal (2003: 131) argues that narratives need to be understood as embodied processes, where external information is received, processed and ordered by individuals into 'stories'.

However, it is important to recognize that the body, and our ideas of it, are similarly socially constructed. Sjöblom (2008: 132), citing the work of Dourish (2001), argues that a focus on embodiment should not stop at simply considering the body in front of the screen, but rather recognize how this is located and constructed within everyday life. As Dourish (2001: 125) writes:

'[E]mbodiment' does not simply mean 'physical manifestation'. Rather, it means being grounded in and emerging out of the everyday, mundane experience … […] … embodiment is a fundamental property out of which meaning, theory, and action arise … […] … embodiment is a participative status, a way of being, rather than a physical property.

Figure 5.2 Using a gamepad (photo: G. Crawford)

This is an argument I would wholeheartedly support, and Chapter 8 of this book specifically seeks to locate video gaming more firmly within the everyday.

Intertextuality and transmedia

Intertextuality refers to the intersection and cross-referencing that exist between texts, where the understanding or 'decoding' of any one text may refer to, or even require, the understanding of another text or texts. The theories of Mikhail Bakhtin, where any text contains 'multiple voices' within it, have been developed by Julia Kristeva (1969) in relation to intertextuality. Here, Kristeva suggests that any text can be analysed in terms of the other texts that it has absorbed and transformed. This in turn relates to the ideas of Roland Barthes (1978) and others, which assert the 'death of the author', as all texts are constructed from a 'mosaic of citations' (Kristeva 1969) where texts quote, borrow, echo, allude to, parody and pastiche other texts.

Intertextuality is evident in many media forms, such as novels, television and radio. One contemporary example of intertextuality would be the Wayans brothers' *Scary Movie* series of films. The comedy in these movies, as with many recent 'spoof' films, comes primarily from their references to other films and popular culture texts. In particular, the *Scary Movie* series particularly draws on, and makes reference to, the *Scream* series of films, which in turn contain a high number of intertextual references to other films, such as *Halloween*. However, Marshall (2002) suggests that intertextuality is particularly apparent in new forms of media, such as video games, which frequently draw on the narrative of, or make reference to, other texts. As Murray and Jenkins (n.d.) write:

> [A] high proportion of the digital media on the market are second-order phenomenon, adaptations of texts that gained their popularity through film and television. In a horizontally integrated media industry, characters, plots and images move fluidly across various media, participation in what Marsha Kinder (1991) has called the entertainment supersystem.

At least part of the appeal of many video games is their links and references to other texts. For instance, Conway (2010) suggests that many sport-themed video games, such as *Pro Evolution Soccer* and *FIFA* draw on the presentation style of television sports coverage. This provides video gamers with a sense of familiarity and also authenticity (see also Chapter 8), allowing them to feel that they are engaged in a competition, which is very much like playing association football.

A concept closely associated with intertextuality is that of 'transmedia'. Transmedia relates to the 'horizontal integration of the entertainment industry' (Jenkins 2006a: 147). That is to say, themes and narratives are more consciously spread across a wide variety of texts and media forms. One of many examples of this might be *The Matrix*, where stories set in this universe can be found in many different media forms, such as film, video games, novels, comic books and animation. Here, certain narratives run across and intertwine in multiple texts. For example, the video game *Enter the Matrix* includes cinematic scenes and gameplay that follows a narrative that runs parallel with, and helps inform the understanding of, the final two instalments in *The Matrix* trilogy of films. Jenkins (2006a: 147) suggests that the increase in levels of transmedia evident in the contemporary entertainment industries is partly a 'marketing strategy [to] promote a sense of affiliation and immersion in fictional worlds'. However, he suggests that this also reflects the changing nature and development of a more active audience, who are more willing, and want, to seek out and follow narratives and themes across multiple texts and media forms – a point addressed in Chapter 8.

Narrative and content analysis

Diane Carr (2006a: 35), drawing on the work of Chatman (1978: 19), defines a narrative as consisting of two interlinked elements: a story (*histoire*), which is the contents, the chain of events, characters and settings, and a discourse (*discours*), which refers to the meaning, its expression and how the content is communicated. That is to say, a narrative is a text that tells a story (Kücklich 2006), but in understanding this story, it is important to consider not just its content, but also its forms, expression and meanings, and both how they were intended and received.

The presence of narratives in video games, and hence the relevance of narrative analysis to video game studies, has been, and continues to be, challenged by many writers. For instance, as shown in Chapter 1, Lantz (2009) provocatively argues that video games are not a process of communication between a sender and receiver; they do not possess a predetermined and readable narrative, but rather meaning is created through the active participation of the video gamer.

It is evident that not all video games have a traditional (canonical) narrative structure, in that many do not tell a typical linear story with a beginning, middle and an end. For instance, the classic example used by many authors is that *Tetris*, or similar 'puzzle'-style games, do not contain a discernible narrative structure. Similarly, Juul (2001) suggests that many video games, such as *Space Invaders*, do not have a conclusion. *Space Invaders* does not have a 'story' that ever ends, as the gamer is confronted by wave after wave of 'invaders'. Even when video games do have some resemblance to a traditional narrative structure, they tend to have fairly limited stories, which often operate only as vehicles for stringing together action sequences or environments within a game. For instance, in video games such as *Gran Turismo*, highlighted by Kücklich (2006), the fictional worlds in which they are located provide only a prop or a setting for the game action and have no significant story development. Hence, Juul (2001) underscores how traditional narration is the telling of a story that *already* exists, while in video games, much like sport, the story is happening right *now*, as the gamer plays through the game.

However, Carr (2006a: 39) argues that just because a video game does not appear to have a traditional narrative structure, it does not necessarily mean that they are devoid of all narrative elements. Applying the work of Genette (1980), Carr (2006a) suggests that sports have narratives, but that these are 'simultaneous narratives' (that is to say, they are constructed as the 'action' takes place) as opposed to the 'classical [canonical] position of the past tense narrative' (Genette 1980: 217). Similarly, Genvo (2009), applying the work of Greimas (1992), argues that all video games can be understood as possessing a form of narrative. For Greimas (1993) a narrative needs to be understood as the realization of a project; where a subject (individual) goes through a number of conflicts to achieve an object (a goal). Genvo (2009) thus argues that most, if not all, video games, which frequently require the gamer to complete a number of tasks to reach a specific goal, could be seen to involve a narrative.

Grodal (2003: 131), as noted above, argues that narratives need to be understood as an embodied process where external information is received, processed and ordered by individuals into 'stories'. They can thus be both contextualized and made sense of. Most films and books do not follow a necessarily linear past-tense narrative structure, but it is the reader or viewer who constructs the information into logical narratives in their own imagination (Jenkins 2004). Just as the reader of a book *actively* assimilates the information on the page into a coherent story, it can similarly be argued that players of a video game construct narratives of play. Andrew Burn (2006: 77), drawing on the work of Janet Murray (2000), suggests that video games provide players with a repertoire, or a series of textual elements, which they put together to form a narrative sequence.

It has also been suggested that all forms of gaming can form the basis of narratives constructed and recounted after the event. For instance, Kirshenbaum (2009) suggests that players of tabletop wargames will often recount gaming episodes as a narrative of events, to create a kind of 'war story' (cited in Randall 2011). Albrechtslund (2008) discusses similar practices by players of *World of Warcraft*, who create and write narratives that recount and elaborate on their video gameplay (discussed further in Chapter 7). Even those who argue against a narratological analysis of video games, such as Juul (2001), recognize that video games can form the basis of stories told by gamers. As Juul (2001) acknowledges, 'games may spawn narratives that a player can use to tell others what went on in a game session'. These narratives of play can form a useful social bond, joining players together in the creation and telling of these stories, which also feed into individuals' sense of identity, a theme discussed further in Chapter 7.

Though there are many drawbacks to the outright denial that video games contain narrative elements, as the above arguments highlight, I would agree with Mäyrä (2009: 9) that the counter-narratology arguments of ludic-focused scholars have helped make visible important differences between video games and other media forms. Once more, it is important to recognize that theories and concepts developed in one field cannot necessarily be easily applied to another (Jenkins 2004). This does not necessarily mean, however, that all previous knowledge, theories and tools need to be completely rejected, just because a new case appears somehow different from what has gone before. In particular, I would argue that narrative analysis still has a useful place in the study of video games, their play and culture.

However, the fixation of narrative analysis, both in terms of its rejection and defence, might appear quite odd to many media and cultural studies scholars. Narrative analysis is just one of a plethora of forms of content analysis they regularly employ. What seems strangely under-represented in video game studies is the use, or debates concerning the relevance of, other forms of content analysis, such as quantitative content analysis, discourse analysis and semiotics.

While it may still be debatable to some degree whether video games contain narratives, most scholars would readily admit that video games do contain representational elements; that is to say, texts or textual elements that can be associated with meanings, ideologies and discourses. As Mäyrä (2009: 18) argues, even if players choose to ignore or skip past story elements of a video game, 'it is likely that all players are to some degree influenced by the representational parts of the game'. Furthermore, as argued in Chapter 1, our understanding of a video game is not just constructed from the game itself, but, additionally, magazine articles, newspaper stories, advertising campaigns, instruction manuals, the box the game came in, reviews, discussions with friends, as well as numerous other paratextual elements, contribute to the representational system of a video game (Jones 2008). It may be that other forms of content analysis, such as semiotics (discussed below), might prove more useful in the analysis of video games, particularly those with weak narrative elements, as well as the study of associated video game texts, such as advertising campaigns or packaging. See, for example, Randall's (2011) discussion of online boardgames.

Of course, it is not to say that other forms of content analysis are completely absent in video game research, but the use of analytical tools such as semiotics does appear far less common than narrative analysis, and these methods are not regularly discussed in the majority of (video) game studies textbooks. However, I would argue that content analysis, in all its many forms, could, and probably should, be included in the arsenal of the video game studies scholar. Let us consider briefly two further tools: quantitative content analysis and semiotics.

The traditional technique of quantitative content analysis was developed by Berelson (1952) and simply involves counting the frequency of certain elements within a text. There are some, but few, examples of quantitative content analysis in video game studies, and most commonly they are focused upon the representation of race and gender within games. For instance, Dietz (1998) conducted quantitative (and some qualitative) content analysis of the 33 most popular Nintendo and Sega Genesis video games at the time of her research, such as *NHL 95*, *Paper Boy 2* and *Earthworm Jim*. In her findings Dietz (1998: 425) reports:

> [T]here were no female characters in 41% of the games with characters. In 28% of these, women were portrayed as sex objects. Nearly 80% of the games included aggression or violence as part of the strategy or object. While 27% of the games contained socially acceptable aggression, nearly half included violence directed specifically at others and 21% depicted violence directed at women.

Quantitative content analysis allows for large quantities of media to be analysed quite quickly and easily to determine the relative levels of attention particular items or themes receive. This can tell us, therefore, what video game designers deem as suitable content for games, for example, as well as reveal dominant industry trends in the portrayal, of say, women or black and minority ethnic groups. However, for a more detailed analysis of content, we need to turn to qualitative analysis, such as narrative, discourse, or frame analysis or semiotics.

Semiotics, or semiology as it is frequently referred to in Europe, is the study of 'signs'. The simplest way to understand what a sign is, is to consider the components or parts that make it up. At its simplest, semiotics suggests that a sign consists of two components. First, there is a spoken, written or visual symbol, such as a word, or a road sign or a video game character; this is known as the 'signifier'. Second, associated with this symbol there will be a certain concept or idea; this is the 'signified'. For example, the video game character Lara Croft (the signifier) and our understanding of who, and what, Lara Croft is (a female adventure, a video game character, a collection of pixels – the signified) together provide us with an understanding or meaning of Lara Croft. This, then, is the sign, the sum of both the object and the meanings we attach to it. Semiotics teaches that a sign will have both a level of denotation, that is to say, its obvious and literal meaning, and connotation, which is what is implied by the sign. In this way the ideological nature of signs can be exposed and considered. For instance, at its simplest level, Lara Croft is a video game representation of a female English aristocratic adventurer, but Yates and Littleton (2001) suggest that Lara Croft is viewed and portrayed from the perspective of a male gaze; she is a sexualized portrayal of a woman, who is watched by (predominantly) male video gamers. Content analysis recognizes that a text will have an 'implied reader', which Carr (2006a: 37) suggests is not necessarily a 'flesh-and-blood' individual, but rather 'a structural entity, and organizing principle within the text' that privileges one reading over others. However, video gamers can (as can other audiences) disrupt dominant readings, for as Yates and Littleton argue, Lara Croft is not just watched, but also played, which could allow female players to challenge 'preferred' readings of the *Tomb Raider* video games. In this respect, semiotics is not only helpful to video game analysis, but, similarly, video games can help us to understand how patterns of play may, or may not, alter textual readings.

Geography

It is evident that discussions of new technologically mediated virtual and ephemeral spaces such as 'virtual reality' and 'cyberspace' have influenced not only ideas on the changing nature of identity (as discussed above), but also those relating to the nature of space within a contemporary networked society.

Many of these ideas, and in particular the concept of 'cyberspace', were born out of 1980s cyberpunk literature, and most notably the work of William Gibson. In his novels and short stories, Gibson describes a fictional geo-political system, characterized by weak nation-states and dominant transnational organizations. His work explores the forms of hybrid 'cyber' consciousness that arise from the use of new technologies as a means of domination. Though inspired by the development of new technologies like virtual reality, personal computers and the Internet, Gibson's work focuses as much on the social contradictions thrown up by technology as the machinery itself. It is on the one hand resolutely post-humanist, but also represents a counter-culture romanticism (Longhurst *et al.* 2008).

Nitsche (2008: 17) argues that the concept of cyberspace has 'never totally shed the element of the fictitious'. He continues: '[A]lthough there are conceptual parallels, today's internet does not work or look like the original vision of cyberspace as William Gibson introduced it in 1984, yet the term seems to work as a reference to the web and numerous other digital formats.' The singular cyberspace envisioned by Gibson and other writers has not (yet) materialized, and the possibility of escaping the body and reality remains firmly in the realms of science fiction.

For many writers, though, video gameplay continues to be seen as occupying a kind of borderland space, between the human and the machine, ordinary life and play, or an intersection of all of the above. It is this attitude that has informed the literature on the 'magic circle' (as discussed and critiqued in Chapter 1) as well as references to video gaming occupying a 'liminal space'. For writers such as Salen and Zimmerman (2004), the magic circle constitutes a space where gameplay takes place. It is a temporary place and time where the players of games establish, negotiate and maintain the rules of play specific to that particular time, place and game; rules that do not necessarily apply outside of the circle. Similarly, several authors, such as Wright *et al.* (2002), Dovey and Kennedy (2006) and MacCallum-Stewart (2011), refer to video gameplay as occupying a liminal or liminoid space. A liminal space is often understood as a threshold, a space 'betwixt and between' normal social relations which transcends the limitations of class, gender, race, nationality, politics, religion, even geography (Blackshaw and Crawford 2009).

However, as detailed in Chapter 1, there are a number of weaknesses with such arguments and conceptualizations. The work of Johan Huizinga, from whom the concept of the magic circle is taken, has been described as overly romanticized (Jones 2008), and the fact that many games (of all forms) are often played in a state of only partial attention, and that play is increasingly diffused into our everyday lives, makes the argument that this exists in a magic circle, which is separate and distinct from ordinary life, difficult to maintain (this is discussed further in Chapter 8). Similarly, Thompson (1981) argues that liminality remains a rather insubstantial concept, with little evidence of its existence, the idea being largely based upon commonsensical assumptions and anecdote. Indeed, as Martin (1981) argues in relation to the difference between work and play, 'like switching over the TV channels or changing the script; everyone knows his part in both channels and both scripts' (cited in Blackshaw and Crawford 2009: 134).

My biggest concern with the use of concepts such as the magic circle, cyber-space, virtual reality and liminality is that they are often taken as an excuse to ignore wider social issues and patterns. Sometimes an acknowledgement is made that there is a 'world outside', which can carry over its influence into the magic circle, liminal space and so forth, or that what happens in the play space could have some implications outside of it, but still the world away from play is largely left as an unexplored and distant land. What is needed is a discussion of video gaming that firmly places this within the ordinary and everyday, where it belongs. As Shields (1996a: 3) argues: '[I]t is essential to treat telecommunications and computer-mediated communications networks as *local* phenomena, as well as global networks ... [and] embedded within locally specific routines of daily schedules and the "place-ballets" of individuals' (emphasis in original).

This, however, is not to say that space, both within video games and where play takes place, is not important, as place and space matter very much. For instance, Nielsen *et al.* (2008: 102) suggest that video gameplay can be defined by the 'dynamics emerging from the interplay between rules and geography'. What a video gamer can do in-game, where they can go, what they can see and hear, as well as numerous other in-game dimensions, shape the nature of gameplay. Furthermore, where a video game is played, such as on a bus, in an arcade, in a bedroom, what it is played on, who it is played with, as well as a range of other social, physical and technological factors, also shape the nature of video gameplay.

Space is an important element of the video game experience, and continues to be central to many debates within video game research. In particular, video game space can be defined physically, in terms of the on-screen or space in front of the screen, for example, or more conceptually, as when spaces are understood as rule-based or fictional.

A good discussion of the physicalities of video game space is offered by Nielsen *et al.* (2008). They suggest that video game spaces are as follows. First, by their dimensions, that is to say, if they are two- or three-dimensional. Second, by space type: does the game space wrap around, so that, as in *Defender*, it can be circumnavigated, or is it more abstract, such as in *Spacewar!*, where the spaceship leaving one side of a screen simply appears on the other? This relates to their third element, that of game scrolling. This refers to questions such as whether the game space is revealed by horizontally scrolling, as in *Ghosts'n'Goblins*, or vertically, as in *Commando*, or is scrolling possible both virtually and horizontally, as in *Time Pilot*, or restricted by objects like walls, as in *Gauntlet*? Fourth, and related to this, is the idea of off-screen space. In some video games, the only game space that exists is what is visible, as in games like *Pong*. Other video games have an off-screen area, but this is inactive until the gamer finds and explores it, while in other video games, as in many real-time strategy video games, the off-screen is very much active and changing, even though it is not all on-screen. Fifth, Nielsen *et al.* suggest that time, and how it is portrayed, also contributes to the aesthetics of a video game. 'Play time', which is out-of-game clock time, is not necessarily the same as 'event time', which is the in-game time. For instance, many video games will use cut-scenes to signify the passage of a significant period of time in-game, such as cutting to the next day in the game narrative. Sixth, similarly, game audio contributes to the game experience and its sense of geography. For example, sound effects and ambient sounds can provide a sense of place or distance. Seventh, graphical style can also provide this. A photorealistic game, such as *The 7th Guest*, caricatured characters and spaces, such as in the *Zelda* game series, or a more abstract game environment, such as in *Tetris*, all provide a different gaming experience and geography. Finally, the number of players a video game is designed to be played by shapes its geography and how this is interacted with. For instance, with two players on a single video game console, playing a first-person-shooter like *Call of Duty*, the television screen will most commonly be divided into two halves, showing different perspectives and geography.

Michael Nitsche, also writing in 2008, provides a more conceptual consideration of video game space, and presents this as a consideration of five planes. These planes are:

1   Rule-based space as defined by the mathematical rules that set, for example, physics, sounds, AI and game-level architecture.
2   Mediated space as defined by the presentation, which is the space of the image plane and the use of this image, including the cinematic form of presentation.
3   Fictional space that lives in the imagination, in other words, the space 'imagined' by players from their comprehension of the available images.
4   Play space, meaning space of the play, which includes the player and the

video game hardware.

5   Social space defined by interaction with others, meaning the game space of other players affected (such as in a multiplayer title). (Nitsche 2008: 15–16)

Each of these planes is defined by its own particular qualities, but all have to work in combination in order to provide a fluid game experience, which, Nitsche suggests, players understand as a narrative of space. As Nitsche (2008: 3) writes:

> Through a comprehension of signs and interaction with them, the player generates new meaning. The elements that are implemented in the game world to assist in the comprehension will be called 'evocative narrative elements', because they do not contain a story themselves but trigger important parts of the narrative process in the player. These processes can lead to the generation of a form of narrative.

This is a similar argument to that set out by Henry Jenkins (both alone in 2004 and with Fuller in 1995). In particular, Fuller and Jenkins (1995) suggest that there are striking similarities between the centrality of the exploration of space in video games and that found in sixteenth- and seventeenth-century literature on New World travel and discovery. Hence, what characterizes both gameplay and this New World literature is an exploration and a mastery of space and geography, and to further illustrate this similarity they draw on de Certeau's (1984, 1986) idea of a 'spatial story':

> For de Certeau ... narrative involves the transformation of place into space (117–118). Places exist only in the abstract, as potential sites for narrative action, as locations that have not yet been colonized. Places constitute a 'stability' which must be disrupted in order for stories to unfold ... Spaces on the other hand, are places that have been acted upon, explored, colonized. Spaces become the location of narrative events.
>
> Fuller and Jenkins 1995: 66

This argument Henry Jenkins continues and broadens in 2004, where he suggests that video games not only provide spaces for exploration, but also spaces that facilitate 'different kinds of narrative experiences' (2004: 122). That is to say, video games provide gamers with an environment in which they find their own path and story; a 'map' and a 'tour' to use de Certeau's terminology (see Chapter 8). This also takes narrative analysis beyond merely textual, game-based analysis, towards a consideration of how individual gamers use, interact and play with games. However, what is quite surprising, is that though Jenkins employs the work of Michel de Certeau, who is most famously associated with his writing on everyday life, Jenkins does not carry his consideration of spatial narratives beyond the instance of play and does not fully explore how gaming narratives are embedded within the everyday. It is crucial to recognize that the geography, the place and space, that video games are played in will have a significant influence on how they are played – and this is explored further in Chapter 8.

Chapter summary

- Though some early debates within video game studies revolved around whether emphasis should be placed upon play (ludic) or representational (such as narrative) elements, most contemporary scholars recognize that analysis of both, along with a consideration of the role of the social, is important.
- Contemporary literature identifies a number of important video gameplay elements that are relevant to this book's focus on video gamers and video gamer culture. These are: rules, effects, interactivity, immersion, engagement and flow, performance, identity, roles and embodiment, intertextuality and transmedia, narrative and geography.
- Rules are considered to be one of the key defining features of a game, if not indeed the key feature, and authors such as Salen and Zimmerman suggest that rules are what unite all games. However, others such as Liebe (2008) suggest that the nature of rules in video games is fundamentally different from that in other games.
- A key area that was prominent in early video game analysis, and continues to be a popular topic of debate, is video game violence effects. Authors such as Dill and Dill (1998) suggest that links between video game violence and levels of aggression are more worrying than those seen with other media forms, as video games are more 'participatory'. However, video game violence effects research is deeply flawed, most notably thanks to its inconsistent methodologies and small and unrepresentative sample groups, and because video gamers are seen as passive and vulnerable.
- Interactivity is often held up as another key defining feature of video games. Authors often argue that video gamers are interactive participants, compared to the passivity of audiences of other media forms, such as television and radio. However, other writers question the overuse, misuse and lack of clarity of terms such as 'interactivity'.
- Carr (2006b) suggests that a video gamer's 'absorption' in a game can be understood in terms of their 'immersion', 'engagement' and 'flow'. Immersion can be sensory, where the video gamer is immersed in the gameplay, or a more psychological immersion, where they are immersed in the game world. Sometimes video gamers can be 'engaged' with an activity, but not necessarily immersed in the game, such as when a video gamer has to repeat a task to complete a game goal. Flow is a concept introduced by the psychologist Csikszentmihalyi (1988) to describe a state of heightened awareness, focus and concentration on a goal.
- Crawford and Rutter (2007) identify four key forms of video game performance. They are: where the gamer primarily performs for their own pleasure; when they perform to others in-game; when they perform to those who are in the same location as them; and where video gaming can act as a resource to fuel social performances away from the game screen.
- Early literature on new technologies, such as the Internet, was often concerned with the opportunity technologies afforded individuals to play

with their identities. Though themes of identity play are important in video game studies, most scholars recognize that the out-of-game and offline also play a key role in shaping in-game and online identities.

- Intertextuality refers to how texts reference and borrow from other texts. This is apparent in all media forms, but it is suggested that this is particularly apparent with new media, such as video games. A related concept is trans-media, which refers to the horizontal integration of media, where themes and narratives cross-cut a variety of media texts and forms.

- The presence of narratives within video games continues to be a key battle-ground in video games studies. It is evident that many video games do not have a traditional narrative structure. However, several authors suggest that video games can involve narrative elements, or act as a resource for narrative construction.

- Geography is another key element of video games and gameplay. Many early writers on new media were interested in the opportunities they afforded to explore new spaces away from the everyday. However, video gameplay is not located outside of the everyday or ordinary life, it is built from and within it, and the physical location of video gameplay is important in shaping its nature.

Further reading

Barthes, R. (1978) *Image, Music, Text*, London: Hill and Wang.

Cover, R. (2006) 'Audience Inter/Active: interactive media, narrative control and recon-ceiving audience history', *New Media and Society*, 8 (1), 139–58.

Goffman, E. (1969) *The Presentation of Self in Everyday Life*, Harmondsworth: Penguin Books.

Juul, J. (2005) *Half-Real: video games between real rules and fictional worlds*, Cambridge, MA: MIT Press.

Trend, D. (2007) *The Myth of Media Violence: a critical introduction*, Oxford: Blackwell.

Wright, T., Boria, E. and Breidenbach, P. (2002) 'Creative Player Actions in FPS On-Line Video Games: playing *Counter-Strike*', *Game Studies*, 2 (2). Online. Available HTTP: http://www.gamestudies.org/0202/wright/.

6 Conceptualizing video gamer culture

Introduction

Though the traditional image, often encountered in the popular press, is of an isolated and anti-social video gamer, sitting alone in front of a video game screen, ignoring the world around them and everyone in it (a stereotype discussed in Chapter 1), research on video game culture, time after time, has highlighted its social nature. In particular, Hand and Moore (2006) argue for the consideration of video gamers as a 'community' with extensive and complex patterns of social interaction, culture and norms. This is an argument supported by many video game scholars, and in Crawford and Gosling (2008) we suggest that the majority of video gamers we interviewed readily and willing labelled themselves as being part of some form of video gamer community. This we illustrate with a typical statement from one of our interviewees ('David'):

> [Y]ou know it's [video gaming] important to me because it's another group of friends and I can sort of like you know meet up with people and know people and whatever else, but it is like important. It's a difficult thing [video gaming] … to talk about to people who aren't sort of really aware of it. So although it's an important part of what I do … I know that non-gaming friends know about it, occasionally ask about it, but we talk about other [non-game related] stuff, you know.
>
> Crawford and Gosling 2008: 131

For 'David' video gaming provided him with a group of friends and community separate from his other social networks, such as work and family connections. Though for many, those they share video game interests and conversations with may be the same as, or cross-cut with, other social networks, for 'David', what separated his video gaming friends from other social groups was a shared culture and understanding, which those who did not play video games may not have fully understood. It is certainly evident that those who play video games will commonly share certain knowledges and practices. For instance, video gaming has its own language, or at least set of terms associated with it, such as MMORPGs, FPS, afk, mappers, modders, crackers, hackers, mobs, noob, grinding, bio and many more terms. Chapter 8 will look in more detail at how video gaming is located within social networks and everyday life, but before this, I wish to first address a more fundamental question. That is, if we label, and seek to understand, video gaming as a culture and video gamers as part of a community, then what theoretical tools can we use to categorize and understand this?

Within the existing video game literature a number of concepts have been used to describe video gamers and video game culture. The degree to which these terms are critically reflected upon differs greatly from paper to paper, and author to author, but the main concepts that have been advocated as useful in under- standing video game culture and communities include: *subcultures, neo-tribes, fans, knowledge community, players, Otaku, gamers, scenes* and *habitus*. It is to these terms, their meanings and usefulness in understanding video game culture and communities that I now turn.

Subcultures and neo-tribes

Probably the most obvious concept to turn to when considering video gamer culture is that of a 'subculture'. Many authors, such as Wright *et al.* (2002), Griffiths *et al.* (2004), Yee (2006), Crawford and Rutter (2006), Mäyrä (2008), as well as numerous others, refer to video gamers as a 'subculture', while others, for instance Schleiner (2001) and Cavin and Noguchi (2006), label specific types of gamers, such as 'hackers' or 'modders' (see Chapter 7), as a subculture. However, in most of this literature, there is little real attempt to explain or theorize what this label means or entails.

The term 'subculture' is one that has leaked out of academia into common parlance. To most, it has come to refer to any loosely identifiable, most often youth, group that appears to share some kind of common culture, such as music or pop culture tastes or fashion choices, which is in some way different from what would be deemed 'mainstream' culture. So any interest in goth music, comic books, video games, even ballroom dancing, can be deemed a subculture, as have all of these at one time or another.

It is fairly easy to make the case that video gaming has an identifiable culture, maybe even style, of its own. For instance, Mäyrä (2008) makes a good case, certainly one of the better, for considering video gamers as a subculture by iden- tifying the presence of certain shared traits and practices. Mäyrä suggests that by playing together video gamers develop a shared *language*, and also engage in shared *rituals* of play. Video game culture, Mäyrä proposes, includes the use of similar *artefacts*, like game devices, which may carry memories for the player and others, possibly becoming an item of *memorabilia*. Finally, Mäyrä suggests, video gamers frequently occupy a *shared space*, such as playing together in the same room, or online in the same game environment.

Subcultural theory, however, certainly as it was first proposed, is about much more than shared practices and common spaces. The origins of subcultural theory can be found in two sociological or cultural studies 'schools'. The first is the 'Chicago School', which consisted of a group of scholars at the University of Chicago who, from the 1920s onwards, began studying urban, institutional, interactional and deviant patterns, among others. In particular, the work of, for example, Howard S. Becker (1963) on marihuana users and dance musicians and Albert Cohen's *Delinquent Boys* (1955) provide a foundation for understanding how deviant groups can hold and express different norms and values from those of the wider society. In particular, in his 1955 book, Cohen suggests that working-class boys, deprived of social status and opportunities, would commit 'deviant' acts, which contrasted with middle-class dominant values. This then results in 'pressure' and the formation of 'subcultures', with their own value system, in which members can find in-group status and rewards.

However, subcultural theory was developed most notably by a group of scholars working at the University of Birmingham's Centre for Contemporary Cultural Studies (CCCS or the 'Birmingham School') from the late 1960s onwards. In particular, the Birmingham School were responsible for associating the idea of subculture with particular style groups, such as, mods, punks, skinheads and Teddy boys. Of most note here is the work of Dick Hebdige (1979), who suggests that subcultures engage in a process of 'bricolage', whereby groups draw on existing consumer goods (such as Vespa and Lambretta scooters and smart tailored suits, for mods), but redefine and combine these to develop a distinct style, which marks them out from the general public, and acts as both a means and identifier of social subversion and resistance.

Hence, and crucially, for both the Chicago and Birmingham scholars, subcultures were first and foremost a youth and working-class reaction to their disempowerment. This is an important point, often overlooked by many, and not just those writing on video game culture. As Shaw (2010: 410) argues, Birmingham School scholars such as Dick Hebdige move beyond simply iden-tifying patterns of musical and fashion taste to locate this within, and as an expression of, class identities and tensions. Shaw (2010) argues that a short-coming in the application of this concept by many video game scholars is that it encourages a limited focus on the video gamers themselves. Hence, as Shaw (2010: 410) argues, many video game scholars are 'not looking at this subcul-ture as part of a larger culture'.

Subcultural theories have been extensively criticized, however. The weak-nesses of subcultural theorizations include their failure to consider the internal diversity, the overlaps and movement between subcultures, the instability of these groups and their often permeable and ill-defined boundaries (Blackshaw and Crawford 2009). In reading many subcultural studies there is a sense that the individuals under scrutiny are primarily, if not solely and immovably, a punk, skinhead or other subcultural 'type', almost caricatures set in stone. Adopting a traditional subcultural approach also suggests that these groups form as a response to structural social processes, and most notably their class-derived alienation. This overlooks levels of personal choice and agency. A traditional theorization of subcultures also overlooks the role and influence of the mass media and consumption in helping form and define subcultures. In the work of Birmingham School authors, the mass media tend to be viewed as part of the state apparatus, and, hence, detached from and even opposed to the subcultures rather than playing an important role within their creation (Hodkinson 2002).

There is also a general belief, even by subcultural writers such as Dick Hebdige himself, that subcultures were tied to a particular era, and are less applicable to understanding contemporary forms of youth culture or social groupings. As Hebdige (1988: 8) writes: 'Theoretical models are as tied to their own times as the human bodies that produce them. The idea of subculture-as-negation grew up alongside punk, remained inextricably linked to it, and died when it did' (cited in Hodkinson 2002: 13).

It is suggested that many of the former certainties of life, such as work, social class, locality and religion, have become less important in defining our identities and allocation to social groups. Where once our identities and social belonging were largely assigned to us, it is suggested that 'elective belongings' (Savage *et al.* 2005) become increasingly significant, and in particular that these are facilitated through the rise of consumer choice and culture.

Zygmunt Bauman (1998: 22) suggests, then, that 'ours is a consumer society'. He suggests that all societies are consumer societies, to a greater or lesser extent, but there is something 'profound and fundamental' about the nature of contemporary consumer society that makes it distinct from all other societies (1998: 24). Most significantly, Bauman argues that all prior societies have been primarily producer societies, but in 'our' (consumer) society, an individual 'needs to be a consumer first, before one can think of becoming anything in particular' (1998: 26). According to Bauman, it is consumption that defines who we are and who we can be.

Hence, Bauman argues, social groups, identities and hierarchies become less stable and fixed as traditional markers, such as regional identity, social class and family, become less certain. Moreover, in a quickly changing and 'liquid' world, fixed identities become less useful, so our identities and social groupings similarly become fluid. The concept Bauman employs here to theorize the nature of contemporary social formations is 'neo-tribes'.

Neo-tribes is a term borrowed by Bauman (1990, 1992a, 1992b) from the French sociologist Michel Maffesoli (1996). Bauman, and before him Maffesoli, argue that individuals, increasingly detached from traditional (assigned) social categories, engage in new and fluid (elective) groups (neo-tribes) out of a search for community and belonging. Therefore, 'neo-tribe', or to use Maffesoli's original term 'tribus', refers to the loose, fluid and multiple groups individuals participate in and move in and out of several times a day. Rob Shields, in his introduction to Maffesoli's *The Time of the Tribes* (1996) provides a number of examples of tribus: 'Typical examples of *tribus* are not only fashion victims, or youth subcultures. This term can be extended to interest-based collectives: hobbyists; sport enthusiasts; and many more – environmental movements, user-groups of state services and consumer lobbies' (Shields 1996b: xi).

For Bauman neo-tribes signify a loss of, and a desperate search for, community. Individuals flit between social, consumer and leisure groups out of a search for a belonging that can never be obtained. Hence, for Bauman, neo-tribes are less a theorization of community than part of a wider critique of contemporary consumer culture and the rise of individuality. This, however, is in contrast to Maffesoli's original use of the concept, which sees neo-tribes more as a transformation, and hence the continued resilience, of social belonging and networks, which bind people together in tribalism (Blackshaw and Crawford 2009).

In Crawford and Rutter (2006: 153) we propose that rather than being understood as a subculture, Maffesoli's theorization of neo-tribes might prove 'a more profitable theorization of gamer communities'. This concept would seem to better reflect the fluid, permeable and increasingly diverse nature of video gamer culture, which appears to be a social grouping or identity most gamers move in and out of regularly, such as playing a round of *Call of Duty* with friends online in-between doing homework or discussing tactics for *Football Manager* during a coffee break at work, before moving on to other duties, identities and, possibly, neo-tribes.

But an important aspect of neo-tribes that both Maffesoli and Bauman emphasize is that as a result of their fluid and often changing nature and membership, they possess little social power, apart from the possibility of integration and inclusion, displayed through the habits and rituals of the group, and still able to 'elicit a strict conformity among its members' (Maffesoli, 1996: 15). That is to say, the norms, values and culture of these social groups have the power to define what, and who, can belong to them. For example, Wright *et al.* (2002) discuss how video-game-specific language can operate as an important mechanism of video gamer inclusion and exclusion. But the fluidity of neo-tribes means that they can exert little political power or wider social influence.

There have, however, also been attempts to redefine and salvage the concept of subculture, and most notable here is the work of Paul Hodkinson (2002) on goths. Hodkinson rightly points out that we, as academics, are often far too quick to throw out existing theories in an ever-spiralling attempt to justify our subject areas as 'new' and invent concepts to explain this – something video game studies has often been guilty of.

Hodkinson (2002) argues that subcultural theory does need some adaptation, in that it needs unpacking from ideas of social class structure, resistance and youth. Goths, as well as members of other subcultures, can come from different social class backgrounds, are of varying ages and not necessarily resistant to dominant social values. Hodkinson recognizes that there do exist more fluid and temporal communities within contemporary society which can be defined as 'ephemeral', but others, he argues, can be defined by their 'substance' and relative stability and coherence. In particular, Hodkinson suggests goths constitute a group characterized by substance, in that they have specific identifiable and coherent characteristics and culture, and hence can be understood as a subculture.

Nevertheless, there are a number of weaknesses with Hodkinson's reformulation of subcultural theory. This includes, first, the fact that Hodkinson studied participants at goth festivals, which are likely to have been attended by individuals particularly invested in this culture. Participants at these events may thus reflect only hardcore members and not necessarily the whole culture; an important point to consider if studying video gamers at game conventions, LAN parties or similar. Second, stripping away ideas of youth, class and resistance takes away the very core of what this concept was created to understand, and therefore it leaves the term largely hollowed out and lacking as a useful analytical tool.

Fans

Another term frequently applied to video gamers, or more commonly to certain types of gamers (a point I return to shortly), is that of 'fans'. Again, it is quite easy to find many authors, such as Newman (2004), Burn (2006), Dovey and Kennedy (2006), Crawford and Rutter (2007) and Dormans (2010), who label video gamers as fans, or at least compare them. However, the classification of video gamers as fans, or at least as similar to fans, proves problematic, chiefly because there is little agreement, even within the fan studies literature, as to what or who constitutes a fan.

Most people have a general understanding of what a fan is (Hills 2002). A fan is usually seen as someone with a strong interest in, maybe even loyalty to, a particular sport, team, celebrity, television show, band or similar. However, even this simple definition starts to raise more questions than it answers, such as what makes someone a fan, does this involve a minimum level of interest, dedication or loyalty? These kinds of questions, and more, have perplexed scholars for many years. Hence, beyond everyday or generic definitions (such as that found in the *OED*), defining what is meant by the term 'fan', in a way that can be operationalized and set as a subject area for study, proves quite problematic. As Hills (2002: xi) suggests: 'fandom is not simply a "thing" that can be picked over analytically'; being a fan is not just a label or category, it is also tied into individual and group identities and social performances, which are rarely set or coherent. This problem of definition has led many writers to avoid defining precisely what they mean by the term.

In terms of video game studies, probably the most referred to literature on fan culture is the work of Henry Jenkins, and most notably *Textual Poachers* (1992). This was a particularly influential book in fan studies, but its applicability to video games has been aided by Jenkins himself providing extensive and important writings on video games, gamers and game culture. The early work of Jenkins follows similar lines of argument to the work of his former teacher John Fiske (1987, 1989a, 1989b, 1992), in that both find their theoretical inspiration in the work of Michel de Certeau (1984), and through this they seek to emphasize the potentially creative, and even subversive, nature of certain aspects of consumer culture.

In particular, Jenkins (1992) draws a distinction between ordinary media audiences and fans. Jenkins argues that while general audiences are happy to simply consume popular culture texts, such as television shows, fans will engage with them in a more active and creative way, such as 'poaching' from media texts. The idea of 'textual poaching' is drawn from de Certeau (1984), but here Jenkins specifically uses this concept to describe the ways media fans will take characters, scenarios or narratives from existing texts, such as a television show or film, and use them to produce their own cultural artefacts, such as art, poetry, stories, performances and so on.

The similarities between the kinds of fan creativity outlined by Jenkins (1992) and that of certain video gamers, such as modders, hackers, walkthrough writers and so forth (discussed in more detail in Chapter 7) provides an obvious parallel, and hence the applicability of Jenkins's fan work to video gamers similarly seems a logical step undertaken by many video game scholars. Just as Jenkins's *Star Trek* and *Dr Who* fans take storylines and characters and use them to create art and poetry, *Doom* or *Quake* modders may take game codes and use them to create game add-ons or adaptations, or *EverQuest* gamers take narratives and settings to write new fictions around them. Moreover, just as there have been struggles between fans and official producers of television shows and films over the use of intellectual property, such as characters and storylines, similarly video gamers have frequently encountered legal challenges to their production of game modifications, stories and so forth. One example among many is that of a player of *EverQuest* (known in-game as 'Mystere') who in 2000 was ejected and banned from the game for posting stories based upon the *EverQuest* mythos on the online forum EQVault (Parker 2000). Of course, the relationship between producers of game mods, walkthroughs, guides and similar and the publishers of video games is far from straightforward or conflictual, just like the relationship between media fan producers and television and film companies. For example, many video game publishers are quite supportive of certain aspects of video gamer productivity. A case in point is Value, the makers of *Half-Life* and *Half-Life 2*, who have actively encouraged amateur-produced game modification, but, again, this is an area considered in more depth later in Chapter 7.

It would seem, then, that the activities and position of at least some video gamers does appear to be very similar to that of media fans, as outlined by authors such as Henry Jenkins and John Fiske. However, there are a number of problems with both Jenkins's and Fiske's theorizations of fans, and also their applicability to video gamers. For instance, such theorizations tend to categorize 'types' of people and assign particular activities and attributes to them. Fans are thus always seen as active, and the wider population as invariably passive, but such over-generalizations rarely hold true for all fans, or wider audiences, all of the time. Moreover, it is only the 'active' type of audience, that is to say, 'fans', that are seen as worthy of consideration and study, dismissing the majority of the population as either irrelevant or not of interest. Such categories are often based upon subjective and romanticized ideas of 'authenticity', which see the celebration of one form of audience and the rejection as 'consumerist' of all that is seen as mainstream. As Grossberg writes (1992b: 52): 'while we may all agree that there is a difference between the fan and the consumer, we are unlikely to understand the difference if we simply celebrate the former category and dismiss the latter one'.

Furthermore, in applying fan studies literature to video gamers, the problematic question is raised whether to categorize all or only some video gamers as fans. As mentioned above, it is tempting to see parallels between the productivity of fans and certain video gamers who produce game mods, cheats, hacks, walkthrough, guides and so forth. It is to these types of video gamers that the literature on fans has most commonly been applied (see for example Newman, 2004). Other writers, however, apply fan literature much more broadly to consider a range of gamers and activities, such as Dormans (2010), who advocates the usefulness of applying fan culture literature to the analysis of the players of MMORPGs like *World of Warcraft*, tabletop wargames such as *Warhammer* and Live Action Role Play (LARP).

The claim is frequently made that *all*, not just a minority of, video gamers are 'active'. As argued earlier, video gamers are often viewed as (inter)active participants, even co-authors, in the video game experience. For instance, as cited earlier, writers such as Chris Crawford (1982) highlight gamer 'activity' as a key feature that distinguishes them from wider ('passive') media audiences. This, then, brings us back to the difficulty (outlined in Chapter 5) of operationalizing what we mean by terms such as 'activity' and 'interactivity'. Are only some video gamers active, and hence 'fan-like', or are all gamers active? While it might seem applicable to refer to an individual who produces and maintains a website dedicated to the *Final Fantasy* video game series (of which there are many) as a fan, can we say the same for every player of a video game, even the most uninterested and unimpressed? I certainly see no issue with describing some individuals, such as walkthrough and mod producers (see Chapter 7), as fans, but this may be an ill-fitting label for all video gamers.

Knowledge community

The problem of resolving how media users', including video gamers', creativity compares to, and maps onto, fan cultures is approached by Henry Jenkins in his consideration of the changing nature of fan cultures, most notably his 2006 books *Fans, Bloggers and Gamers* and *Convergence Culture*. Here, and particularly in the essay 'Interactive Audience?' (first published in 2002, but reprinted in *Fans, Bloggers and Gamers* 2006a), he shifts his theoretical inspiration away from Michel de Certeau towards the work of (another French scholar) Pierre Lévy (1997) on 'collective intelligence'; however, there are many continuities with the arguments he sets out in his earlier work, such as *Textual Poachers* (1992).

Jenkins (2006a: 135) argues that rather than focus on whether particular technologies, such as video games or the Internet, are interactive, we need to instead consider the 'interactions that occur among media consumers, between media consumers and media texts, and between media consumers and media producers'. In particular, he argues that we need to consider the rise of what he sees as a new participatory culture of media users. Jenkins, drawing on Lévy (1997), argues that this participatory culture has developed thanks to three key, interconnected factors. First, the advent of new tools and technologies that 'enable consumers to archive, annotate, appropriate, and recirculate media content' (Jenkins 2006a: 135). Obvious examples here would be computers, the Internet, mobile telephones and so forth, which enable users more readily to create, collect and distribute information. Second, the rise of a number of 'subcultures' (to use Jenkins's term), which promote DIY media production, such as video game modders or Internet bloggers. Third, 'horizontally integrated media conglomerates encourage the flow of images, ideas, and narratives across multiple media channels and demand more active modes of spectatorship' (Jenkins 2006a: 136). Here, Jenkins is referring to the rise of 'transmedia', where media narratives increasingly cross-cut, and sometimes require engagement with, different media forms (see Chapter 5). For Jenkins, transmedia requires and presumes the existence of a more active and participatory consumer, who will seek out and actively engage with narratives across a variety of media texts and forms.

Setting out arguments similar to many writers on contemporary community, such as Zygmunt Bauman (as discussed above), Lévy (1997) argues that there has been a decline in the power and pull of what he terms 'organized' social groups, such as nation and religion, as well as 'organic' groups, such as the family and clans, which have been replaced by 'self-organized' groups. These self-organized groups are similar to what Maffesoli (1996) calls neo-tribes, and, Lévy suggests, are held together by shared patterns of production and mutual knowledge, or what Lévy terms a 'collective intelligence'. Jenkins (2006a: 140) argues that this collective intelligence is not the same as the dystopian image of the 'hive mind', where individual thought and voices are suppressed, but rather this is more egalitarian, and 'far from demanding conformity, the new knowledge culture is enlivened by mutual ways of knowing', and this Lévy (1997) terms a 'knowledge community'.

Jenkins (2006a) argues that key examples of new participatory knowledge communities, include (as the title of his book suggests) fans, bloggers and gamers. Here, Jenkins discusses several examples of what he sees as productive, participatory and democratic forms of popular culture use. Again, he revisits arguments about fans poaching from media texts, but to this he adds several contemporary examples, such as the involvement of video gamers in game testing and production. For example, Jenkins (2006a) highlights how LucasArts included 'would-be' players of their new *Star Wars* MMORPG, *Star Wars Galaxies*, in its development process. He also recounts how Maxis encourages 'grassroots' production of game skins and add-ons for their *The Sims* game series, as well as the (often-cited) example of the hugely successful 'player-created' game modification (of the Valve game *Half-Life*) *Counter-Strike*.

These individuals and groups Jenkins sees as at the vanguard of contemporary consumer practices, but argues that active and participatory engagement with media is becoming increasingly mainstream. This Jenkins (2006b) suggests is part of an increasing 'convergence culture'. 'Convergence' is a term that has frequently been used to describe the blurring of media boundaries, and usually in terms of media forms and technologies, such as mobile telephones that can play and record video and music, or televisions that allow users to surf the Internet, or any number of other contemporary examples (considered in more detail in Chapter 8). But for Jenkins, convergence culture is also about a blurring between user and producer patterns and new forms of collaboration and participation; not just for a minority, but, increasingly, for a majority of media users. As Jenkins (2006b: 246) writes: 'participation is understood as part of the normal ways that media operate'. In particular, Jenkins (2006a) argues, gone (or at least added to) is the concept of the passive media-consuming couch potato, replaced (or accompanied) by the image of the (invariably) young male, media- and technology-savvy consumer. 'No longer a couch potato, he determines what, when, and how he watches media. He is a media consumer, perhaps a media fan, but he is also a media producer, distributor, publicist, and critic. He's the poster child of the new interactive audience' (Jenkins 2006a: 135).

Jenkins adds further weight and voice to the argument for considering a wide variety of media users as active and participatory; an argument I would certainly endorse. However, Jenkins is rather optimistic and celebratory of the power of user groups, and Ross and Nightingale (2003: 148) go as far as to describe him as 'utopian' in his outlook. Occasionally, Jenkins does offer cautionary notes. For example, he argues that convergence culture is both 'top-down' as well as 'bottom-up' (Jenkins 2006b: 257), and he writes that 'it would be naïve to assume that powerful [media] conglomerates will not protect their own interests as they enter this new media marketplace' (Jenkins 2006a: 136). However, such statements are usually followed by a countering and wholly positive '*but ...*', such as that concluding this (2006a: 136) quotation: 'but at the same time, audiences are gaining greater power and autonomy as they enter into the new knowledge culture'. Jenkins's occasional cautionary statements are greatly outweighed by his overall optimism, which may at times overplay the power of consumers.

For instance, and as cited above, Jenkins (2006a) uses the much-referenced creation of *Counter-Strike* as an example of participatory video game culture. But as Dovey and Kennedy (2006) argue, this is also a much-romanticized example, which usually portrays the game as the product of a lucky and plucky Canadian student, Minh 'Gooseman' Le. However, *Counter-Strike*, as with most examples of so-called amateur-produced software, such as share- or freeware, was created by an organized and highly skilled team of programmers.

May (2002) argues that this form of 'gift-giving', that is to say, producing goods such as software for free, is not an example of an increasing democratization, but rather a key feature of a new capitalist economy. It is through the production of cultural products such as video game modification and add-ons that amateur or semi-professional producers demonstrate and audition their skills in a corporate marketplace. This productivity, May (2003: 98) argues, is therefore largely driven by the 'promotion of self-interest'. It is, moreover, also a culture readily exploited by media corporations, who are happy to select and use, free of charge, the fruits of the labour of amateur producers, and occasionally elevate some to positions within their companies once they have proved their worth, such as happened with Minh Le.

Additionally, video game publishers legally enforce their relationship with modification producers through End User Licence Agreements (EULA). EULA are the legal blurb users often click to 'accept' and skip past when installing new software, but such agreements ensure that game modifications and add-ons cannot be produced as standalone products, but must remain an add-on to the original, which remains the commercial property of the video game publishers (Newman 2008) (see the more detailed discussion in Chapter 7). As Balnaves *et al.* (2009: 273) write: 'the digital game industry, is therefore, a fascinating example of a profit driven environment that benefits from the non-profit activities of its fan programmers and writers – modders, mappers, skinners and textual poachers'.

Therefore, Jenkins's more recent work may expand his scope beyond media fans and draw in theoretical inspirations beyond Michel de Certeau, but his arguments remain very similar to those set out in *Textual Poacher*, and also suffer from many of the same weaknesses, such as celebrating certain forms of consumption and marginalizing consideration of structural inequalities. Hence even this updated consideration of fan culture does not seem to adequately map onto or fully explain video gamer culture.

Players, gamers and Otaku

It is for the reasons above, and others, that Newman (2008) rejects the concept of 'fan' as a suitable theoretical framework for understanding video gamers and video game culture, and he suggests that we need to look elsewhere. Newman therefore considers a number of other concepts and associated theoretical tools which could be, or have been, used to understand video gamers and video game culture. First, Newman (2008) considers the term 'player'. In Chapter 1, we saw how theories and literatures of play have become probably the most dominant and frequently employed theoretical tools for understanding video gaming. Consequently, referring to video gamers as 'players' is a simple extension of the idea that video games can first and foremost be understood as instances of play. However, Newman argues, focusing merely on the instances of play tells us little about the broader culture of video gaming, or the wide variety of ways individuals can use and engage with video games. As Newman (2008: 17) writes: '"player" is clearly an inadequate term for our purposes'.

Newman (2008) also considers the applicability of the term 'Otaku', a Japanese word which in English means something like 'geek', but is used specifically to describe individuals obsessed with manga or anime. However, given its similarities to the concept of 'fan', Newman feels that this, too, is not an appropriate term to describe the diversity of video game culture.

The term Newman decides upon as most useful for understanding video games and video game culture is simply that of 'gamer'. At a most basic level this is fairly unproblematic. As suggested in Chapter 1, the use of the term 'game' seems fairly ubiquitous; whether we use the prefix 'computer', 'digital' or 'video', the one constant here is the word 'game'. Most people would admit that the 'things' that we are talking about here are 'games', and hence it seems logical that those who play them could be termed 'gamers'. Certainly 'video gamer' is my term of preference, and is used most frequently in this book. However, even though it is not always necessary to use the prefix 'video' before 'game' every time, I would argue that it is still important for authors to be clear when they are referring to gamers of any kind, generally, and when specifically referring only to video gamers. As discussed in Chapter 1, the argument is frequently made, for example by Salen and Zimmerman (2004), that video games are the *same* as older game forms, such as boardgames. However, I disagree with this perspective. Though there are certainly similarities and continuities with video games and other game forms, like boardgames, there are enough differences to suggest that video games are not simply an electronic version of a boardgame (Randall 2011). Hence, the term 'gamer' may be a little too ambiguous and broad.

In addition, there is a second, deeper problem with Newman's (2008) use of the term 'gamer', in that he does not locate this within any wider theoretical framework. We are left simply with a label, a term, for describing those who play video games. This term does not impart, or even suggest, any theory or literature that could be used to understand and analyse this culture and its practices. This therefore leaves us still with the question of how we understand and theorize video gamers.

Scenes

A further term that has sometimes been used to describe video game culture, and one we advocate in Crawford and Gosling (2008) and Gosling and Crawford (2011), is that of 'scene'. As with other, similar labels, such as subculture, the term 'scene' has been used by writers such as Rambusch *et al.* (2007) with little consideration of the specific meaning or theoretical underpinnings of this concept.

In Gosling and Crawford (2011) we suggest that the concept of scene has been used most typically to describe music-affiliated cultures. In particular, Hesmondhalgh (2005) suggests that the concept has been primarily applied in one of two ways. First, as used by authors such as Shank (1994), to describe place-specific music cultures, such as in the UK the 'Mersey Beat' of the 1960s or the Manchester-based 'Madchester' scene of the late 1980s to early 1990s; second, as employed by writers like Straw (1991), to describe non-place-bound flows of music affiliations, such as in the global 'goth' scene (Longhurst 2007). Though Hesmondhalgh highlights the two separate usages as incompatible, and therefore questions the validity of 'scene', Longhurst (2007) suggests that they are not necessarily conflictual, and, in fact, highlight the usefulness of this concept. There are two main reasons for this: first, scene allows for an understanding of how elective belongings are lived out and experienced in our 'ordinary' lives, but, second, of how they may take on 'extraordinary' meanings at certain times and in specific locations. Hence, 'scene' usefully combines an understanding of the importance of place with a consideration of the everyday and ordinary.

The goth scene provides an illustration of this. Goths are part of a wider society and culture, most have jobs, interests and friends outside of the goth scene, but they remain part of this scene in their ordinary lives, primarily through a sense of identity and their music and fashion choices. However, this scene becomes 'extraordinary' and takes on increased significance at certain times and in certain places, such as at goth clubs or, most visibly in the UK, at the bi-annual goth weekends in Whitby in North Yorkshire (see Hodkinson 2002). Focusing on the ordinary lives of goths may lead one to highlight the 'ephemeral' and fluid nature of elective belonging and identity, while concentrating on 'extraordinary' events may lead one to emphasize the stability and 'substance' of this group, as Hodkinson does.

It is possible to understand video game culture in a similar way. The meaning, nature and importance of video gameplay depends significantly upon the physical location in which it takes place, an argument discussed in more detail in Chapter 8. Space and place, both in-game and out-of-game, help determine what is, and what is not, possible, and shape the very nature of play. For instance, playing a video game in a NAMCO arcade in a shopping mall is very different from playing at a LAN event (see Figure 6.1), which in turn is different from playing in a bedroom or living room; each will shape the nature of gameplay in different ways. Location matters, and location is what helps make video gaming take on extraordinary significance for the video gamer. It is possible to understand video game spaces and play as located within a specific 'frame' (Goffman 1961, 1974) or even a 'magic circle' (Huizinga [1938] 1949), and doing so can make video gaming

Figure 6.1 Video gaming at a LAN event (photo: G. Crawford)

seem out of the ordinary, and hence extraordinary, as, in these locations and times, it is. But the concept of scene allows us to understand extraordinary moments as located within a wider, everyday, and at times mundane, culture.

However, the argument made earlier on in this book (see Chapter 4) is that video gaming seems now to be an activity engaged in by a majority, rather than minority, in many countries, such as the UK and the USA. Furthermore, Chapter 8 makes the case that video gaming is, increasingly, an ordinary and mundane activity for many. Therefore, though the term 'scene' theoretically has its uses, it seems somewhat counterintuitive to describe a pastime undertaken by the majority of the population, often in relatively ordinary and mundane ways, as a 'scene', a term most commonly associated with marginal, often spectacular, cultures, such as goths. Moreover, probably only a minority of those who play video games would see themselves as belonging to any kind of 'scene'. Therefore, what might prove more fitting is to understand video gaming as *habitus*.

Habitus

A further theoretical body of work that has sometimes been drawn on in the analysis of video game culture is the work of French sociologist Pierre Bourdieu, and in particular his work on habitus, and more specifically cultural capital, and also its expansion to include discussions of 'game culture' (Consalvo 2007).

Wacquant (2004) tells us that the term 'habitus' originates in the work of Aristotle, but its modern usage was introduced by the French sociologist, and nephew of Émile Durkheim, Marcel Mauss (1934), and developed further by Norbert Elias (1978). However, it is a concept that is today mostly associated with the work of Pierre Bourdieu.

Bourdieu (1977) argued that social life can be understood as consisting of numerous, and interrelated, social spaces or 'fields', examples of which include the fields of art, politics, sport and economics. For Bourdieu, each of these fields has its own habitus. Habitus is similar to what other authors have described as the 'culture' of a particular group or society. However, key to Bourdieu's understanding of habitus is that this is embodied. This, Richard Jenkins (1992: 74) argues, is manifested in three ways. First, habitus exists only 'inside the heads of actors'; for instance, ways of behaving and modes of practice are learned and internalized by social actors. Second, habitus exists only through the practice and actions of social actors, their ways of talking, moving, acting and behaviour. Third, the 'practical taxonomies' actors use to make sense of the world are all rooted in the body: male/female, hot/cold, up/down are all linked to our senses and physicalities.

Bourdieu's theory of habitus has been critiqued by some as being a largely structuralist, and hence rigidly deterministic, model which does not necessarily account for agency and flexibility (see R. Jenkins 1992). However, it is important to recognize that habitus is not a set and inflexible culture, which remains static throughout people's lives. As Bourdieu and Wacquant (1992: 133) suggest:

> Habitus is not the fate that some people read into it. Being the product of history, it is an open system of dispositions that is constantly subjected to experiences, and therefore constantly affected by them in a way that either reinforces or modifies its structure.

In Crawford and Rutter (2006), we argue that the work of Bourdieu is easily applicable to video gameplay and culture, specifically because Bourdieu, an ex-rugby player, often used games as examples and metaphors for understanding social patterns and order, as when describing habitus as being like a 'feel for the game' (Webb *et al.* 2002: 94). Moreover, we argue that habitus is particularly useful in understanding video game culture, and play specifically, because of its emphasis on embodiment. It is evident that playing any game is not just a matter of knowing the rules and acting upon them, but rather video gaming is located within a wider social context and order. However, most of this is not consciously recognized, but rather expressed and experienced through our embodied encounter with the video game, which comes to feel like 'second nature' or an almost automatic response. As Crawford and Rutter (2006: 155) write: 'part of being a successful player of a deathmatch in *Quake* is not just a matter of being an accurate shot, but rather having a *feeling for the game's* development and different strategies that inform when to shoot and how to get into the right position to do this' (emphasis added). Bourdieu can therefore provide important insights into the embodied nature of video gameplay, which, as discussed in Chapter 5, authors such as Grodal (2003),

Sjöblom (2008) and Westecott (2008) have called for greater focus on. Bourdieu also offers an understanding of how our cultural and physical behaviours are learned processes. For instance, though many video gamers may assume, and even argue, that their understanding and feeling for a game is innate and natural, Bourdieu would argue that this is part of a cultural understanding and skill that is *taught* to us. Bourdieu is thus also useful in understanding a video gamer's career (see Chapter 4).

Crucially, Bourdieu's (1977, 1984) theorization is connected to, and an attempt to understand, social class relations and structures. In doing so, he identifies three key types of social resource, or 'capital', which he terms 'economic', 'cultural' and 'social' capital. These three resources then become socially effective, and their ownership is legitimized, through the mediation of a fourth form of capital: 'symbolic' capital (Siisiäinen 2000: 1). Symbolic capital is a development of Max Weber's idea of 'status', in that it refers to a person's, or group's, social standing and prestige (Calhoun 2002) and is the result, and in turn legitimization, of the unequal distribution of economic, social and cultural capital.

Economic capital relates to ownership of and control over economic resources, such as wealth, property and other financial assets. Economic capital can play a direct and obvious role in shaping video gameplay and culture. Video gaming is undoubtedly an expensive pastime, requiring not only the purchase and use of expensive game equipment, such as consoles or computers, but also their updating or replacement as a result of technological advances, the purchase of video game software, which in turn is replaced by newer games or newer versions of games, as well as associated video game cultural activities, such as surfing the Internet or buying magazines and so forth, all of which are underpinned by a capitalist economic system.

As argued in Chapter 4, there is currently very little empirical research on the relationship between economic wealth and video game culture, much-needed though this is, but it is evident that there is not necessarily a simple and proportionate relationship between income and media use. That is to say, it is not simply the case that the more money an individual has, the more video game hardware and software they will own, and the more they will play with this, or, similarly, the more television or films they will watch, and so forth. For instance, even though ownership and monthly subscription rates for satellite television in the UK are relatively high, Van der Voort *et al.* (1998) illustrate that working-class families are more likely to own and subscribe to satellite services than their middle-class counterparts, and also, on average, watch more television. Moreover, Facer *et al.* (2001) in their survey of 855 children found that though working-class children were less likely to own personal computers (PCs), they were more likely to own game consoles than their middle-class counterparts. There appear to be other factors, other forms of capital, beyond the economic, at work here, shaping patterns of media use.

However, economic capital does not only play a role in influencing access to video gameplay, but video gaming may also act as a means of economic capital generation itself. For example, Malaby (2007) highlights how players in 'synthetic worlds', also known as 'virtual worlds' or MMORPGs, can produce or acquire items and wealth which both have value in-game and can also be sold and transferred into out-of-game economic capital. Furthermore, recent years have seen a rise in competitive video gaming, also known as e-sport, which has not only introduced prize money for competition winners, but also seen competitive video gaming become an area of increased sponsorship and gambling. Unfortunately, to date, their still remains little research on e-sports and their participants, but what research does exist, such as the work of Rambusch *et al.* (2007), suggests that this is likely to be a fertile area for further analysis (Crawford and Gosling 2009).

A second form of capital discussed by Bourdieu is what he terms 'social capital'. Social capital can be defined as 'the social networks and relationships associated with civic virtues and social responsibility which involve social communities and other social groups establishing common values, trust and cooperative ways of being and working together for mutual benefit' (Blackshaw and Crawford 2009: 192). Therefore, social capital involves social ties and relationships, but it is more than this; it is about communities, or similar groups, who have shared beliefs and values and who work together for their mutual benefit.

Though not discussed extensively by Bourdieu, social capital is a term that has come very much into vogue in recent years, and in particular with authors such as Robert Putnam. In his book *Bowling Alone* (2000) Putman argues that contemporary American society has seen a general decline in beneficial forms of social capital. The title of his book is not to be taken too literally. Very few people bowl alone, but Putman is arguing that neither are people regularly participating in the public leagues and competitions that were once common throughout America; rather people bowl with those they already know. This, then, simply reinforces what Putman calls their 'bonding' capital, with 'like people', but does nothing to obtain more profitable 'bridging' capital, with those outside their normal social networks. This, Putman argues, is important for both the individuals concerned and the stability and health of society (Blackshaw and Crawford 2009).

Putman provides several reasons for this supposed decline in bridging capital within contemporary America. These include the fact that more women are now in paid employment and so have less time for organizing and socializing, and that more people spend their leisure time in solitary leisure pursuits, such as watching television and playing video games. In particular, at several points in *Bowling Alone* (2000) Putman uses video games as a key example of declining sociability, for example in the comparison he draws between what he sees as the sociable activity of playing card games with others, such as in a casino, and the solitary activity of playing a card game like Microsoft's *Solitaire* on a computer.

Of course, within recent years there has been a fervent argument, particularly from within game studies, against the idea of video games as isolating, anti-social and as a contributor to the decline of social capital within modern America and beyond. It is evident that video gameplay can be, and frequently is, a very sociable activity. This is also a sociability that can at times extend beyond intra-group ties to include the kinds of intergroup relations Putman outlines as necessary for establishing and maintaining bridging capital. In particular, the creation of strong and profitable social bonds is often attributed to playing online video games, and in particular MMORPGs (see Malaby 2007), and also attending video-game-related events such as game conventions or LAN events. For example, Steinkuehler and Williams (2006) conducted a study of the players of the MMORPGs *Asheron's Call* and *Lineage*. From the results of these studies, they concluded that:

> [B]y providing spaces for social interaction and relationships beyond the workplace and home, MMO[RPG]s have the capacity to function as one form of a new 'third place' [between work and home (see Oldenburg 1999)] for informal sociability. Participation in such virtual 'third places' appears particularly well suited to the formation of bridging social capital – social relationships that, while not usually providing deep emotional support, typically function to expose the individual to a diversity of worldviews.
>
> Steinkuehler and Williams 2006: 885

Similarly, Fern Delamere (2011) argues that *Second Life* is a computer-generated 'third place' where people with disabilities can come together beyond work and home life. Third places are, to some degree, a 'neutral' ground, and, therefore, can be a site of community beyond locality. Whilst Delamere points out that digital technology can present some limitations and prove challenging for people with certain disabilities, it can also provide opportunities, acting as a useful source of information and communication for disabled video game players and their family and friends. *Second Life*, in this context, acts as a potential source of social capital, allowing people to build their confidence, learn new communication and technical skills and providing them with the opportunity to socialize with others. To this end, Delamere argues that *Second Life* might lead to a blurring of social capital between 'virtual' worlds and 'real' worlds.

The most widely used and discussed form of capital, both by Bourdieu himself and others, is that of cultural capital. Cultural capital refers to the cultural knowledge, competencies and understanding that people develop, or more specifically are *taught*, through their socialization and their educational experience. Individuals are taught the cultural practices, values and beliefs that correspond to their social class, and this equips them with the tools necessary to operate in society and their place within it (Bagnall 2009).

In his book *Distinction: a social critique of the judgement of taste* (originally published in French in 1979, and first published in English in 1984), Bourdieu sets out an impressive study of cultural tastes and patterns of consumption, derived from his detailed studies of French social and cultural life in the 1960s. Bourdieu argues that all culture is not equal; it is not equally valued and not equally useful as a social resource. In particular, people's cultural beliefs, practices and their 'tastes' are closely linked to their social position, class and educational level. Though individuals may assume that their beliefs, and in particular their tastes, are in some way natural or even innate, as when arguing that they simply have 'good taste', Bourdieu (1984: 7) suggests that these are learned preferences, which play a 'social function of legitimating social differences'. That is to say, knowledge and expertise in certain respected forms of culture, such as high cultural forms like opera or art, are frequently used as a social marker and form of distinction.

Cultural capital is not secondary to either social or economic capital, as each may be important in different contexts, and, furthermore, each capital is potentially convertible into other forms of capital. One example, cited by Bagnall (2009: 49), is that 'people working in certain jobs, may earn high wages [economic capital] yet may not be able to appreciate or understand classical music or fine art [cultural capital]. Whereas, there are some people who are high in cultural capital but comparatively low in economic capital, such as teachers.'

Within the field of video gaming, it is evident that there are patterns and hierarchies of cultural capital. Possessing certain video game skills and knowledges can be very valuable and respected by peers, and, Malaby (2007) argues, can therefore be understood as a form of cultural capital. As Newman (2004: 157) writes: 'sharing and trading knowledge is an important part of the social interactions that take place amongst videogame fans. The complexity of videogames and the wealth of secret features in most titles mean that information as to the whereabouts of a particular key, the solution to a particular dungeon, the technique for defeating a particular Boss character, is immensely valuable.' Chapter 3 considers video gaming as a social career, in which certain gamers will be seen to claim a higher social status and greater gaming knowledge than others, whom they may instruct or share their expertise with. Furthermore, Chapter 7 discusses how various forms of video gamer productivity, such as modding, can also bring with them social status and respect. These examples also demonstrate the interplay between forms of capital, as it is evident that video gamer knowledge can also be seen as a form of social capital, because gamers will often draw on their networks and the knowledge within them.

At the same time, it is questionable whether video gaming carries much convertible cultural capital beyond its own field, as it is very apparent that video games are a frequently condemned and rarely respected cultural form, often categorized as a 'low', or at best 'pop', culture. Searching most, particularly right-wing, newspapers will produce a list of stories denigrating video games. For instance, a simple search (in November 2010) on the website of the British newspaper the *Daily Mail* (dailymail.co.uk) generated links to a long list of alarmist stories about video games, such as 'Average Video Gamer Is 35, Fat And Depressed', 'Children Who Play Video Games for Two Hours a Day May "DOUBLE Risk of Getting ADHD"', 'Violent Video Games Make Children Lose Self-Control'. These stories, and others, would certainly seem to suggest that video games are not generally seen as a useful, creative or artistic cultural form. Certainly, in Crawford and Rutter (2006) we suggest that the critical theorist Theodor Adorno would probably have a lot to say about the contemporary video game industry and its culture. Adorno, writing most notably in the 1930s and 40s, famously criticized the popular culture of his day, and in particular Hollywood cinema and popular jazz music. For Adorno (1991), popular culture, or what he termed the 'culture industry', to emphasize its capitalist industry-based nature, was devoid of any real human creativity, expression or innovation. The purpose of the culture industry was not to disseminate art, to engage or challenge audiences, but rather produce and reproduce easily digestible products. The culture industry produces simple, standardized and formulaic products, based upon what has successfully sold before, and designed to wash over audiences, requiring them not to think too deeply, but rather just consume more. This is an argument that could easily be applied to video games. As we argue:

> [A] limited number of game genres, such as first person shooters and sport-related games dominate North American and European markets. Moreover, the industry is increasingly dominated by a limited number of large companies and numerous games will share the same or similar engines, reducing the need and cost of innovation and so maximizing the risk to profit ration. Further sport games such as EA Sport's *FIFA* get minimal updates and are repackaged and resold each year, while classic games such as *Doom* and *Quake* get simply updated and remade ... rather than creating new games and titles.
>
> Crawford and Rutter 2006: 151

However, there are those, such as Henry Jenkins (2005), who argue that video games do involve high levels of creativity and could be considered as art. There are certainly a number of books on to the subject of video game art, such as Kelman (2005), Jenisch (2008) and Tavinor (2009), to name but a few. There are video game art exhibitions, such as Into the Pixel. As part of the Edinburgh International Festivals in August of each year, video games have their own festival, Edinburgh Interactive; which sits alongside numerous other art festivals, including theatre, comedy and literature. Since 2003 the British Academy of Film and Television (BAFTA), the UK equivalent of the American Academy Awards (the 'Oscars'), has offered a separate annual video game academy award, to complement their existing awards for film and television. There are also many video games produced by small and independent companies which show high levels of originality and creativity. These and other indicators would seem to suggest that video games are increasingly becoming seen as a respected form of culture and, possibly, an art form, at least by some, and therefore might carry at least some form of convertible cultural capital. In particular, Dovey and Kennedy (2006: 78), applying and updating the work of Bourdieu, argue that certain technology-focused professions, such as web design and video game programming, have 'maximum cool' and therefore carry with them symbolic capital. This, therefore, questions whether simple hierarchies of 'high' versus 'low' cultural forms still hold true today.

In particular, in recent years there has been an increasing questioning of whether the conclusions Bourdieu formed, based upon research conducted in 1960s France, can be said to hold true for contemporary societies. One attempt to address such questions is the literature on the 'cultural omnivore', which developed, most notably, out of American sociology in the mid-1990s. The general premise of this literature is that in contemporary society there is occurring a diffusion of cultural tastes, with members of society's elite acquiring more interest in middle- and lowbrow tastes, and, to a lesser degree, those further down the social spectrum developing tastes in high- and lowbrow culture, and middle- and highbrow culture, depending on their position on the spectrum.

Peterson and Kern (1996) suggest that this move from snobbishness to omnivorousness is occurring because of five main societal shifts. First, they point towards structural changes within society such as broadening of education, geographical and social mobility and the growth of the mass media, all of which have reduced cultural distinctions. Second, Peterson and Kern discuss how value changes have led to the tolerance of other cultures, outside of what is traditionally seen as the dominant culture, and we might include here the example of the increased acceptance of video games as a creative, possibly even artistic, form. Third are changes within the art world, where market forces have opened up art to a wider market and broadened its scope. Fourth, they point to generational politics and the liberalization of culture since the late 1960s. Finally, they look towards status-group changes and suggest that increasingly dominant social groups have sought to gentrify aspects of popular culture and incorporate into their own cultural domain. These changes, Peterson and Kern (1996) suggest, have led to a blurring and breaking down of cultural distinctions and hierarchies, and are leading to an increase in cultural omnivorousness.

Erickson (1996) argues that no longer can we talk of a universal culture and universal cultural hierarchy on which cultural capital is based. The most useful cultural resource, Erickson argues, is a wide variety of tastes and 'omnivorousness', which is closely linked to social network variety. Hence, for Erickson, it is social networks which define an individual's cultural resources, and the level of social prestige that they can obtain from these. It follows from Erickson's argument that social advantage is not just achieved and maintained through, for example, the middle classes talking high culture, but also their ability to talk pop culture. The company director may be able to talk about the merits of Toscanini to fellow board members, but is equally equipped to discuss strategies in *World of Warcraft* with the company's IT technician. Warde *et al.* (1999) suggest, therefore, that though a diverse cultural knowledge may be a useful form of cultural capital, Bourdieu's original work should not be overlooked, as expertise in forms of high-brow culture can still operate as an important mark of social distinction.

A development and application of the work of Pierre Bourdieu to video game studies is Mia Consalvo's (2007) concept of 'gaming capital'. In many respects, Consalvo follows a similar path to that set out by Sarah Thornton (1995), in that both Consalvo and Thornton seek to develop Bourdieu's ideas to understand the culture of a specific social subgroup. In the case of Thornton, the group under consideration is the dance music club scene of early 1990s England, while Consalvo focuses on video game players. Both argue that knowledge acquisition, through direct socialization or from secondary sources, such as fanzines, magazines or websites, establishes a form of in-group cultural capital, what Thornton terms 'subcultural capital' and Consalvo 'gaming capital', which is employed and exchanged to establish position within this culture. Consalvo (2007: 4) describes the formation and maintenance of gaming capital as such:

> Games aren't designed, marketed, or played in a cultural vacuum. I would argue that it is somewhat futile to talk about the player or a game in the abstract, as what we know about players can change over time, and be dependent on such elements as player skill and age. Likewise, even the most linear game can be experienced in multiple ways, depending on a player's

knowledge of past games in that genre or series, including previewed information from magazines or Web sites, and marketing attempts at drawing attention to certain elements of the game. All of that knowledge, experience, and positioning helps shape gaming capital for a particular player, and in turn that player helps shape the future of the industry.

This is useful, as it links the study of video gameplay and its culture with a wider media ecology, as well as providing a dynamic understanding of the development of this culture, its membership and internal power relations (Walsh and Apperley 2008).

Though Thornton uses the term 'subculture' to understand clubbers, this is a concept rejected by Consalvo in the context of video game culture. Consalvo (2007: 3) argues that 'a subculture, to be identified as such, must share common symbols, through such things as fashion, music or aesthetics'. This, she suggests, could potentially see the player of certain MMORPGs such as *EverQuest* categorized as a subculture, but it is far more doubtful that this is a term that could apply to all gamers, such as players of a first-person-shooter like *Counter-Strike*. Given the discussion of the limitations of the concept of subculture outlined above, I would agree with Consalvo in avoiding its use. However, equally, I would question both Consalvo's (2007) and Thornton's (1995) need to add to the vocabulary of Bourdieu's work. Bourdieu's concepts of economic, cultural, social and symbolic capital seem perfectly adequate to describe both club and video game cultures. Bourdieu's central argument was that each field has its own habitus, and hence systems of capital, but we lose the sense of interplay and interchangability of capital *across* fields if we continually develop specific concepts for each and every field.

Chapter summary

• This chapter considers a variety of conceptualizations that have been offered in understanding video game culture, and in particular those of *subcultures, neo-tribes, fans, knowledge community, players, Otaku, gamers, scenes* and *habitus*.
• The most widely used concept to describe video gamers is probably 'subculture'. This concept was developed most notably by a number of academics at the University of Chicago in the 1950s and 60s and at the University of Birmingham in the 1970s.
• The uniting theme for all of these writers was that subcultures were understood as a result of, and response to, working-class alienation. This is a fundamental factor that is often lost in contemporary applications of this concept, and devoid of its class basis, this concept becomes hollow and lacking in real analytical value.
• Several authors, such as Bauman (1997, 1998), suggest that changes in the nature of society make social grouping based upon old certitudes such as class less common. What becomes increasingly important are elected, rather than assigned, belongings. To theorize this, Bauman and others utilize the concept of 'neo-tribes' to describe the fluid and flexible elective groups people belong to.

- Another term frequently applied to video gamers is that of 'fans'. However, this is a very ambiguous one and is often poorly defined. It is possible to see parallels between the activities of some video gamers, such as those who make mods and manage websites, and media fans. However, this term is probably ill-equipped to describe all video gamers.
- In the development of his work on fans, Jenkins (2006a, 2006b) proposes the use of the term 'knowledge community' to describe contemporary media users, including video games. For Jenkins, changes in the nature of audiences, consumer patterns and new technologies have led to more cooperative and participatory forms of consumption. However, his arguments concerning the democratizing trends of new media can be seen as rather optimistic, if not utopian.
- Newman (2008) considers the concepts of 'player', 'gamer' and 'Otaku'. Newman dismisses 'player', as he suggests this is too closely aligned with a play-focused approach to video game studies. 'Otaku' he also finds unhelpful because of its specific association with Japanese manga and anime. 'Gamer', he suggests, therefore is probably the most useful term here. However, he offers no real conceptualization or theoretical tools for understanding what a gamer is and what they do.
- Other authors, such as Gosling and Crawford (2011), describe video gamers as a 'scene'. 'Scene' is useful as it recognizes that while elective belongings can take on greater significance at certain times and places, they also diffuse into, and are part of, everyday life. However, if we accept that video gaming is now an activity undertaken by a large proportion of the population, it seems problematic to describe this mainstream culture as a scene.
- 'Habitus' might be a more profitable way of understanding video game culture. Habitus, put simply, is the culture of a particular area or 'field' of social life, but crucially it does not exist outside of social actors, but is rather an embodied system.
- Within social fields there will operate social hierarchies, determined by various forms of capital. For instance, economic capital refers to economic and material wealth. Social capital refers to the strength, type and value of social bonds and networks. Cultural capital is the utilization of taught cultural tastes and knowledges.
- These forms of capital are useful in understanding video game cultures. For instance, social capital can be applied to considering the importance and value of video game and online communities, and cultural capital allows for an understanding of the varying levels of value placed upon different cultural pursuits and industries.
- Some have suggested that strict hierarchies of taste may no longer exist, but it is evident that cultural tastes and knowledges can still operate as important forms of social distinction.
- Consalvo (2007) adapts the work of Bourdieu in her theorization of 'game capital', which is useful as it locates video game culture within a wider of media and cultural framework. However, it is questionable whether there is a need to develop terms for specific fields, as the usefulness of Bourdieu's

model is that it recognizes interconnections of forms of capital across fields, as well as within them.

Further reading

Bourdieu, P. and Wacquant, L. (1992) *An Invitation to Reflexive Sociology*, Cambridge: Polity Press.
Hebdige, D. (1979) *Subculture: the meaning of style*, London: Methuen.
Hodkinson, P. (2002) *Goth: identity, style and subculture*, Oxford: Berg.
Jenkins, H. (1992) *Textual Poachers*, London: Routledge.
Longhurst, B. (2007) *Cultural Change and Ordinary Life*, Maidenhead: McGraw-Hill.

7   Video gamer productivity

Introduction

Chapter 3 recounted Fiske's (1992) argument that audience production can be seen to take three key forms: textual, semiotic and enunciative. Textual activities refer to the creation of new texts, semiotic activities are processes of cognition, such the interpretation and reinterpretation of texts, and enunciativity relates to social and interpersonal activities. While there will inevitably be a great deal of crossover between forms of audience productivity, this tripartite model does provide a useful analytical tool.

This chapter considers various forms of video gamer productivity, but focuses most notably on forms of textual production, and specifically the production of websites, mods and hacks, private servers, game guides, walkthroughs and FAQs, fan fiction and forms of fan art. It is evident that video gameplay involves various forms and levels of semiotic and enunciative productivity. However, this chapter specifically looks at video gamers' production of meanings, community and narrative identities.

Textual productivity

Video gamer textual activity refers to the productivity of secondary or video-game-related texts, such as video game mods, walkthroughs, fan fiction, art, cosplay and so forth. A consideration of such practices is important in video game studies, as it expands the area of study beyond the sight of the screen, and recognizes that video gaming is so much more than simply the interaction of one or a few individuals with a video game machine. The consideration of this form of textual productivity more closely also aligns the analysis of video gamers with previous research on media audiences and fan cultures, and it has been the argument throughout this book that this literature can provide important insights into video games' extended culture. As Burn (2006: 88) writes: 'particularly committed [video game] fans go further, joining online communities of fans, and contributing to message boards, art galleries, writing groups and other forms of expansive embroidery of the game and its components'. In particular, this section focuses on several key forms of textual video gamer productivity, but as with all areas covered in this book, this list should not be seen as necessarily exhaustive.

Websites

The first area of fan productivity under consideration is the creation and maintenance of video-game-related websites. The Internet, and in particular the World Wide Web, have played a key role in the development of video games and video game culture. As we argue in Crawford *et al.* (2011a), video gaming and the Internet have, to a certain extent, had a long relationship. Video games and the Internet are both products of the same era and environments, and their developmental histories are closely intertwined. For instance, early video games, such as *Spacewar!*, were distributed across fledgling computer networks which enabled programmers to play, modify and redistribute games. This sharing and collaboration in video game development, in turn, provided one of the first non-military and non-corporate uses of the Internet, which helped cement the usefulness of this new technology beyond the domains of work and war. Today, the Internet continues to play a significant role in the development of video games, as well as video game culture (Crawford *et al.* 2011a).

Some of the most popular websites on the Internet continue to be search engines such as Google and Yahoo! and major corporate sites like those of Microsoft and the BBC, but recent years have seen the rise in popularity of sites based around some degree of user-generated content, such as Wikipedia, YouTube, Blogger, Facebook and MySpace. This has led some to suggest that the World Wide Web has now evolved into what is sometimes referred to as the 'Web 2.0'. This evolution is supported by changes and developments in technology and the structure of the Internet, but also refers to the more 'interactive' and 'user-controlled' nature of the web, incorporating many more social networking sites such as Facebook, blogs (short for web-logs), wikis (websites that allows users to edit and add to contents, such as online encyclopaedias like Wikipedia) and so forth (Longhurst *et al.* 2008). Forms of Web 2.0 user participation and creativity are, as discussed in the previous chapter, key examples of what Jenkins (2006a, 2006b) sees as the increasing control of the Internet by users, their 'collective intelligence' (Lévy 1997), and democratization trends in information communication technologies. In particular, Jenkins (2006b) points to Wikipedia as an example of a collective and democratic knowledge base, which Jenkins (2006b: 255) claims: 'works because more and more people are taking seriously their obligations as participants to the community as a whole'.

It was the hope of many that the Internet would provide alternative means for the distribution of information and ideas, of creativity and expression; and to some extent it has. The Internet does provide a greater opportunity for user contribution and participation than probably any other form of mass media, such as print media or television. It could also be argued that the nature of the Internet has had a significant effect on shaping the development of other mass media forms, such as television, which have moved to include more user interaction and user-generated content.

In particular, websites provide video gamers with a means to access and distribute information and content, as well as interact with fellow video gamers and, occasionally, video game producers. For instance, Boellstorff (2008) discusses the web activities of *Second Life* players (known as 'residences'), which include the creation and maintenance of *Second Life*-related blogs, guides, galleries of pictures and videos, and much more beyond. However, the creation and maintenance of the video-game-related websites themselves is a surprisingly under-considered area of video game culture. Many popular and successful video-game-related websites are created and maintained by video game fans. However, academic focus is often placed most specifically upon what the sites host, such as walkthroughs, mods and fan art, but it is important to recognize that websites are, in themselves, examples of video gamer productivity.

However, it is important not to get too carried away with the idea of the Internet as a form of democratization, as, of course, Jenkins's and others' somewhat optimistic reading of the empowering and revolutionary nature of the Internet can be challenged – for instance, see the arguments of information society sceptics such as Christopher May (2002) that are touched upon in Chapter 5. Dick Hebdige (1979), writing on subcultures, argues that capitalism has an ability to incorporate, sterilize and sell back to consumers ideas of resistance. A sizeable proportion of user-generated content is enabled, hosted, censored and ultimately owned by profit-making corporations such as YouTube and Facebook. Even non-profit-based organizations such as Wikimedia, who own Wikipedia as well as numerous other websites, are not beyond the editing and censorship of user-generated content. Furthermore, even the argument that Wikipedia is 'more' democratic than traditional offline print encyclopaedias like *Encyclopaedia Britannica* is questionable. Though websites such as Wikipedia are supposedly open for all to create content, the ability to do so is severely restricted by access to relevant technology and knowledge, and only a very small percentage of users actually generate content. Furthermore, Wikipedia is not generally accepted by many as a 'legitimate' repository of knowledge and 'truth', particularly by those who are traditionally seen as the guardians of knowledge, such as academics. Similarly, many video-game-related websites are owned by capitalist corporations, and, most commonly, video game production companies themselves. It could be argued that the creation and maintenance of video-game-related websites, as with mods (discussed below), adds to the popularity and profit-making longevity of many video games. For instance, websites offering advice on how to complete tasks in MMORPGs like *World of Warcraft* help ensure that video gamers do not get stuck, bored and drift away from the game, taking important subscription revenue with them. Video game companies can also be quite controlling of online content related to their particular products, removing or censoring user-generated content on official sites, or issuing cease and desist orders to third-party websites they deem to be infringing their intellectual property rights and profitability.

Mods and hacks

Probably the most-cited and -discussed example of video gamer productivity is software and hardware 'modification', or as it is frequently known, 'modding'. Video game modifications, or 'mods', most commonly refer to a modification to an existing video game program or a game add-on; such as the popular game add-on *Atlas* in *World of Warcraft*, which adds additional maps and user inter-faces. These kinds of video game add-ons are also sometimes called 'plug-ins'. Other types of mods include 'mapping', the development of new video game environments, most commonly in first-person-shooters ('mapping' is also used to describe the act of creating maps (or a complete atlas) of the in-game area, such as those provided in game guides), or 'skinning', which is where 'in-game char-acter graphics are altered and replaced with scans of figures from other games, other cultural texts, or images of gamers themselves' (Newman 2008: 163). These forms of video game fan creativity, Wright *et al.* (2002) suggest, are 'not unlike creating works of art'.

Another form of modding is video game subtitling or translation, where some modders will add subtitles or change audio in imported video games (usually Japanese) to allow them to be played by non-native-speaking video gamers (most commonly English-speaking). Here, Newman (2008) draws parallels with the activities of fans of anime and manga who translate or subtitle texts, often referred to as 'fansubbing' or 'fanslation'.

More extensive video game modifications are sometimes referred to as 'total conversions'. This is where the modification of the video game is so extensive as to render its origins almost invisible. The most frequently referred to example here is *Counter-Strike*, which, though built out of the program code of *Half-Life*, provides a very different video game and game experience.

Video game modification is as old as video games themselves. *Spacewar!*, which is often seen as the 'first' video game, was freely and widely distributed between the creators' friends, colleagues and beyond, some of whom added to, adapted and modified the game (King and Borland 2003). Those skilled in programming have been adding to and modifying program codes throughout video game history. However, video game modding became much more widespread with the release of *Doom* by id Software in 1993. The designers of *Doom*, Carmack and Romero, were particularly adept at seeing the opportunities afforded by allowing users to add to, modify and develop their games further (Dovey and Kennedy 2006). *Doom* was easily modifiable thanks to the innovation of game WADs. WAD refers to the file suffix '.wad', which supposedly stands for 'where's all the data?' WAD files are packages containing video game data, such as graphics and levels, and therefore creating new WAD files allows users to modify the content and nature of the video game. Notable *Doom* WADs include the *Eternal Doom* WAD, which was created by TeamTNT and first released in 1996. The *Eternal Doom* WAD introduces a time-travelling subplot and changes the original *Doom II* levels to reflect a variety of historical settings, including a medieval fortress and crypt.

The reasons for producing video game modifications are manifold. Like many hobbies, there is an inherent pleasure to be obtained from the act of production itself, whether in making a video game mod or building a model airplane. It is also apparent that video game modding is part of a 'gift-giving economy', where modders produce video game adaptations and add-ons and freely distribute them to others (such as to friends or over the World Wide Web), which is likely to bring the mod creator a sense of achievement, if not pride, in their endeavours. As discussed in Chapter 6, Jenkins (2006a) sees modding as one example of an increasingly participatory culture of media consumption and 'DIY aesthetic', which also sees video gamers actively involved in the design, testing and further development of video games. Jenkins argues that this DIY (counter)culture was born out of a 1960s revolutionary mentality, which saw the production of alternative media forms, such as posters and radio, which challenged the dominance and legitimacy of mainstream media. He continues:

> The DIY aesthetic got a second wind in the 1980s as punk rockers, queer activities, and third wave feminists, among others, embraced photocopied zines, stickers, buttons and T-shirts as vehicles for cultural and political expression. These groups soon recognized the radical potential of videotape for countersurveillance and embraced the 'digital revolution' as an extension of earlier movements towards media revolution.
>
> Jenkins 2006a: 149–50

This DIY aesthetic, Jenkins argues, manifests itself in the forms of the 'cultural jammer', who seeks to subvert, block or opt out of mainstream media consumption, and the 'poacher', who is 'dialogic rather than disruptive, affective more than ideological, and collaborative rather than confrontational'. He continues: 'poachers want to appropriate their content, imagining a more democratic, responsive, and diverse style of popular culture' (Jenkins 2006a: 150). Examples of poachers, as the title of his 2006 book suggests, include, fans, bloggers and gamers. As proposed in Chapter 6, Jenkins provides a rather enthusiastic, if not utopian, reading of the opportunities and empowerment afforded poachers and jammers by digital technology: 'the new digital environment expands their [consumers'] power' (Jenkins 2006a: 151). However, modding is not just about user participation, empowerment or the democratization of video game production.

As noted above, May (2002) argues that the gift-giving economy of video game modding, as well as other forms of online productivity, are primarily about building individual reputations and status. According to May: 'this new information community is individualized in the sense that the reasons for electing to join are the promotion of self-interest' (2002: 98). Aphra Kerr (2011) argues that key motivations for producing video game mods frequently include building status through social capital within the video gamer community and demonstrating skills, which will enable the individual to get a job within the video game industry. Moreover, the production of mods is a gift economy that the video game industry can transform into a profitable commodity through their use and enforcement of End User Licence Agreements (EULA). As suggested earlier, EULAs usually insist that mods exist only as an addition the existing video game, and hence cannot be played without a legally owned version of the original video game. Moreover, most EULAs ensure that any mods or add-ons are automatically the property of the company that owns the original video game source. This means that the modder is not allowed to (economically) profit from their endeavours, but, if the video game developer sees fit, they can incorporate any mods into the video game and sell it on. But even if the video game manufacturer does not decide to directly profit from the work of unpaid mod developers, they often reap indirect benefits, as the existence of mods adds to the longevity of a video game's playability and hence its continued sales. It has also been suggested, by the likes of Newman (2008), that often modders can be more creative and innovative than those already employed in the video game industry, because modders have more freedom to take risks and experiment. Hence, here again, the video game industry can benefit from the creativity and innovation of the unpaid modders. However, on balance, both Jenkins (2006a) and May (2002) overstate their arguments. As Mactavish (2008) maintains, the modder is simultaneously both submissive and resistant to the video game industry. Everyday life is rarely, if ever, wholly controlled or free, as Michel de Certeau (1984) remarked, but will, often at the same time, involve strategies of regulation and tactics of subversion (see Chapter 8).

Modding is sometimes conflated with 'hacking', and the two terms are often used interchangeably. For instance, Newman (2008) discusses modding as a subcategory of hacking. However, hacking is often used to specifically refer to illegally breaking into a computer program code, or similarly breaking through computer security systems. Forms of video-game-related hacking include 'homebrew' and 'cracking'. Homebrew refers to users making software changes to hardware that is not usually adaptable or programmable by users (often known as 'proprietary hardware'), such as video game consoles, like the PlayStation Portable (PSP). This usually involves editing the firmware, which are small fixed programs integral to the operation of hardware, or developing emulators, which are programs that allow computers to run software not specifically designed for that platform, such as running Commodore 64 games on a Nintendo DS. Cracking is the act of removing or circumventing software security systems. This usually involves hacking a program to remove, for example, anti-piracy mechanisms or regional coding, which prevents the video game from being played on a game machine purchased in a different geographical region (Newman 2008). Cracking therefore is often used in the illegal copying and distribution of video games.

Furthermore, modding can also refer to the modification of hardware as well as software; and two key examples of this are 'case modding' and 'chipping'. Case modding refers to the modification of hardware, usually PC casing, often in unusual or artistic ways (see Figure 7.1). For examples, the European trade fair for video games, Gamescon, held annually in Cologne, has a case modding competition. In 2010 submissions included PC cases that looked like a military radio, a minimoto (small motorbike), as well as various wooden 'steampunk'-inspired PC and laptop cases. Chipping usually refers to the act of adding a physical component to an existing piece of hardware, such as an additional microchip, which is most commonly done to circumvent video game security systems, for example to enable the playing of copied games.

Private server gaming

Another form of video gamer productivity is the creation and maintenance of online 'private servers'. Private servers are unauthorized, usually illegal, servers set up to run alternative versions of commercially available, most commonly MMORPG, video games, such as *World of Warcraft*, *Lineage* or *Ragnarok Online*.

Figure 7.1 A modified PC casing (photo: G. Crawford)

Lin and Sun (2011) argue that the typical view, certainly from the larger video game companies, whose games these servers replicate, is of private servers as akin to music or software piracy and, hence, ultimately criminal. Those who play on private servers are also often seen as a small minority of deviants, who exist on the periphery of mainstream video gaming.

However, Lin and Sun suggest that this is a far more complex relationship. In particular, they highlight a plethora of reasons for using private game servers. These include allowing 'nostalgic' players to play video games that are no longer officially supported (such as was the case with the *Uru* players discussed by Pearce 2009, 2011 – see later in this chapter), or video gamers who are dissatisfied with the way official servers are managed or structured. A key example here would be that some private game servers allow rapid level progression, enabling players to move quickly through the more tedious parts of an MMORPG. Private servers also frequently offer greater levels of customization and individualization of the video game experience, rather than the sometimes 'one-size-fits-all' attitude to how video games should be played evident in many official game servers.

Lin and Sun (2011) therefore demonstrate that there is a much more complex relationship between official and private servers, where this is not necessarily the one-dimensional parasitic draining of video gamers away from official servers commonly assumed by many. Private servers are a form of gamer productivity, which allow players an alternative game experience where they can circumnavigate the parts of the official game that they do not enjoy, or experiment with new styles of play, which, they suggest, may actually help keep players on the official servers, rather than drifting away from the game altogether.

Game guides, walkthroughs and FAQs

Video-game-related user productivity is not restricted solely to software or hardware modification, and can extend beyond this, as well as beyond those related to direct interaction with the video game itself. In particular, I want to turn now to 'secondary' texts constructed to complement gameplay, such as 'guides', 'walkthroughs' and 'FAQs'.

Terms such as 'game guides', 'walkthroughs' and 'FAQs', as well as some others, are frequently used interchangeably, or at least their meanings often overlap significantly. This is because there are often no clear divisions between these types of texts, but generally we can make some loose distinctions here. FAQs are answers (often user-produced) to specific issues or questions (FAQ standing for 'frequently asked question') about a particular video game. For example, an FAQ might address where to find specific items in a video game, such as the location of all of the vault bobbleheads in *Fallout 3*, like that produced by Nick Zitzmann and available online at gamefaq.com. Walkthroughs are usually more comprehensive and provide a more detailed guide to how to 'complete' a video game. (I use the term 'complete' here loosely, as what 'completing' a video game means varies greatly from video game to video game, from walkthrough to walkthrough, and even from gamer to gamer, playing the same game.) Walkthroughs usually provide specific and procedural steps needed to get to the end of a video game; that is, if the particular video game has an 'end'. Some walkthroughs ignore any activities that are not necessary to reach the end point (whatever that is deemed to be) of a video game, such as ignoring side quests, while others aim to be more 'completist', offering a guide on how to, for instance, explore all aspects of a video game map or achieve a '100 per cent' completion rating. Related to walkthroughs and FAQs are 'cheat' or 'cheat code' lists. Some video games will include aspects that the video gamer can use to their advantage. This may include exploiting game bugs (errors in the video game's coding), which are in the game by mistake, or at times programmers put commands into video games which when entered by the gamer (such as typed commands or pressing a certain combination of gamepad buttons at a specific point in the game) will produce certain predetermined results. For instance, on the PlayStation 3 version of *Grand Theft Auto: San Andreas*, the gamer pressing the gamepad buttons, triangle, L1, triangle, R2, square, L1, L1, in that order, turns all the cars in the game invisible. There are many more codes like this, in this video game and others. Additionally, the introduction of game 'achievements' on the Xbox 360 and 'trophies' on the PlayStation 3, which are token rewards given to video gamers for completing certain in-game acts, has produced a new kind of user-produced list: the achievement/trophy list (or FAQ), which details achievements/trophies for a particular video game and (usually) how to obtain them.

Walkthroughs, FAQs and game lists usually contain only text, and are most commonly saved as simple text-only files, like plain text (files with the suffix '.txt') or rich text ('.rtf') files. In contrast, some users produce maps or atlases that chart the geography of a video game; which is often referred to as 'mapping'. These maps can be quite detailed and colourful, and are sometimes constructed from in-game graphics or screen shots, such as the detailed maps of *World of Warcraft* featured on the website mapwow.com.

In contrast to walkthroughs, FAQ, cheat, achievement and trophy lists, maps and so forth, 'game guides' is a term, Newman (2008) suggests, which should be used more specifically to refer to, usually more complex, multi-component texts. That is to say, game guides are texts that provide a more comprehensive guide to a video game than just a walkthrough, FAQ, list or map, but may include these components, along with other elements, such as, for instance, background to the video game's design and development. Many game guides are produced by professional publishing companies, probably the most notable example being the BradyGames series, a division of Penguin Books, which produces thousands of video game 'strategy guide' books. However, hardcopy books are not the only example of video game guides, and there are also many websites that could be classed as online game guides providing a variety of information on video games, including maps, FAQs and walkthroughs. Again, these online guides are sometimes 'professionally' produced, BradyGames, for example, also produce 'eguides', but there are also many examples of user-produced online guides.

It is evident that most guides, walkthroughs, FAQs and so on are written in a dispassionate, procedural style, relaying detailed information on what actions need to be undertaken step-by-step in a video game, for instance. However, Burn (2006: 91) argues that this dispassionate style hides motivations that are 'full of passion'. Burn (2006: 90) argues that for the producers of walkthroughs, and other similar gameplay aids, the thrill comes from their 'exhaustive expertise'. Walkthrough authors, FAQers, mappers and the like get pleasure from demonstrating their video gaming skill and knowledge, and it is also a demonstration of expertise that can bring them acclamation and esteem from other gamers. As Burn (2006: 92) writes of Kao Megura, a producer of several video game walkthroughs:

> We can see the social motivation of walkthrough authors like Megura as a kind of advanced version of the 'expert' ... he wins social standing among the player community by specializing in the stripped-down, efficient sequence of commands that gets the player through the game system. He goes on to build a kind of career for himself as expert, however – a career which is characterized by the excessive, excited, language of the obsessive amateur on the one hand, and by the cool, detached tones of the professional on the other.

Therefore, we can again see elements of both resistance and inclusion in the acts of amateur game aid producers. By producing detailed walkthroughs, maps or similar, 'amateur' producers are subverting the 'dominant' ways the video games were, most probably, intended to be played. They allow, for instance, video gamers to circumvent certain aspects of the game, or avoid having to explore or take wrong turns (literally and metaphorically), or exploit bugs in game code. This can also be seen as a way of empowering video gamers, and Newman (2008: 112) suggests, applying Jenkins's (2006a) arguments, that the production of video game aids of this sort could be understood as an example of collective intelligence. It is evident that there is often a dynamic relationship between video gamers and video game aid producers, where gamers will not only use, but also contribute to, guides and often enter into an ongoing dialogue with the authors, who are, in turn, invariably video gamers themselves. However, as with video game mods, the impetus for producing video gameplay aids, at least to some, may be about selfish ends, and specifically about developing individual reputation and status. Game guides extend the playability and hence profitability of games. Furthermore, video gamers have differing opinions on the legitimacy of using video game aids of this nature. In particular, Newman (2008) argues that for many video gamers, the assistance provided by these kinds of tools is tantamount to cheating, and therefore undermines the challenge of playing and mastering a video game.

Fan fiction and art

Where the primary focus of authors of video gameplay aids, such as walkthroughs, FAQs, cheat lists and so forth is the mechanisms of the video game, Burn (2006: 92) suggests that these elements are largely ignored by the producers of video-game-related art, fiction and so forth. For the makers and authors of video-game-related artistic work it is most commonly video game narratives that act as their primary inspiration and resource. Here, it is obvious, and probably just, to draw parallels between the production of video-game-related artistic and fictional texts and those produced by fans of other media forms, such as television and cinema, on which there already exists an extensive literature (such as Radway 1984; Bacon-Smith 1992; H. Jenkins 1992). For writers such as Newman (2004, 2008), Schott and Burn (2004), Burn (2006), Dovey and Kennedy (2006) and others, the producers of video-game-related art, poetry, fiction, music, machinema, cosplay and so on (see below) can clearly be considered as 'fans', and their activities understood using the same theoretical tools and approaches developed in the study of other media fan culture (see Chapter 6).

Fan fiction, a term sometimes abbreviated to 'fanfic' or 'fic', has a very long literary pedigree. Since antiquity, readers have drawn on, reinterpreted, reworked or built upon the work of others. This is a common literary practice. In particular, the Bulgarian critic and philosopher Julia Kristeva, in her use of the term 'intertextuality' (see Chapter 5), suggests that any text can be analysed in terms of the other texts that it has absorbed and transformed, as all texts are constructed from a 'mosaic of citations' (Kristeva 1969), where texts quote, borrow, echo, allude to, parody and pastiche other texts. The lines between originality and imitation, as well as professional and amateur production, have always been somewhat blurred. However, fan fiction, as we know it today, probably developed most significantly in the late twentieth century. What is often identified as a key development here is the growth of fan fiction inspired by science fiction television programmes from the 1960s onwards, and in particular *Star Trek*. Television series such as *Star Trek* inspired a multitude of fans to start writing stories and poetry and producing art and music and so forth. These fan productions were sometimes distributed individually or compiled, perhaps in fanzines, and distributed via mail or at science fiction conventions. However, the Internet has undoubtedly added new possibilities to fan fiction production and distribution. The Internet provides a means of easily distributing fan-produced texts, as well as greater access to resources and information, such as databases of scripts, characters, show-listings and so forth, allowing fans more easily to link into networks of fellow fans and fan writers, who in turn can contribute to work, as well as provide ideas and information.

It is to this rich, and well-researched, culture, that video game fan productions are added. Of course, there are notable and sizeable crossovers between the production of science fiction and video-game-related artist endeavours. For instance, in an era of increasing media convergence (see Chapter 8) and transmedia forms (see Chapter 5) we see key 'brands' such as *Star Trek*, *Star Wars*, *Harry Potter* and *The Matrix* expanded across a variety of formats such as books, films, television and video games, all of which become resources that fans draw on in the construction of their own artistic outputs.

Burn (2006) discusses the production of fan fiction inspired by the *Final Fantasy* video game series, posted on the website Final Fantasy Shrine (ffshrine. org). Burn argues that the fan fiction he considers has nothing to do with the systems or mechanisms of the video games or their gameplay, but instead draws on their characters and narratives. In particular, Burn considers a specific story which seeks to fill in the gaps and develop the stories of key characters from the *Final Fantasy* series, such as Cloud and Aeris. Here, Burn draws on the work of Hodge and Tripp (1986), who consider the reading of television cartoons by children. Burn argues that like the children in Hodge and Tripp's study, fan writers selectively draw on elements of a narrative and construct them into their own version of events. Hodge and Tripp, drawing on literary theory, refer to this as 'paratactic'. Parataxis places together events or acts side by side in short, simple forms, such as one thing happened, then another and another. Hodge and Tripp argue that this is how children read and recounted the narratives of cartoons; not as complex and whole, but rather a series of events. Burn argues that fan fiction writers similarly draw out key events, characters and so forth from narratives and use them to construct their own paratactic stories. For Hodge and Tripp, this kind of paratactic construction is a form of oppositional reading. It is the children ignoring the intended dominant reading of the cartoon and constructing their own alterative version of this. However, Burn argues, for his *Final Fantasy* fan writer, this is not necessarily oppositional in its reading and representation of video game characters and narratives, but, rather, portrays them in this story in ways that adhere to a 'conventional' reading of the characters and narratives. As Burn (2006: 94) writes: '[W]e might modify Hodge and Tripp's rather idealistic view of paratactic readings, then, to suggest that such readings produce interpretations of the text to fit the reader's singular preoccupations, but that these may or may not be closely aligned with the representational strategies of the text.'

For Newman (2008), what he sees as particularly significant about fan fiction is the collective and collaborative nature of this. Newman suggests that fan fiction is rarely produced alone. At its most simplistic, writers will draw on others' stories and ideas for inspiration, but also by posting work on fan fiction websites (such as fanfiction.net), other contributors will review and offer feedback, advice and encouragement on work. Websites such as fanfiction.net harbour a community of writers, who often work together, offer guidance and enable the sharing of knowledge, and like Jenkins (2006a), Newman here turns to the ideas of collective intelligence (see Chapter 6) in theorizing patterns of collaboration.

However, it is important not to be too utopian in considering such patterns of fan collaboration. An important aspect of fan production involves the establishment and maintenance of 'the canon'. The canon refers to what are seen as acceptable and legitimate characters, stories, events and so forth, and therefore, by extension, what is outside of the canon. For example, Newman (2008) draws attention to the fact that *Sonic the Hedgehog* fan fiction writers frequently deem only video games produced by Sega as part of the acceptable *Sonic the Hedgehog* canon. Fiction that draws on video games that feature Sonic, but are not a Sega production, are judged not to adhere to the accepted and legitimate knowledge surrounding Sonic and his fellow characters. Though Newman and, more so, Henry Jenkins (1992, 2006a) are keen to emphasize the supportive and collaborative nature of fan writers, it is in relation to the idea of the canon that Newman (2008: 63) acknowledges that fans can be a 'highly critical community'. What writers such as Newman and Jenkins, in their search to emphasize the democratic nature of fan production, do not fully explore is that fan communities are often very hierarchical and can be very critical and judgemental. As Schott and Kambouri (2006: 122) argue:

> [G]ame culture can serve as an arena for the creation of hierarchies and for the bullying of weaker members of a group; and it can be a vehicle for the 'border-work' that marks the boundaries between boys and girls, and thereby prevents girls form gaining access to technology or the knowledge that is required to use it.

Maffesoli (1996) (see Chapter 6) writes of neo-tribes that the one power communities of this nature have is to differentiate who and what falls within their group and what constitutes legitimate forms of knowledge and patterns of behaviour. For instance, Newman (2008: 59) discusses how fan fiction writers obtain respect and status from innovation, but only within certain boundaries, as defined by the canon and fellow writers. This is very similar to the activities highlighted by Paul Hodkinson (2002) in his consideration of goth culture in the UK. Hodkinson similarly argues that goths obtained respect and standing from pushing at the boundaries of their 'subculture', in terms of dress or musical tastes, for instance. However, those deemed to be overstepping the mark were ridiculed and marginalized by others within the group. But what writers such as Newman, Jenkins and Hodkinson fail to fully articulate is the importance of power relations. That is to say, certain individuals, or groups, have more power than others to define what is and what is not acceptable and legitimate knowledge. This is something Anthony King (2001) recognizes in his consideration of football hooliganism and collective memory, arguing that within this particular culture, there are only certain individuals who are deemed to have the right to define what is legitimate knowledge and the accepted version of events. Who has the right to establish legitimate knowledge and behaviour is usually determined by owner-ship of capital, whether economic, cultural or social capital (see Chapter 6). Fan communities, of all kinds, therefore need to be understood not as democratic and utopian spaces but, rather, socio-cultural fields with hierarchies and patterns of inclusion and exclusion.

Closely linked to fan fiction is the production of video-game-related fan poetry. For example, Burn (2006) discusses fan poetry that draws on the *Final Fantasy* video game series as its inspiration. What Burn finds most interesting here is the use of a first-person perspective in many of the poems present on the *Final Fantasy* Shrine website, where the poem places the reader in the role of a video game character by using the first-person pronoun 'I'. This is a common strategy in many media fan texts, such as poetry and fiction, but Burn argues that here it also replicates the video game system. It is the video gamer who controls the in-game avatar and plays the game, hence it is they who undertake the actions, and this, Burn suggests, is replicated in video-game-inspired poems, which are most commonly written from the perspective of the protagonist. This, then, seems, to some extent, to contradict Burn's earlier point in relation to fan fiction, that they do not consider the video game system. Burn is suggesting here that the act of playing the video game, in the role of the protagonist, does have an influence on how video-game-inspired poetry and fiction is written. This is a point made by Newman (2008: 53), who suggests that writers of fan fiction inspired by video games have a different range of experiences and types of engagement to draw on than fans of other media forms. This includes not only the video game's narra-tives, but also its systems and how it is played and performed.

The next key area of fan productivity I wish to consider is that of video-game-inspired fan art. The most obvious, and probably common, form of video-game-related fan art is static visual artworks, such as paintings and drawings. Video games have provided particularly fruitful sources of inspiration for the creation of visual art. For instance, a quick search of the World Wide Web for art relating to popular video games and game series, such as *Final Fantasy*, *Grand Theft Auto*, *Gears of War*, and especially MMORPGs, such as *World of Warcraft* and *EverQuest*, to name but a few, produces a vast array of fan-produced pictures and artwork. Once more, authors such as Schott (2006) and Newman (2008) empha-size the communal nature of fan production, suggesting that fan artists frequently collaborate and help others develop skills and techniques. However, though occa-sionally some fan art may challenge the heteronormativity of mainstream media, such as by depicting male homosexuality, a much larger proportion often conforms to highly sexualized fantasy depictions of women. Here again, Newman high-lights the importance of the canon, and the need for artists to work within certain accepted parameters of legitimate knowledge and styles. In particular, Newman suggests that a lot of fan art is reverential, mimicking the styles of, usually profes-sional, video game artists, such as those employed to produce artwork for adver-tising campaigns, official books or game boxes. This can lead to some narrowing of artistic styles and expression, and while some fan art is impressive and at times even innovative, Newman (2008: 74) argues that 'it would be wrong to create the impression that videogame fanart exclusively comprises rich, playful work that is executed with consummate technical skill. Much videogame fanart, just as much fanart inspired by other media forms, is derivative and lacking imagination.'

Burn's (2006) consideration of Yaoi art is of interest here. Yaoi, Burn tells us, is an acronym taken from the Japanese words for 'no climax, no point, no meaning'. Yaoi is a subgenre of Japanese 'amateur' (*doujinshi*) manga comics, which focus specifically on homoerotic and homosexual relationships between male characters, and are most commonly produced by women. Yaoi is therefore the production of both visual art and fiction, in comic book format. The inspiration for Yaoi comic books is therefore not just video games, but also the histories and traditions of manga. Burn suggests that this style of video game fan production tends to be the most removed from the original video game themes and narratives, and it is therefore more subversive than many traditional fan-produced stories and artwork, particularly since Yaoi challenges the common heteronormativity and male-gaze perspective of most video games (Newman 2008).

Obvious parallels can be drawn between Yaoi and the 'slash fiction' writing of, predominantly American, science fiction fan groups, and, again, most notably female writers. Contemporary slash fiction has its origins in 1970s *Star Trek* fan writing, where this subgenre began to surface through (largely) female fans producing homoerotic literature focusing on the relationships between key characters from the *Star Trek* television series (Sandvoss 2005). (The term 'slash' is taken from the slash between the characters' names depicted in these stories, such as Spock/Kirk.) As with other forms of fan fiction, slash began as photocopied and hand-distributed stories, but has been greatly enhanced and expanded by the advent of the Internet and the World Wide Web. Studies of slash fiction can be illustrative in helping us understand Yaoi, and, in particular, Sandvoss's comparisons between the work of Henry Jenkins (1992; also Tulloch and Jenkins 1995) and Camille Bacon-Smith (1992) are helpful here. Though the focus of both Jenkins and Bacon-Smith is *Star Trek* fandom more generally, both consider slash writing within their studies. A significant difference here is the degree to which Jenkins and Bacon-Smith interpret fan writers and writing as resistant to the male hegemony of mainstream science fiction writing. For Jenkins, slash fiction presents a key example of the renegotiation of gender roles and challenges dominant power relations. As Tulloch and Jenkins (2005) argue, the polysemic nature of *Star Trek* proves a fertile ground for slash fiction writers to subvert traditional ideas of gender. As they write: 'the generic multiplicity and ideological contradictions of *Star Trek* invite fans to construct their own utopias from the material it provides ... By rethinking the utopian vision of Star Trek, [slash writers] ... rescue the female characters from the stereotypical on-screen behaviour' (Tulloch and Jenkins 2005: 212, cited in Sandvoss 2005: 26). By contrast, in Bacon-Smith's study of the female fans of *Star Trek* there is much less evidence of a struggle for a utopian future (Sandvoss 2005). For these particular female fans and slash writers, their activities were much less concerned with ideas of challenges to dominant gender relations and hegemony, but much more about their own everyday struggles and deprivation (Sandvoss 2005: 26). Though it is Henry Jenkins who most notably draws on the work of Michel de Certeau in theorizing the activities of the fans he considers, it is actually the activities of the group of female fans that Bacon-Smith studies that fit most closely to de Certeau's (1984) ideas of 'making do'. As discussed in greater detail in Chapter 8, for de Certeau, resistance is not necessarily about obvious and grand challenges to visible power relations, but rather social resistance can be found in mundane and everyday activities, such as the adaptation and personalization of what life presents individuals with. This, in many ways, is what Bacon-Smith's women were doing; not engaging in some kind of subversive 'guerrilla' warfare (to use Fiske's 1989a description of fan activities), but rather 'making do', and making sense of what life gave them. This is important: for fan art and other forms of productivity to have significance, they do not necessarily have to be about utopian ideas of visibly challenging and subverting dominant power relations, ideas and ideologies. Michel de Certeau teaches us that there is significance, human creativity, and even beauty, in the minutiae of everyday life – an area explored further in the following chapter.

Static visual artwork, such as paintings, drawings and Yaori comic books, are not, of course, the only forms of video-game-related fan art. For Newman (2008), fan art also includes the production of music, crafts and costumes, and to this Dovey and Kennedy (2006) also add 'machinema'. For instance, Newman (2004, 2008) highlights how some video game fans will carefully and meticulously transcribe and re-perform video game soundtracks, sound effects and theme tunes, or remix them into new musical creations; many of which can be found posted on video game fan websites. However, here I wish to focus on just two further examples of fan artistry, those of machinema and cosplay.

The term 'machinema' is a contraction of the words 'machine' and 'cinema', and, put simply, denotes the act of film-making using video games. In machinema video characters and objects are manipulated to 'act out' scripts, with a soundtrack, such as actors' voices, either dubbed on afterwards or provided in real time by actors voicing over the actions of the in-game characters. Probably one of the most successful and well-known examples of machinema is the comical science fiction series *Red vs. Blue* (or *RvB* for short) produced by Rooster Teeth from 2003 onwards using the video game *Halo*. *RvB* is mainly filmed using linked Xbox video game consoles. The audio soundtrack is usually recorded beforehand and the controllers of the in-game characters (the actors) move their characters to correspond with the prerecorded dialogue. This is then recorded by an additional player who acts as the 'cameraperson' for the production. The action and dialogue are then put together and the whole film edited using video editing software, in a final post-production stage, all of which produces often impressive-looking and sometimes very humorous short films. Newman (2008) finds machinema particularly significant, arguing that this is an example that challenges game studies' primary focus on the act of gameplay. Machinema is the use of video games, not as a tool of play, but rather as performance. As already highlighted, play and performance do not need to be mutually exclusive, as all video gameplay is in itself an act of performance, particularly (but not necessarily only) when gameplay involves other individuals. But I accept, and ardently support, Newman's general tenet here, that video games have other uses and significance beyond merely the act of play. Therefore, as Newman (2008: 147) argues, academic consideration should expand beyond game studies' narrow focus on playing video games, to consider, what he refers to as 'playing *with* videogames' (emphasis in original). This therefore includes what individuals do with video games, beyond simply playing them: writing walkthroughs, producing mods, making machinema or, another area considered by Newman, using video games as an inspiration for costume production and dress, often termed 'cosplay'.

'Cosplay' is a contraction of the words 'costume' and 'play' or 'role-play'. The meaning and boundaries of cosplay can vary, but generally cosplay involves wearing costumes, which have usually been made by the individuals themselves, to depict a specific fictional character, most commonly from Japanese popular culture; such as manga, anime and video games, such as the *Final Fantasy-*inspired cosplayers pictured in Figure 7.2.

Cosplay remains primarily associated with Japanese culture, but in North America and Europe, Japanese-inspired cosplay is increasingly blurring with Western fan traditions of dressing up as science fiction television and film characters, such as those from *Star Trek*, along with live-action role-players (LARP) and historical re-enactment participants, such as those involved in civil war (most commonly English or American) battle re-enactments. Hence, there is a significant blurring in cosplay between the culture of video gaming and other fan cultures.

*Figure 7.2 Final Fantasy-*inspired cosplayers (photo © Russell Fenton; foxseye.com)

Newman (2008) suggests cosplay is subversive as it challenges and plays with ideas of identity, and it is also a place within fan culture significantly populated by women, who frequently find themselves marginal and marginalized in other areas of fan culture, as well as video gaming. Furthermore, Lamerichs (2010) suggests that cosplay can also involve more 'transformative' forms of play, such as engaging in 'gender play', with, for example, women dressing up as female *Mario Bros*.

Cosplay costumes are usually made by the individuals themselves, or sometimes cosplayers commission others to make costumes for them. However, Lamerichs (2010) argues that most respect is given to those who make their own outfits, and shop-bought costumes are usually frowned upon. Newman (2008: 88) suggests that 'what is particularly interesting about cosplay is that, despite the inference in its name, it does not typically involve role-playing'. Newman may not be clear enough here in relation to what he classifies as 'role-playing', but Lamerichs in her study of cosplayers certainly suggests that part of cosplay is about adhering to character traits, and cosplayers receive encouragement for acting like the character they are portraying.

However, following Hills's (2002) consideration of the 'performative consumption' of cult media fans, it is important that the dressing up in character is not understood merely as imitation. For instance, Hills cites Henderson's (1997) discussion of a Japanese Elvis impersonator, Mori Yasumasa. Henderson (1997: 251–2) suggests that this impersonator, and others, are not simply trying to be, or even replicate, specific characters or celebrities, but rather they are using them 'as a platform for their own personality' (cited in Hills 2002: 165). Hills therefore suggests:

> The Elvis impersonator's remaking of the flesh is ... not a denial of the body, but exactly part of that process which Baudrillard (1993: 23) believes we no longer have time for: 'to search for an identity for ourselves in the archives, in a memory, in a project or a future'. The fan's writing of Elvis upon his or her (see Henderson 1997: 125) body *is* that search, not for a 'look' or visuality (an 'I want to look like Elvis') which Baudrillard (1993: 23) diagnoses as the condition of contemporary consumer culture, but for a being (an 'I want to be (like) Elvis'). Elvis impersonation is a project; it represents recourse to an archive (the precise catalogue set of jumpsuits and outfits worn on stage by Elvis; images of Elvis; set-lists and conventionalised details of his stage show), and recourse to a powerful set of memories; those of the fan's lived experience *as a fan*.
>
> Hills 2002: 164–5; emphasis in original

Hills's (2002) discussion of 'performative consumption' offers an understanding of how consumer goods and resources are frequently drawn on by fans, along with their own lived experiences and other influences, in the construction of their identities. Identity, then, is not something simply bought off the shelf, as the likes of Bauman and Baudrillard would suggest, but rather needs to be understood as a 'project', where consumer goods and mass media resources may be drawn on by fans to fuel their performances and the construction of their identities.

Newman (2008) argues, as with fan fiction and artwork (both discussed earlier), that cosplay is a largely supportive and cooperative community, where, through websites, conventions and meetings, cosplayers offer advice, guidance and encouragement to others within their hobby group. However, he also highlights the importance of 'the community's agreed practices' and of 'externally verifiable' authenticity (Newman 2008: 86). Lamerichs's research hints at a community that can be at times very critical, maybe even exclusionary, of those who do not adhere to an accepted canon. It therefore seems, as with other fan cultures, that cosplayers operate within a dynamic code of practice, which frequently rewards innovation, but equally chastises that, and those, deemed to have transgressed its social boundaries.

Semiotic and enunciative productivity

So far this chapter has focused most keenly on the textual productivity of video gamers, such as the creation of video game mods, fan fiction, art and so forth. These forms of productivity are probably the most visible and obvious forms of video gamer creativity, as they produce tangible outputs, such as written stories or cosplay performances. However, Fiske (1992) alerts us to the fact that productivity can also take the form of cognitive and social processes, what he refers to as semiotic and enunciative production.

Semiotic production

It is evident that playing a video game will most often involve forms of semiotic productivity. Contrary to media effects theory (see Chapter 5), video gamers are not passive recipients of media messages, but are active participants in the creation of meanings and social values. It is evident that the meanings and social norms surrounding play are not wholly, or necessarily, inbuilt in the video game's code, but rather are, to a large degree, constructed through processes of cognition and social interaction. For instance, players will construct and maintain rules beyond those inherent in the video game's program, and, as discussed in Chapter 5, Grodal (2003) points out that all narratives need to be understood as embodied processes. Here, video gamers receive only partial information, which they process, interpret and make sense of, all of which can be understood as forms of semiotic production.

Examples of semiotic production of this nature can be understood using Charles S. Peirce's ([1909] 1998) distinction between icon, index and symbol (Randall 2011). Icons refer to a likeness or resemblance of an object. For instance, in a *Mario Bros.* video game, the pixels that constitute Mario depict an Italian-American plumber. The video gamer is presented, not by a real plumber, a flesh-and-blood Mario, but rather an icon, which the gamer takes to represent an Italian-American plumber. Indices demonstrate the influence of an object. For example, a video game cut-scene may feature the sound of a gunshot and a game character falling to the floor in a pool of blood. The sound of the gunshot and the action of the falling character are indices that refer to the person being shot. A symbol is a referent of an object or action, but has no direct likeness to it. A good example of this would be achievement points on the Xbox 360, where achievement points refer to the completion of particular in-game actions, but the points do not resemble the particular action undertaken. Icons, indices and symbols, of this nature, are present in all video games, and require the video gamer to engage in a process of semiotic productivity to link the particular icon, index or symbol to particular meanings and appropriate responses. The video gamer has to understand that the sound of a gunshot refers to a gun, or that the strangely shaped pixels moving down a game screen in unison are *Space Invaders*. They need to then process, order and make sense of this information, and react accordingly. However, the meanings we attach to objects and how we react to them, are not natural or innate, but rather learned patterns (a habitus or frame) that the audience has to tap into and process to make sense of the particular text they are presented with. Furthermore, the reading and interpretation of a video game are not restricted to information present in the game text itself. As highlighted in Chapter 1, Jones (2008) argues that what constitutes the meaning of a video game is also constructed from paratextual sources, such as the complex web of advertising, reviews, media, understandings, interpretations and interactions surrounding video games and their culture. Furthermore, as highlighted in Chapter 5, the reading of a video game will also invariably involve intertextual, and possibly transmedial, links to other texts and media forms.

Producing community

Enunciative production refers to the social and interpersonal activities of audiences. This can take the form of, for example, conversations, such as meanings and interpretations communicated between individuals, or in the display of particular associations, as when Fiske (1992) discusses football supporters wearing team colours or Madonna fans dressing up like their idol. Enunciative production is important in the formulation and maintenance of communities, and in turn, individuals' identities as part of a particular community. The enunciative activities of video gamers are a greatly under-researched area, but a crucial part of video game culture.

The previous chapter suggested that video gamers can be understood as a community (Hand and Moore 2006); however, as with all forms of elective belonging, communities of this nature are not spontaneous, rigid or constant, but rather they are dynamic and fluid structures that are, at least to some extent, created and maintained by their members. A video game community can therefore be understood as an enunciative production.

A key example of the enunciative production of video gamers is Celia Pearce's (2009, 2011) discussion of players of the MMORPG *Uru: Ages beyond Myst*, which provides important insight into the creation and maintenance of a video game community. *Uru* was the only online game in the popular *Myst* video game series. It was released as a beta version in 2003, and was quickly populated by up to 10,000 players; however, at least at that point, *Uru* did not make it to full release, closing after less than six months. What, to that point, had primarily been a single-player game series, played, Pearce suggests, by many who would describe themselves as 'loners', with *Uru* it became an online communal experience. Once the closure of this game was announced, players began almost immediately to discuss and make plans to migrate to another online game world. Though players eventually moved to a number of different online worlds, the most significant migration was to There.com. What was particularly significant about this migration was that the gamers did not simply give up on a now-dead game and move on, but rather engaged in a purposeful attempt to maintain and continue the identity and community established within *Uru*. This involved creating avatars, landscapes and objects in There.com, similar to those seen in *Uru*, and maintaining close social ties to fellow *Uru* players. The case of *Uru* thus provides a revealing example of patterns of video gamer community, creativity, loyalty and identity formation. This Pearce (2006, 2011) refers to as 'productive play', where play transgresses into creative and worklike activities – in this case *Uru* players working at maintaining this community and identity.

Of course, there will also be crossovers and interplays between forms of textual, semiotic and enunciative productivity, a good illustration of which is the work of Anne-Mette Albrechtslund (2008, 2010). Albrechtslund considers video gamers' online storytelling. She suggests that video gamer storytelling is similar to fan fiction, as this is a form of video-game-related narrative written out and posted on websites. However, for Albrechtslund this is not exactly the same; where fan fiction simply draws on video games for inspiration in creating new narratives, video game storytelling is more closely associated with telling a story about video gameplay. This therefore has more in common with the 'war story' recounted by tabletop wargamers, as discussed by Kirshenbaum (2009), and highlighted here in Chapter 5.

Albrechtslund discusses a particular *World of Warcraft* guild website, an area of which is dedicated to the telling of stories about the guild's history and members' adventures playing *World of Warcraft*. Though this history of the guild and its members does include some fictitious elaboration, to make it more story-like, Albrechtslund suggests that the focus of the narrative still remains primarily on actions that have been played out in-game. Therefore, this form of video game storytelling is both textual and enunciative, and will also inevitably involve elements of semiotic productivity, such as the use of icons, indices and symbols.

Albrechtslund (2008) suggests that video-game-related stories are important in questioning the rejection of narrative as a useful tool of video game analysis. As reported in Chapter 5, several contemporary writers, such as Eskelinen and Tronstad (2003) and Frasca (2003), have sought to distance video game analysis from media and literary studies, suggesting that the theoretical tools used in the study of media texts, like narrative analysis, are not applicable to the study of video games. Probably one of the most influential papers to make this case is Jesper Juul's 'Games Telling Stories?' (2001). In this paper, Juul argues that not all video games have traditional narrative structures (see in Chapter 5). For example, puzzle-style video games like *Tetris* have no identifiable narrative, while in many other video games, the fictional world in which they are set provides only a backdrop for the action. In a challenge to these and similar arguments, and in a play on the title of Juul's original paper, Albrechtslund in 2008 presented a conference paper at the University of Southern Denmark entitled 'Gamers Telling Stories' which went on to form the basis of an article, of the same name, published in *Convergence* in 2010. In these papers, Albrechtslund argues that the work of the French philosopher Paul Ricoeur on narrative identity is particularly useful in understanding the stories that video gamers tell, and, in particular, the relationship between individuals and community narratives, and fiction and history within them, an argument we similarly make in Crawford and Gosling (2008) and Gosling and Crawford (2011).

Narrative identity

For Ricoeur (1988) the idea of 'narrative identity' suggests the idea of a self as a 'storied self'; made up of stories told by the person about themselves and their lives, stories told by others about them and wider social and cultural narratives. Similarly, Giddens (1991) suggests that the 'narrative of the self' is a modern social construction linked to our contemporary ideas of romantic love, which requires the active construction of a shared history. The role of narrative in identity and group construction is also taken up by Longhurst (2007), who argues that within an increasingly media-drenched society, the mass media operate as a resource on which individuals actively draw in constructing narratives, identities and social performances. Therefore, media, including video games, not only help inform what people talk about, but also how they appear and perform to others.

Each individual thus develops a life narrative and sense of who they are; an identity, through narratives. This then recognizes the temporal nature of identity, for, as with a never-ending story, this is always being constructed and developed and so is ever-changing. This theorization also overcomes the dualism of fiction and history, recognizing that personal narrative identities are a construct of both of these. Likewise, narrative identity mediates both 'sameness' and 'selfhood', locating individuals within a wider community and cultural narrative, but identifying the individual's specific location and personal narrative within this. For instance, in an argument that replicates King's (2001) study of football hooligans (discussed above), Albrechtslund (2008, 2010) suggests that only certain individuals in the *World of Warcraft* guild she considers had the right and power to dictate what was deemed the authoritative story of events. Both individual and group narratives invariably shape individuals' identities, therefore. As Giddens writes:

> A person's identity is not to be found in behaviour, nor – important though it is – in the reactions of others, but in the capacity *to keep a particular narrative going*. The individual's biography, if she is to maintain regular interaction with others in the day-to-day world, cannot be wholly fictive. It must continually integrate events which occur in the external worlds, and sort them into the ongoing 'story' about the self.
>
> Giddens 1991: 54; emphasis in original

Other authors have effectively used the idea of narrative identity in considering different aspects of contemporary leisure, and of particular note here is the work of Tony Blackshaw (2003). Blackshaw provides an insightful ethnography of the leisure lives of a group of working-class men in Leeds (UK). He suggests that in an increasingly 'liquid modern' (Bauman 2001) world, where the certitudes of life such as social class, occupation and family become increasingly fragile, identities similarly become more fluid and flexible, out of the need to negotiate one's identity and social position within this ever-changing world. Blackshaw suggests that for the group of men in his study, as with many others, this 'liquid' world creates anxieties and a sense of dislocation, which they seek to combat through the creation of narrative identities played out in certain (hyperreal) 'solid' masculine environments, such as the local pub. It is in these locations that the men draw on each other's constructed identities and narratives in (re)asserting and (re)defining their own masculine identities and narratives.

The idea of increasingly fluid identities within contemporary society is related to video gaming by Miroslaw Filiciak (2003), and in particular how MMORPGs allow individuals to play with their identities and construct what Filiciak refers to as 'hyperidentities'. However, though Filiciak (2003) acknowledges that in-game identity formations draw on and influence what he refers to as 'real life' emotions, Filiciak's main focus is upon in-game identity formations and he does not fully explore the location or implications of video-game-related identities within a wider social setting. However, as argued earlier, there is little doubt that not only is video gameplay influenced by its location with everyday social practices, but that video games' importance extends far beyond the sight of the screen, helping to shape the individual's sense of identity, life narratives and social networks – and it is to the question of the location of video gaming in everyday social life that the following chapter turns.

Chapter summary

- This chapter utilizes Fiske's (1992) three key forms of audience production (textual, semiotic and enunciative), but focuses most closely on video gamer textual productivity, considering the production of websites, mods and hacks, private servers, game guides, walkthroughs and FAQs, fan fiction and art.
- The growth of a wider distribution of web-content generation has led to the creation of more websites dedicated to video games and video gameplay, and the creation and maintenance of these sites can be understood as a form of video game textual productivity.
- Probably the most discussed forms of video game user productivity are mods and hacks. Mods describe modifications to existing software or hardware. They can be simple, such as a game plug-in, or more extensive, such as completely remodelling a game's appearance and play-style.
- Though modding is sometimes seen as a form of democratized, participatory and collaborative community, some would argue that modders are often driven by selfish ends and in turn are frequently controlled and exploited by a capitalist video game industry.
- Private server games are the running of online video games on unofficial, usually illegal servers. Though often dismissed as a marginal act, this again

could be understood as a form of video game fan productivity, which displays a wide range of significant content generation and play patterns.

- Game guides, walkthroughs, FAQs and so forth describe texts produced to assist others in their video gameplay. Though 'official' and professionally produced game guides exist, most player aids of this nature are usually produced by video game fans and freely distributed online.

- Parallels are frequently drawn between the producers of fan fiction and art inspired by video games and those who draw on other forms of media, such as science fiction films and television shows.

- Fan fiction and art are often seen as a form of collaborative and supportive production, which is sometimes subversive in its use and challenging of mainstream media; for many, an example of Lévy's knowledge community. However, it is important to recognize that fan communities can also be very exclusionary and hierarchical and are not necessarily subversive.

- The consideration of fan fiction and art, as with other forms of fan productivity, such as mods and game guides, is important, as this recognizes that the significance of video games extends far beyond the sight of a game screen.

- It is evident that playing a video game, as well as consuming associated paratexts, involves, at times, significant levels of semiotic productivity. Semiotics teaches that meanings are never uncomplicated, but are always arbitrary. That is to say, there is not a simple relationship between object and meaning. Rather, meanings are learned, and understanding is an active and social process of interpretation and reinterpretation.

- Forms of social, or enunciative, production include the creation and maintenance of video gamer communities and gamer identities. In particular, the work of Albrechtslund (2008) and Crawford and Gosling (2008) suggests that video games can be used to create social narratives, which gamers construct in creating and maintaining social networks and identities.

Further reading

Burn, A. (2006) 'Reworking the Text: online fandom', in D. Carr, D. Buckingham, A. Burn and G. Schott (eds) *Computer Games: text, narrative and play*, Cambridge: Polity, 88–102.

Dovey, J. and Kennedy, H. (2006) *Games Cultures: computer games as new media*, Maidenhead: Open University Press.

Newman, J. (2000) *Playing with Videogames*, Routledge: London.

Pearce, C. (2009) *Communities of Play: emergent cultures in multiplayer games and virtual worlds*, Cambridge, MA: MIT Press.

Ricoeur, P. (1988) *Time and Narrative*, vol. 3, trans. K. Blamey and D. Pellauer, Chicago: University of Chicago Press.

8   Video gaming and everyday life

Introduction

The argument of this book is that video gaming needs to be understood not as a solitary leisure activity that occurs only at certain isolated times and locations, but rather as a culture which extends far beyond the sight of a video game machine or screen. As Burn (2006: 88) writes:

> [E]ngagement with the game does not finish when the game session ends and the computer or console is switched off. Players continue to think about, imagine, even dream about, the events, landscapes and characters of the game.

Video gaming is not just the act of playing a game, but also a source of memories, dreams, conversations, identities, friendships, artwork, storytelling and so much more. In turn, video gaming is located within and is part of and shaped by a wider society. Hence, an academic focus merely on the instance of video gameplay touches on only a very small part of what video gaming is, and as Newman (2004: 153) argues, greatly 'impoverishes the study of video games'.

It is to this end that authors such as Jenkins (1993), Newman (2004) and Crawford and Rutter (2007) have repeatedly called for the study of video games to significantly widen its scope beyond a primary, if not sometimes sole, focus upon video gamers' direct and immediate use of the game text and interface. This is a call that has recently started to be heeded, as more and more writers, such as Dovey and Kennedy (2006), Nielsen *et al.* (2008) and Newman (2008), are considering in more detail what video games mean in a wider social setting and what a video game culture entails.

In particular, Nielsen *et al.* (2008) apply the work of Aycock (1988) on chess to video game culture. Aycock argues that chess involves a culture beyond the instance and psychology of play, which includes a wide variety of social and cultural practices and meanings, such as tournament rules, equipment, organizations, publications and so forth. This Aycock calls the 'metaculture' of the game. Adopting this perspective, Nielsen *et al.* similarly argue that video gameplay has both a gameplay-culture and meta-culture, and similarly that there are gameplay communities, such as those who play together online, and metaculture communities, which include out-of-game online discussion boards, magazines and gamer discussions. This theorization is useful in recognizing that the social significance of video games extends far beyond the instance of play, and that, in turn, there are wider social and cultural influences upon this practice. However, creating a dichotomy of play culture and a wider (meta) culture is not necessarily helpful, and the argument in this chapter, as throughout the book, is that it proves more useful to understand video gameplay as part of the fabric of everyday life, rather than seeing wider culture as a separate culture beyond the instance of play.

Therefore, where Chapter 6 considered theoretical tools that could be used to understand video game culture, and Chapter 7 discussed examples of video gamer productivity, this chapter deals much more specifically with the nature of this culture and its location within wider society and patterns of everyday life. It begins therefore with a brief introduction to theories of everyday life before reflecting more closely on how such theories have been applied to the study of video gaming. However, the argument is made here that very few theorists have considered video gaming as located within patterns of the everyday away from the video game screen. This is particularly significant when, as this chapter argues, video gaming is increasingly becoming a relatively ordinary and everyday, at times even mundane, activity. The chapter finishes with a consideration of a body of literature on the domestication of technology, which I suggest may prove particularly profitable in understanding the location of video gaming in ordinary and everyday life.

Theorizing everyday life

Gardiner (2000: 2) refers to 'everyday life' as 'the largely taken-for-granted world that remains clandestine, yet constitutes what Lefebvre [1991] calls the "common ground" or "connective tissues" of all conceivable human thoughts and activities'. That is to say, the routines, habits and mundane patterns, including our 'ordinary' consumption, which underlie and link together our lived experiences. In particular, the term 'everyday life' is most commonly used to describe life and practices outside of work and education, and most frequently those that take place within the home (Haddon 2004).

Though the everyday consists of the relatively mundane, it is frequently 'the most overlooked and misunderstood aspect of social existence' (Gardiner 2000: 1). However, in the past couple of decades there has been an increased awareness of and interest in the routine, and sometimes mundane, activities of everyday life, such as eating, cooking, using the telephone or watching television. Henri Lefebvre was one of the first writers to argue that the everyday was important and should not be taken for granted. However, when first published (in French) in the 1940s his work was largely ignored in English-speaking academia and quite recently received attention. Lefebvre, applying a neo-Marxist perspective in *Critique of Everyday Life* ([1947] 1991), highlights everyday life as an important site of oppression and social control, recognizing that dominant power relations operate not just in formal social institutions, such as in the workplace or educational system, but also shape the minute and routine details of our everyday lives.

In contrast, other authors have highlighted the everyday as a site of social resistance and possible empowerment. Authors such as Mikhail Bakhtin ([1968] 1984) and Michel de Certeau (1984) suggest that everyday life is not fully controlled by dominant forces, and within daily routines there will be opportunities for individuality, expression and even resistance against controlling social forces. Though de Certeau (1984) recognizes social life as constraining and oppressive, where individuals are largely 'marginalized' and have little say or control over factors such as market forces, he suggests that everyday life is extremely complex and multifaceted, allowing room for manoeuvre and individuality. Where sociological grand narratives tend to strip away the mundane, seeking some hidden and deeper truth or meaning, for de Certeau this stripping away of the everyday hides what is truly important, as it is only at the level of the everyday that we can understand how social relations are experienced and lived out.

In theorizing everyday practices, de Certeau employs the concepts of 'strategies' and 'tactics'. Strategies for de Certeau are, in many respects, similar to Erving Goffman's frames (as discussed in Chapter 2) or Pierre Bourdieu's habitus (as discussed in Chapter 6), in that strategies are linked to places and the appropriate manners and actions specific to that particular time and place. However, in contrast to Bourdieu and Goffman, de Certeau sees no 'single logic' to the social practices within these places, as there will always be room for multiple actions and practices, even if these are often 'unsigned, unreadable and unsymbolized' (Gardiner 2000: 170). These multiple actions de Certeau refers to as 'tactics' which involve the disguises, deceptions, bluffs, stubbornness and personalization of experiences that take place within socio-cultural spaces. However, de Certeau is not suggesting that tactics exist outside of strategies; tactics are not a magic circle, but rather a constituent part of strategies and the two may often be indistinguishable.

Before moving on, it is important to note that some authors reject the term 'everyday life' or seek to limit its use. Grossberg (1992a) draws a distinction between what he refers to as 'everyday' and 'daily' life. For Grossberg, an individual's daily life consists of the routine and subsistence practices of eating, sleeping and generally getting by in life. In contrast, everyday life, for Grossberg, refers to individuals' cultural and leisure pursuits, and what people do with their time beyond their subsistence needs. This is useful in that it recognizes that not everyone has access to the cultural and leisure pursuits enjoyed by the majority of the population, and that social class, gender, age, ethnicity and various other social factors may restrict the opportunities open to some. However, the work of writers on the everyday, and especially de Certeau, emphasize the blurring and intertwining of social patterns, and this makes establishing a distinction between 'daily' and 'everyday' life hard to determine or maintain.

Longhurst (2007) rejects the concept of everyday life altogether, preferring instead to utilize Raymond Williams's term 'ordinary life'. Longhurst argues that everyday life is most often employed in one of two main ways: either to highlight the exploitative and repressive nature of the everyday (see for example Lefebvre [1947] 1991) or, second, as the site of potential resistance and subversion (see for example de Certeau 1984), both of which, he suggests, are too limited in their focus. However, Longhurst overlooks the criticism frequently directed at Williams for being overly celebratory of ordinary creativity, something he rejects de Certeau for; de Certeau in fact is not necessarily as celebratory of everyday life as Longhurst, and others, often take him to be.

Video games and everyday life

The work of Michel de Certeau has been used extensively in fan studies, and most notably in the work of John Fiske (for example 1989a, 1989b) and Henry Jenkins (for example 1992). In particular, Jenkins has carried over his enthusiasm for the work of de Certeau into his work on video games. For instance, as discussed in Chapter 5, Fuller and Jenkins (1995) utilize the work of de Certeau in understanding how video gamers navigate in-game spaces, and in doing so develop 'spatial stories'. Furthermore, Jenkins (2004) employs de Certeau's terms 'maps' and 'tours' to understand video gameplay narratives. For de Certeau maps and tours provide a good illustration of, as well as a metaphor for, the workings of strategies and tactics. De Certeau argues that the built and natural environment provides individuals with only certain paths that can be explored; this de Certeau calls the 'map'. However, within this map each individual is able to find their own route or path, and engage in their own 'tour'. This example provides a key illustration of de Certeau's principal argument. Though we are limited in what we can do or where we can go by strategies, or maps, there is still room for individuality, expression, creativity, tactics and tours. This, Jenkins (2004) argues, can be usefully applied to video game analysis, in that, though video games may limit what is possible within them, through rules, narratives, technologies and so forth, the video gamer is still able to find their own path (tour) through the game, which will probably be different from that of other gamers, enabling the gamer to develop their own specific, and spatial, story.

Timothy J. Welsh (2006) similarly draws on theories of the everyday in his analysis of the video game *Grand Theft Auto: San Andreas* (*GTA:SA*). Welsh argues that *GTA:SA* is a game which like many other recent video game titles, *The Sims* and other instalments in the *GTA* series, for instance, is about the everyday. Video games like *GTA* and *The Sims* engage the video gamer in the responsibility and monotony of everyday life, but give the impression that the everyday can be escaped. The video gamer feels as if they are escaping the everyday, in-game, and this provides them with the sense of escaping their own everyday lives. But Welsh, drawing on Lefebvre (1991), argues that our leisure lives are only perceived as an escape from the mundane and limited nature of the everyday, but are actually merely another part of it. As Lefebvre ([1947] 1991: 233) argues, even the most successful and entertaining leisure activity does not transcend the everyday. Leisure time is just as much a part of the everyday as work; it is merely perceived to be different, for it 'appears as the non-everyday in the everyday' (Welsh 2006: 133).

Even the most extraordinary aspects of video gameplay, such as the extreme violence, stealing cars, flying helicopters and other outlandish acts seen in video games like *GTA:SA*, become mundane and everyday in their repeated play. As Welsh (2006: 134) argues:

[A]ll this violence is the pure appearance of a fantasy world that exists only as long as one keeps playing. Game violence is not real life violence, its fundamental appeal being precisely its non-everydayness. Devoid of sensuality, the brutality of the acts lacks palpability and is thus itself merely simulated. Furthermore, for the most part, it goes unnoticed by players. It is, after all, the everyday of this embellished world where carjacking is as common as driving. The brutal interruption wears off, the fantasy remains just a fantasy, and the everyday resurfaces.

However, Welsh (2006) also offers a more positive, de Certeauian reading of playing *GTA:SA*, suggesting that though video gameplay is restrictive, at times repetitive and mundane and part of our everyday, there is still room for individual narratives and particularities within its gameplay. As he writes, perhaps a little over-optimistically, 'though one cannot escape the everyday, at the level of practice, one can at least play it as one chooses' (Welsh 2006: 141).

In the same volume as Welsh, David Annandale (2006) provides another analysis of *Grand Theft Auto: San Andreas*, drawing instead on the work of another writer on the everyday, Mikhail Mikhailovich Bakhtin, and in particular his writings on the 'carnivalesque'. The idea of the carnivalesque is derived from Bakhtin's ([1968] 1984) work on European medieval carnivals, where he suggests there was a subversion of the normal social order, hierarchies, conventional roles and identities, and a revelling in the obscene, vulgar and grotesque; interestingly, Bakhtin refers to the sites of the carnivalesque as a 'second life'. Though Bakhtin suggests that this type of 'anarchic' carnival died out in the Renaissance, the carnivalesque spirit continued in literature, and Bakhtin's most famous work, *Rabelais and His World* (1984), is a consideration of the sixteenth-century satirical and extravagant (carnivalesque) writings of François Rabelais (Blackshaw and Crawford 2009).

The ideas of the carnivalesque have been applied to many aspects of leisure, and in particular discussions of social transgression and resistance, both in a textual sense and in terms of social phenomenon. For instance, Richard Giulianotti (1991) applies the concept to his consideration of the carnival-like and transgressive behaviour of Scottish football fans. For David Annandale (2006) *GTA:SA* is carnivalesque as it is a funny, playful text which parodies, satirizes and subverts social conventions. As Annandale (2006: 93) writes: '*GTA:SA* transforms huge swathes of American culture and society into ridiculous caricatures'. He continues '[t]he humor of the game, then, is often very sharply edged. For all the lunacy of the improbable events and larger-than-life characters, the game is grounded in a very recognizable reality of poverty, corruption, and violent race relations. *Grand Theft Auto: San Andreas*' primary comedic weapon in addressing these issues is parody' (2006: 95). This is a parody of, and challenge to, social order that can transcend the game itself. As Annandale (2006: 98) writes: '[t]he line between the game world and the real world … is blurred. The parodies … work as crooked mirrors. The laughter may be generated by the behaviour of the game world, but the actual target of the laughter is the real world.'

The work of Fuller and Jenkins (1995), Jenkins (2004), Welsh (2006) and Annandale (2006) cited here shows the usefulness of theories of everyday life in analysing video game texts and gameplay, but this is where these authors stop. Though the authors, at times, point to social relations outside of the video game and incidences of gameplay, such as Annandale's discussion of the power of parody or Jenkins's consideration of the creation of social narratives, there is little consideration of the importance of video games beyond a gamer's direct interaction with a gaming text. What is often lacking is a consideration of video games *within* the everyday, and the culture and productivity of video gamers away from the video game screen.

Probably the most telling example of the everydayness of video gaming is its location within the conversations and identities of millions of people all over the world, as people at work, school, in the pub or elsewhere discuss video games, tactics, cheats or hardware, or read about these in newspapers, magazines or online. As Haddon (2004: 74) suggests of schoolchildren, and in particular young boys: 'they also talked about games at school. They swapped games. They compared notes as regards tactics. And they passed information about ways to cheat or get around games problems.'

The lack of detailed and extensive analysis of the importance and location of video gaming in patterns of the everyday becomes even more striking when one considers that video gaming is becoming, for more and more people, a relatively ordinary and at times even mundane activity.

Video gaming as ordinary

The image of the typical video gamer continues to be, for many, that of the lonely male teenager, but if industry data, such as that produced annually by the Entertainment Software Association (ESA), are to be trusted, then it seems that in many countries, video games are now played in the majority of households (see Chapter 4). Video gaming, so it would seem, is no longer an activity engaged in by only a small and distinct minority, but is increasingly becoming a mainstream leisure pursuit.

As outlined in Chapter 2, there has been a tendency in video game studies to prioritize the direct engagement of the gamer with a video game text or technology. Such research has often emphasized the focus and concentration of the video gamer, and how they problem-solve, manipulate and interact with the text, or even enter a state of 'flow' (see Shaw 2010). However, it is evident that video gaming can be, for many individuals, a relatively ordinary, even at times mundane activity, often undertaken in a state of distraction. Of course, there will be many who, at certain times, pay particular and specific attention to playing a video game, but for others, or at other times, this can be a fairly mundane part of their everyday lives and routines.

In particular, and as cited earlier, Kirkpatrick (2004) argues that playing video games can quite frequently be a relatively mundane and monotonous task. Here, Kirkpatrick (2004) highlights what he refers to as the 'cynicism' of the video gamer, where the gamer recognizes that success comes from completing, and often having to repeat and re-repeat, a series, of at times, routine and tedious tasks. This can be illustrated by an account of video gameplay given by an interviewee ('Mark') in one of our previous studies:

Yeah like gameplay can involve lots of boring stuff, stuff that you just need to do like to get on. Like in *Oblivion* [single-person role-playing game] there is this cheat ... well you don't have to do it, I suppose, but it really helps, where if you put your guy [player-controlled avatar] in this one particular room, where there is this other guy [Non-Player Character] and sneak against the wall, your sneak skill slowly goes up over time. So in the end what I did was taped my Xbox [360] controller stick into an upwards position, so my guy was just constantly walking, sneaking, into a corner and [I] sat there reading a book while it did that for a few hours [laughs].

Crawford and Gosling 2008: 129

Though *The Elder Scrolls IV: Oblivion*, the video game the interviewee 'Mark' is referring to, is a video game that was lauded at the time of release for its stunning visuals and engrossing gameplay, it seems for him, at least at this point, that its gameplay became so repetitive that he was able to read a book at the same time as 'playing' the video game. Examples such as this call into question the idea that 'play', and associated concepts such as the magic circle, are useful in understanding such practices, as here 'Mark' could not be understood as inhabiting an isolated play spot, separate from ordinary life. In particular, this could better be described as what Highmore (2011: 115) terms 'absentminded' media consumption, which refers to the 'blasé attitudes' of many contemporary media audiences.

Furthermore, the quotation from 'Mark' above suggests that this is not an isolated case, but just one example of the 'lots of boring stuff' that video gameplay can involve. In particular, the undertaking of repetitive, even 'worklike', tasks in video games is nowhere more apparent than in the act of 'grinding' needed in many MMORPGs. In many, if not most, MMORPGs, including *Ultima Online*, *Star Wars Galaxies* and *World of Warcraft*, to name but a few, gameplay involves player-controlled avatars progressing, usually slowly, in a number of skills or professions. The mechanism most MMORPGs use in order for characters to advance in a particular skill is repeated practice in that particular activity. For instance, in *Ultima Online* one particular skill a character can have is 'mining'. To become more skilled in this activity, which enables the character to mine increasingly valuable and useful ore, the character has to first obtain a pickaxe or shovel, then find a suitable cave area and then repeatedly 'dig' there until the ore is depleted or the digging implement gives up, both of which occur frequently, and then the first two stages need to be repeated before digging can resume once more. Progressing to a high level of competence in mining, or any other such skill in most MMORPGs, usually requires hours of repetitive and monotonous tasks, which, to use Kirkpatrick's (2004) term, many gamers may 'cynically' undertake, or even do so while distracting themselves with a second activity, such as reading a book. As Pargman and Jakobsson (2008: 232) argue, 'playing computer games (for long hours) can become a routine activity among other everyday routine activities'.

Simultaneously engaging in other acts or using multiple media, such as playing a video game and reading a book, may not be that uncommon. As Lally (2002: 107) writes of her research on the use and location of computers within the home:

'some study participants frequently play a computer game while simultaneously doing something else, either computer-based or non-computer-based'. This is clearly illustrated by Kendal in her consideration of playing the MUD *Bluesky*:

> Online interactions can at times become intensely engrossing ... However ... when mudding for long periods of time, I frequently leave the computer to get food, go to the bathroom, or respond to someone in the physical room in which I'm sitting. If the text appearing on my screen slows to a crawl or the conversation ceases to interest me, I may cast about for something else offline to engage me, picking up the day's mail or flipping through a magazine.
>
> Kendal 2002: 7, cited in Moores 2004: 27

The speed and ability of modern microprocessors also enables personal computers to run numerous programs at once, allowing a user to run a game of *Solitaire* on-screen, for example, at the same time as having other programs open and running, such as Microsoft Word, and easily flip between them. A video gamer's attention might be divided between playing on a video game console and simultaneously having a conversation with a friend on a telephone, or sitting looking at a map or walkthrough on a laptop. Highmore (2011) suggests that in a media- and information-saturated world, our concentration and attention is often divided between multiple tasks and media. Too often studies of video gameplay assume that gamers are solely focused upon the act of gameplay, not recognizing that this can fit into complex patterns and networks of everyday interpersonal communication and media and technology use; patterns that are becoming increasingly intricate thanks to technological advances and patterns of media convergence (considered in more in detail below).

Video gaming is not just an activity invariably linked to a television screen, computer monitor or computer arcade. Video gaming can be, and has for a considerable period been, mobile. Mobile electronic games have a long history. In the 1960s Cragstan introduced a battery-powered handheld game called *Periscope Firing Range*, in 1972 Waco launched a small battery-powered version of tic-tac-toe (noughts and crosses) and in 1976 Mattel introduced a handheld electronic car-racing game called *Auto Race*, followed a year later by another simple sport-based game called *Football*. The late 1970s and 80s saw a plethora of LCD handheld games, as well as similar game-watches, released by companies such as Nintendo. And of course Nintendo revolutionized the mobile video game market in 1989 with the launch of the Game Boy. However, mobile video gaming is becoming increasingly popular as a result of changing patterns of media consumption and convergence.

'Media convergence' has multiple meanings. For instance, it can refer to the convergence of media corporate ownership, which sees certain individuals or organizations owning multiple media outlets; such as Rupert Murdoch, who controls Sky television, the UK-based newspapers the *Sun*, the *News of the World* and *The Times*, the Fox television network, 20th Century Fox Film Corporation and HarperCollins publishers, as well as numerous other media companies. Convergence can also refer to converging media styles and formats. For instance, many video games draw on cinematic styles, such as the *Matrix*-style 'bullet-time' seen in the *Max Payne* games, while many films similarly borrow from video games, such as the beat-'em-up video-game-like scenes in the film *Scott Pilgrim vs. the World*, or the set pieces and level bosses seen in films like *Sucker Punch*. Similarly, convergence can relate to the increasingly multifunctional nature of many media technologies. For example, the Sony PlayStation 3 is a video game console, but it also allows the user to play music CDs and files, it is a DVD and Blu-ray player and an Internet access point, and much more besides. Personal computers become for many the preferred means of storage and player of film and music content, as well as a work and video game station, while mobile telephones have become not just multiple means of communication, but also mobile media entertainment units which allow the playing of music, video and video games. Mobile telephones have enabled video gameplay for many years, such as *Snake*, which appeared on Nokia mobile telephones in 1997, but today's mobile telephone technologies accommodate visually stunning and highly complex games, like *Infinity Blade*, which are now not that far removed from what can be achieved on dedicated video game consoles.

However, there are those who question this idea of media convergence, and in particular technological convergence. For instance, Jesse Schell in his address to the 2010 DICE (Design Innovate Communicate Entertain) summit, an annual gathering of video game executives, suggests that technological convergence is largely a myth. Schell argues that technologies do not converge, they diverge. This can be seen in the way in which more and more new technologies are created to meet specific needs, often followed by a plethora of rivals. Schell cites the example of the Flip video recorder. This small handheld recorder can take only video, not still pictures, performs no other major function and has not replaced existing (larger) video cameras, but rather added another product; in fact several products, when one considers the whole range of Flip cameras available, as well as the multiple competitors that closely followed. It does seem that the utopian dream of one black box delivering all our technology and media needs is a long way off, as homes are filled with more and more, rather than fewer, technologies. However, Schell (2010) suggests that the exception to this rule is the mobile telephone. Schell explains this by suggesting that the contemporary mobile telephone is in many ways a descendant of the Swiss army knife. That is to say, it is a mobile instrument that performs multiple tasks, at best adequately, but individuals accept its compromises and limitations because of its size and mobility. However, just as individuals are unlikely to use a Swiss army knife in their kitchens, in the home, mobile telephones usually become replaced by specialized, and usually more efficient, technologies.

Whether we agree with media and technology convergence arguments or not, what is largely uncontested is that new mobile technologies such as mobile telephones have, for many, made video gaming more readily accessible away from specific locations, such as the home or arcade. However, as Mäyrä (2008) suggests, mobile gaming has largely been ignored in academic research. Schell (2010) submits that the main reason for this is that the video game industry and academia have been caught unawares by the success of mobile games such as

Angry Birds and *Mafia Wars*. Video games of this nature, as well as similar games, are sometimes termed 'casual' games (see Juul 2009). This term is frequently applied to video games that require a gamer to spend a relatively short period of time acquiring the necessary skills and knowledge. For instance, learning how to play *Snake* on a mobile telephone or tennis in *Wii Sports*, is relatively quick and easy, especially when compared with the intricacies and time required to success-fully play video games such as *Call of Duty* or *World of Warcraft*. Mäyrä (2008: 27) refers to this form of video gaming as the 'largely unexamined ... the "invis-ible everyday"', such as 'a businessman playing Tetris with his mobile phone in the airport lounge'. Mäyrä's argument here concurs with those we also made in the same year, when we suggested that 'the increasing mobility of gameplay, coupled with technological convergence, is doing to gameplay what the Sony Walkman did for music' (Crawford and Gosling 2008: 130). That is to say, advances in mobile and media technologies have helped make playing video games a much more simple and everyday activity, for those with access to these kinds of tech-nologies. In our research, the majority of our interviewees suggested that they would often play video games in quite mundane ways: for short periods of time, while doing other activities or in-between other tasks. For example, one of our respondents, 'Natasha', commented that she would often play video games to 'relieve boredom' or 'fill time', particularly while commuting to and from work:

> [W]ell I play *Who Wants to be a Millionaire* because I always like to think I could win one million pounds. But I never do, I never get past thirty-two thousand but also I said it's on my phone so I can just take that with me and it's like mobile basically, so it's something to do once I'm bored on the train.
>
> Crawford and Gosling 2008: 130

This is a point also made by Pargman and Jakobsson (2008: 232), that playing video games is sometimes about 'having something to do when coming home from school, [or] something that takes the mind off homework'.

New trends and technologies mean that the nature of video gameplay is blur-ring with other forms of leisure and entertainment; such as the *Wii Fit*, *Just Dance*, *Singstar* or *Guitar Hero* (see Figure 8.1) to name but a few, which smudge the boundaries between video gameplay and other activities such as keep-fit, dancing, singing and playing a musical instrument, in these cases. The popularity of these kinds of video games, which could be described as *more* physical video games, for want of a better term, Schell (2010) suggests, has similarly taken the industry and academia by surprise. For Schell, the popularity of these kinds of video games lies in their claims to 'authenticity'. Schell suggests that technologies have increas-ingly separated people from what they see as 'real' experiences. Most people in Western consumerist nations, for example, live in a world where food comes prepacked and preprepared, and where their primary connection with the world is through media outlets, such as television; what Raymond Williams (1974) refers to as 'mobile privatisation'. However, rather than abandoning technology and consumerism, individuals are increasingly being offered the opportunity to use them to get back to the 'real' and the 'authentic'. Video games therefore do not

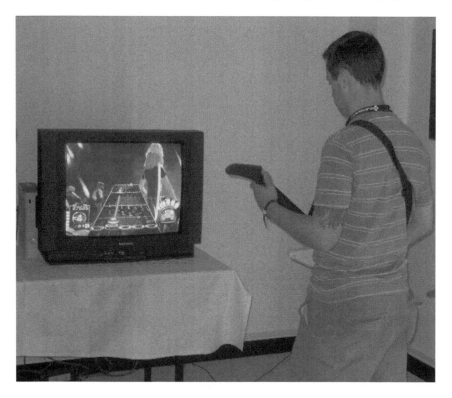

Figure 8.1 A video gamer playing *Guitar Hero* (photo: G. Crawford)

need to take individuals away from 'real' sport, as they can now actively participate in sport in *Wii Sports*, and computers do not necessarily need to be anti-social,
as people can use computers to connect with 'friends' on Facebook and MySpace.

Of course, both the video game industry and academia are quickly realizing the
potential and popularity of 'new' game types and formats, such as mobile, online
and more physical games. In particular, Frans Mäyrä (2011) offers a consideration of various forms of gameplay within, and with, a variety of social media
sites, such as games like *PhotoMunchrs* on the photograph-sharing website
Flickr and *Farmville* on the social networking site Facebook. He makes the case
for the convergence of playful activity in, and among, other activities, such as
online photograph sharing and social networking. Mäyrä thus demonstrates how
gameplay is augmented by other activities afforded by the websites in question.
Status updates, for instance, are made in Facebook while playing games like
Scrabulous. Through this, Mäyrä discusses the possibility for video gaming,
and playful activity more generally, facilitating social networking, and points
to the further blurring of the boundaries within our lives brought about by this
(Crawford *et al.* 2011b).

However, we should not fall into the far too easy trap of assuming that it is
technological developments that have directly, and causally, led to changes in

the nature of video gameplay. In particular, Jenkins (2006a, 2006b) reverses this argument to some degree, suggesting that it is the changing nature of media audiences and consumers which has significantly contributed to the development and convergence of media technologies and practices (Balnaves *et al.* 2009). It would be unjust to suggest that Jenkins sees technological developments and convergence as solely 'user'- led, as he argues that convergent culture is neither wholly bottom-up nor top-down (Jenkins 2006b: 257), but it is fair to say that Jenkins's emphasis is primarily on how audiences have helped drive changes in media technologies.

In particular, Jenkins (2006b) argues that fans were once the avant-garde, or as he terms them 'rogue leaders', of participatory media consumption. Where ordinary audiences simply consumed mainstream mass-market media products, fans operated on the margins, engaging with cult and niche media in ways that were participatory, such as poaching storylines and characters from media texts to produce their own fan art and fiction (H. Jenkins 1992). But Jenkins (2006b) argues that both niche media and participatory culture have become increasingly mainstream. New media technologies such as the Internet and the diversification of television stations and networks mean that consumers have access to a much wider range of media texts. This, Jenkins argues, has helped change the nature of media production and provision. Where once media products such as television shows needed to be successful and popular straight away to ensure their commercial viability, new media technologies allow 'long-tail' consumer patterns. That is to say, media products no longer have such a short 'shelf life'. Easy and instant access to a wide range of media content allows products to be sold over a much longer period of time, and enables users to more readily find products that match their specific niche interests. Passive consumers, for Jenkins, evolve into active users, who seek out niche media texts and follow media flows across a variety of transmedia forms (see Chapter 5) and form links and connections with others with similar interests via new media networks. This is part of Jenkins's wider thesis on the development of 'knowledge communities' and their 'collective intelligence' (see Chapter 6).

It is evident that video games can be played for a variety of reasons, in many different ways and locations, in various states of distraction, slotted into the routines of everyday life. Particularly useful in helping us understand how technologies such as video game machines are located within everyday lives, routines and home life, is the body of literature on the domestication of technology; which is where I now turn.

The domestication of technology

The domestication of technology is the focus of a body of literature and group of academics which emerged in the 1990s, and most notably was inspired and led by the work of the British media scholar Roger Silverstone and his colleagues at Brunel University. The term 'domestication', in its traditional sense, is most commonly associated with the taming of wild animals, and Berker *et al.* (2006: 2) suggest that the term is metaphorically used in this literature to explain how 'new' and 'strange' technologies are integrated into the structures, routines and environments of their users. Haddon (2004) suggests that the main feature of this literature is an understanding of how information communication technologies enter the home, the meanings they have and the relationship technologies have with individual and group identities. In this literature, there is an emphasis on the social relationship between individuals, objects and places, all understood in context, such as the interactions of individuals with pieces of technology and the impact that this has on their interactions with others. This literature, therefore, is particularly useful, as it allows for a consideration of how video games, video game consumption and video game culture are diffused into our everyday lives. As Mäyrä (2008: 6) writes: 'games are the most successful example of information and communication technologies becoming *domesticated*, which means they evidence being integrated into the everyday life and practices of groups of people' (emphasis in original).

Berker *et al.* (2006) suggest that earlier technology studies focused specifically on the nature of the technologies themselves and their impact on users and society more generally. A key example of this is Everett M. Rogers's book *The Diffusion of Innovations*, first published in 1962 (and in its fifth edition by 2003), which views the adoption of technologies as a rational and linear process. However, Silverstone, his colleagues and later writers on the domestication of technology argue that individuals' adoption of, relationship with and use of technologies is far from straightforward, and they seek to move focus away from the technology, the *text*, and towards an understanding of its *context* (Berker *et al.* 2006: 5).

The domestication of technology literature highlights that an individual's relationship with technologies is not set and static, but rather an ongoing and changing process, located within the existing routines and hierarchies of everyday life. For example, Lally (2002: 8) argues that technologies such as home computers are 'brought into a domestic context which is already organized around structures and hierarchies of age, gender and other specific roles, with pre-existing patterns of interaction and activity, and which already contains a large number of objects and other technologies'.

Technologies have to be located within, and fit into, people's homes and lives, both physically and socially. Technologies therefore need to be understood as forming relationships with users, as well as other objects. When a new technology enters a home, it has to fit in with existing objects, or sometimes leads to the acquisition of other objects. For instance, most video game consoles require connecting to a television set before they can be played with, or a personal computer may require the purchase of an accompanying desk and chair, which may require the rearranging of other furniture and the dynamics of a household. Even small objects, such as gamepads and controllers, need to find a place in the home and individuals' lives, whether that means being carefully put away in a cupboard drawer or constantly misplaced under, or behind, an armchair.

The place of objects within our homes, everyday lives and routines is not insignificant, and where an object is located will shape how it is seen and used: a telephone placed in a private bedroom is often used in a very different way from one located in a more communal space, such as a living room or hallway. In particular,

Haddon (2004) suggests that the placing of a telephone in a communal location within a home is often done specifically to control its use and limit access, particularly for younger members of the household. Similarly, where other technologies are located matters and can significantly shape their meaning and use. Green (2001), for instance, suggests that in many households video game technologies, such as computer and video game consoles, are most commonly located within 'male' spaces, such as male siblings' bedrooms and studies. Moreover, McNamee (1998) suggests that even when video game machines are located in shared family spaces, conflict often arises as they continue to be seen as *symbolically* belonging to male household members. Green (2001: 181–2, citing Silverstone *et al.* 1992) suggests that households will often be structured around a 'moral economy' that is expressed through symbolic and material boundaries, which dictate expected gender roles, responsibilities and spheres, and this frequently locates video game technologies as male possessions. Hence, for many households, video game technologies continue to be viewed as culturally not 'belonging' to women, but rather something they are, sometimes, allowed access to.

Considering the everyday and the domestication of technology is important as it allows us to consider how technology is used and fits into the routines and patterns of individuals' lives. This is particularly significant in relation to gendered roles and patterns of play. As we have argued elsewhere (for example Crawford and Gosling 2005) most research on video gaming and gender has focused upon women's, and most commonly girls', marginalization within video gaming culture. However, in recent years there has been a growing and significant literature on how women game, and in particular work such as that by Schott and Horrell (2000), and the ongoing work by Enevold and Hagström (for example 2008, 2009, 2010), highlights the ways in which video gaming is located within women's everyday lives. This research highlights that, contrary to common belief, many women do play video games; however, their patterns of play are often different from those of male video gamers. In particular, it has been suggested that women are more likely than their male counterparts to play 'casual games', such as flash-based games, puzzles or quiz games, and our research (Crawford and Gosling 2005) suggests that the women in our study were more likely to play video games on mobile telephones than men. The most convincing explanation for this probably has to do with the continued constraints placed upon women's leisure time. Research such as Shaw (1994), Wearing (1998) and Aitchison (2004) continues to show that women's leisure time is generally not only more limited than men's, but also more fragmented. Many women, who continue to have primary responsibility for domestic and childrearing chores, find that their work responsibilities do not end at a particular 'clocking-off' point, and hence their leisure time is taken when and where possible, often 'stolen' out of their day and in-between their daily responsibilities (Schott and Horrell 2000). Enevold and Hagström (2008) consequently found in their research that many women, and particularly mothers, who video game do so in fragmented time slots in-between domestic responsibilities. They cite the example of one interviewee (referred to as 'G8M') who suggests that she would often play *World of Warcraft* during the night while trying to get her baby back to sleep. In particular, they cite data from Timecheck (2004) that suggest that of 28 per cent of female video gamers over the age of 40 play video games between the hours of midnight and 5 a.m., a proportion considerably higher than that for their male counterparts (Enevold and Hagström 2008: 151). What is also significant about Enevold and Hagström's argument here is that it is evident that many of the video gamers they interviewed would play video games as a partial distraction or to fill time.

The gendered nature of access to video game technologies is just one example of how existing social hierarchies shape the location and use of objects within households, and beyond. Another key example would be how parents and guardians frequently manage the use of technology by younger family members. For instance, Lally (2002) discusses how children will often be required to ask parents' permission to use certain technologies, such as televisions, computers and video game machines, and parents will frequently monitor and limit their use. Writers such as Morley and Silverstone (1990) argue that access to information communication technologies is often 'double articulated', where not only is access to the technology limited and monitored, but, similarly, the nature of material viewed or used, such as the types of programmes watched or video games played, is also frequently restricted. The meaning of technologies such as televisions, computers and video game consoles is therefore not just determined by what *is* watched and played, but also what *is not*.

A real strength of the domestication of technology literature is that it looks at the intricate, complex and at times even contradictory relationships that emerge and revolve around the location, interactions and use of technologies. As Mackay (1997: 277) writes: 'to understand the consumption of technologies in households, we have to understand the practices of everyday life – how technologies are implicated in household routines and activities'. Technologies do necessarily just fit neatly into existing routines and hierarchies, but can change them, and sometimes can be subversive. For instance, Rakow (1988) highlights that though the telephone was a technology born into a deeply patriarchal world, for many women it provided them with a link to the world outside of the home and for some an escape from their social isolation. Issues of control and access to technology within a household are rarely straightforward and simple. For instance, Buckingham (1991, cited in Haddon 2004), highlights how children will try to subvert parental control and access television programmes their elders have forbidden them to watch. Facer *et al.* (2001), drawing on the work of Michel de Certeau (see earlier in this chapter) describe activity of this kind as 'tactics', where the 'less powerful' seek to use technologies as they wish (cited in Lister *et al.* 2009: 246). The domestication of technology literature is therefore important in revealing, as Lally (2002: 217) writes, that 'the relationship of ownership is one of mutual belonging: we do not simply appropriate objects to the self, but they also "appropriate" each other, and (individually and collectively) they "appropriate" us in turn'.

However, Morley (2006) wonders if we are witnessing a 'de-domestication' of technologies, as a result of the increasing trend towards mobile technologies (as discussed above), such as mobile telephones, personal music players and hand-held video game consoles, which are moving the consumption of technologies out of the home. Mobile technologies are not an area considered in many domestication studies, as the majority of early domestication studies were undertaken in households in the early 1990s, when mobile technologies were very limited in capability and usage. However, more recent research, such as Ling and Haddon (2003), has sought to consider the domestication of portable technologies, such as the mobile telephone, both inside and outside of the home. Domestication is not necessarily just about the home, but rather about how technologies fit into, interact with and transform the routines, practices and structures of everyday life. Moreover, as Morley (2006: 24) argues, mobile technologies have not led to 'the (much advertised) "death" of geography'. Place still matters. Morley argues that levels of Internet connectivity vary greatly with location, for example, and where technologies are used still matters. Nor do hierarchies and social structures, such as gender, age, disability, sexuality, social class and so forth, stop mattering, or shaping social lives, just because an individual takes to playing video games outside of the home. Furthermore, returning to Schell's (2010) argument noted in the previous section, we should not overestimate media convergence or the capabilities of current mobile technologies. For most, watching a film or playing a video game on a mobile telephone is still a very poor relation to doing so on television or a personal computer.

What is needed is an understanding of how technologies are consumed, experienced and located within patterns of everyday life, along with a recognition of the changing nature of media audiences, including video gamers. Audience research, as characterized here by Abercrombie and Longhurst's (1998) 'spectacle/performance paradigm' (see Chapter 3), has moved towards understanding how media consumption is drawn on as a resource in the construction of identities, social interactions, and performances, and Pargman and Jakobsson (2008) suggest that, similarly, video game research needs to look beyond the isolated gamer and video game text to consider its importance and location within everyday life. As Lister *et al.* (2009: 307) write:

> [T]he 'real world' is not left behind for the blinking lights, geometries and disembodiment of a fictional cyberspace. Instead we see a much more complex – and interesting – picture. The communication vectors of the Internet, the dynamic spaces of videogames, the 'technological imagery' of all of these are interwoven, fitting into the architecture of the home, movement through the urban environment, established patterns of gender, family and social life, and dramatised by both the instrumental fantasies of hardware and software producers and the action filled narratives of popular culture.

In many respects, video game studies has been somewhat modest in its focus, as the influence and importance of video games and video game culture extends far beyond the sight of a game screen and console. Video games matter – probably more so than many researchers recognize.

Chapter summary

- Chapter 8 specifically focuses on the role and importance of video games away from the sight of a game screen or machine, and considers how video gaming and its culture extend into everyday life.
- Everyday life refers to the ordinary, and at times mundane, patterns of social life. However, the everyday is a site of complex social patterns, which can be seen as a place of social oppression (see for example Lefebvre [1947] 1991) or of resistance (see for example de Certeau 1984).
- Ideas and theories of the everyday have been applied to video game analysis by a number of authors. For instance, both Welsh (2006) and Annandale (2006) see *Grand Theft Auto: San Andreas* as an example of the everyday in a gaming text. Here Welsh argues that *GTA:SA* gives the player the opportunity to play out the everyday, and, hence, gives an impression of escaping it, while Annandale sees the game as an example of carnivalesque subversion.
- It is evident that playing a video game can be, and is increasingly becoming, a mainstream, ordinary and everyday activity for many. For example, many video games involve elements of tedious and repetitive gameplay, and many video gamers may pay only partial attention to the actions that are taking place on-screen. Advances in technology and changes in audience patterns also mean that video games are now often played on mobile devices, such as mobile telephones, in quite mundane ways, such as while commuting. And changes in video game technology, such as the rise of party-style games, like *Just Dance* or *Rock Band*, and exercise games like *Wii Fit*, further blur the boundaries between video gameplay and other everyday activates.
- A useful literature in considering the everyday nature of video gaming is the domestication of technology literature. This literature shifts focus away from the technology to consider the adoption, relationship and use of technologies. Hence, it moves attention from the text towards an understanding of its context. This is particularly useful in understanding the gendered nature of technologies, as well as how technologies are utilized and drawn on in people's everyday lives, their social networks and identity formations.

Further reading

Bakhtin, M.M. ([1968] 1984) *Rabelais and His World*, Bloomington: Indiana University Press.

de Certeau, M., Giard, L. and Mayol, P. (1998) *The Practice of Everyday Life*, vol. 2, *Living and Cooking*, Minneapolis: University of Minnesota Press.

Gardiner, M.E. (2000) *Critiques of Everyday Life*, London: Routledge.

Silverstone, R. (1994) *Television, Technology and Everyday Life: an essay in the sociology of culture*, London: Routledge.

Postscript

This book provides an overview and introduction to the study of video gamers and moves this debate forward in a number of areas. It does not, however, seek to advocate any one particular perspective or argument. My general thesis is that video games are both new and old. They are a recombinant, combining older media forms, such as video and audio, with gameplay. They are an embodied psychological and social practice, and their influence and importance extend far beyond the sight of the game screen. Video games are many things, never just one.

This book may appear, and probably is, more critical of a ludic approach to video game analysis. This is not because I see this perspective as necessarily less valuable than any other; rather, I am critical of how some (though not all) play-focused scholars have been purposefully narrow-sighted in their approach to video game studies, seeking to utilize only a limited body of literature and analysing only the act and instance of play. But of course, not all ludologists do this, and equally many other approaches to the study of video games, such as advocates of a media or literary approach, have at times been guilty of an equally narrow focus.

My argument throughout is that there are a variety of perspectives and tools that could be used to help us understand video gameplay and its culture. Many of these are already in the domain of video game studies, but others, I suggest, have not yet been fully utilized and exploited in video game analysis. In particular, I point to several key sociological perspectives and theorists who could be more widely used to understand video games and video gamers. Some, such as Goffman and de Certeau, are already used by several writers; others, such as Bourdieu, less so; and other areas, such as work on consumption and audiences, I would suggest, are too undervalued and -utilized here.

Following the arguments of Taylor *et al.* (1973), I make a case for a 'fully social theory' of video game research. Taylor *et al.* in their overview of early criminology research recognized that no one existing theory or body of work provided the 'answer' to understanding crime and deviance. Rather, each literature offers a particular perspective, and a particular angle, which sheds a different light on acts and patterns of deviance and criminality. This is what I am advocating is necessary for video game studies; not the primacy of any one particular approach, but rather a recognition that different perspectives reveal, and similarly overlook, different aspects of video gameplay and its culture.

Of course, I am not suggesting that existing theories can simply and unproblematically be lifted from other areas of research and applied to video games. Video games are not simply another form of media, video gamers are not just another audience and video games are not only another game. But applying different literatures and studies allows us not just to see the similarities video games and their players share with other cultural objects, practices and industries, but also how they differ. In turn, an analysis of video games, and their culture, can add to our understanding of play, media use, audiences, consumption patterns and much more beyond. I do not claim to be the first ever to make these arguments. There is nothing particularly new about advocating a multi-method and multi-theoretical approach to research, but what this book attempts is to add weight to the argument that video game analysis needs to be much wider in its focus and influences.

References

Aarseth, E. (1997) *Cybertext: perspectives on ergodic literature*, London: Johns Hopkins University Press.

—— (2003) 'Playing Research: methodological approaches to game analysis', paper presented at the Melbourne DAC 2003 conference, RMIT University, Melbourne, Australia, 19–23 May. Online. Available HTTP: http://hypertext.rmit.edu.au/dac/papers/Aarseth.pdf.

Abercrombie, N., Hill, S. and Turner, B. (1980) *The Dominant Ideology Thesis*, London: Allen and Unwin.

Abercrombie, N. and Longhurst, B. (1998) *Audiences*, London: Sage.

Adam, A. (2005) *Gender, Ethics and Information Technology*, Basingstoke: Palgrave Macmillan.

Adams, E. (2010) *The Fundamentals of Game Design*, 2nd edn, Englewood Cliffs, NJ: Prentice Hall.

Adorno, T. (1991) *The Culture Industry*, London: Routledge.

Aitchison, C. (2004) *Gender and Leisure: social and cultural perspectives*, London: Routledge.

Albrechtslund, A.M. (2008) 'Gamers Telling Stories: understanding game experience through narratives', paper presented at the Digital Content Creation: Creativity, Competence, Critique, Second International DREAM conference, University of Southern Denmark, Odense, Denmark, 18–20 September 2008. Online. Available HTTP: http://www.dreamconference.dk/nyheder/Albrechtslund,%20Anne-Mette.pdf.

—— (2010) 'Gamers Telling Stories: understanding narrative practices in an online community', *Convergence*, 16 (1), 112–24.

Alexandrov, V. E: (2004) *Limits to Interpretation: the meanings of Anna Karenina*, Wisconsin: University of Wisconsin Press.

Allen, R.C. (1995) *To Be Continued ... Soap Operas around the World*, London: Routledge.

Anderson, D.R. (1977) 'The Effects of TV Program Pacing on the Behavior of Preschool Children', *AV Communication Review*, 25 (2), 159–66.

Annandale, D. (2006) 'The Subversive Carnival in *Grand Theft Auto: San Andreas*', in N. Garrelts (ed.) *The Meaning and Culture of 'Grand Theft Auto': critical essays*, London: McFarland and Co., 127–42.

Appadurai, A. (1990) 'Disjuncture and Difference in the Global Economy', *Theory, Culture and Society*, 7, 295–310.

Armiger, R.S. and Vogelstein, R.J. (2008) 'Air-Guitar Hero: a real-time video game interface for training and evaluation of dexterous upper-extremity neuroprosthetic control algorithms', paper presented at the Biomedical Circuits and Systems conference, Baltimore, MD, USA, 20–22 November 2008, 121–24. Online. Available HTTP: http://ieeexplore.ieee.org/xpl/freeabs_all.jsp?arnumber=4696889.

Arsenault, D. and Perron, B. (2009) 'In the Frame of the Magic Cycle: the circle(s) of gameplay', in B. Perron and M.J.P. Wolf (eds) *The Video Game Theory Reader 2*, Routledge, London, 109–32.

Avedon, E.M. and Sutton-Smith, B. (1971) *The Study of Games*, New York: Wiley and Sons.

Aycock, A. (1988) '"Gens Una Sumus": play as metaculture', *Play and Culture*, 1 (2), 124–37.

Bacon-Smith, C. (1992) *Enterprising Women: television fandom and the creation of popular myth*, Philadelphia: University of Pennsylvania Press.

Bagnall, G. (2009) 'Cultural Capital', in Blackshaw and Crawford (2009), 49.

Bakhtin, M.M. ([1968] 1984) *Rabelais and His World*, Bloomington: Indiana University Press.

Balnaves, M., Donald, S.H. and Shoesmith, D. (2009) *Media Theories and Approaches: a global perspective*, Basingstoke: Palgrave Macmillan.

Barthes, R. (1978) *Image, Music, Text*, London: Hill and Wang.

Bartle, R. (1996) 'Players who suit MUDs', *Journal of MUD Research*, 1 (1). Online. Available HTTP: http://www.mud.co.uk/richard/hcds.htm#Bartle,%201985.

—— (2003) *Designing Virtual Worlds*, Indianapolis: New Riders.

Baudrillard, J. (1993) *The Transparency of Evil: essays on extreme phenomena*, London: Verso.

Bauman, Z. (1990) *Thinking Sociologically*, Oxford: Blackwell.

—— (1992a) *Intimations of Postmodernity*, London: Routledge.

—— (1992b) 'Survival as a Social Construct', *Theory, Culture and Society*, 9, 1–36.

—— (1997) *Postmodernity and Its Discontents*, Cambridge: Polity.

—— (1998) *Work, Consumerism and the New Poor*, Buckingham: Open University Press.

—— (2001) *The Individualization of Society*, Cambridge: Polity.

Bechar-Israeli, H. (1995) 'From <Bonehead> to <cLoNehEAd>: nicknames, play and identity on Internet relay chat', *Journal of Computer-Mediated Communication*, 1 (2). Online. Available HTTP: http://jcmc.indiana.edu/vol1/issue2/bechar.html.

Beck, U. (2002) 'Zombie Categories: interview with Ulrich Beck', in U. Beck and E. Beck-Gernsheim (eds) *Individualization: institutionalization, individualism and its social and political consequences*, Sage: London.

Becker, H.S. (1963) *Outsiders: studies in the sociology of deviance*, London: Free Press.

Benjamin, W. (1931) 'A Small History of Photography', in *One-Way Street and Other Writings* (1979), London: Verso.

Berelson, B. (1952) *Content Analysis in Communication Research*, Glencoe, IL: Free Press.

Berker, T., Hartmann, M., Punie, Y. and Ward, K.J. (eds) (2006) *Domestication of Media and Technology*, Maidenhead: Open University Press.

Berkowitz, L. (1984) 'Some Effects of Thoughts on Anti- and Prosocial Influences of Media Events: a cognitive neoassociation analysis', *Psychology Bulletin*, 95, 410–27.

—— (1990) 'On the Formation and Regulation of Anger and Aggression', *American Psychologist*, 45, 494–503.

—— (1993) *Aggression: its causes, consequences and control*, New York: McGraw-Hill.

Bijker, W.E. (1994) 'The Social Construction of Fluorescent Lighting, or How an Artefact was Invented in Its Diffusion Stage', in W.E. Bijker and J. Law. (eds) *Shaping Technology/Building Society: studies in sociotechnical change*, Cambridge, MA: MIT Press, 75–104.

Blackshaw, T. (2003) *Leisure Life: myth, masculinity and modernity*, London: Routledge.

Blackshaw, T. and Crawford, G. (2009) *The Sage Dictionary of Leisure Studies*, London: Sage.

Boellstorff, T. (2008) *Coming of Age in Second Life*, Princeton, NJ: Princeton University Press.

Bottomore, T. (1980) 'Introduction', in Abercrombie *et al.* (1980).

Bourdieu, P. (1977) *Outline of a Theory of Practice*, Cambridge: Cambridge University Press.

—— (1984) *Distinction: a social critique of the judgement of taste*, London: Routledge.

Bourdieu, P. and Wacquant, L. (1992) *An Invitation to Reflexive Sociology*, Cambridge: Polity.

Brigham Young University (2009) 'Video games linked to poor relationships with friends, family in new study', press release, 16 January. Online. Available HTTP: http://news.byu.edu/archive09-Jan-videogames.aspx.

Bryce, J. and Rutter, J. (2001) 'In the Game – In the Flow: presence in public computer gaming', poster presented at the Computer Games and Digital Textualities conference, IT University of Copenhagen, Denmark, 1–2 March. Online. Available HTTP: http://digiplay.info/Game.php.

—— (2002) 'Killing like a Girl: gendered gaming and girl gamers' visibility', paper presented at the Computer Games and Digital Cultures conference, Tampere, Finland, 6–8 June. Online. Available HTTP: http://digiplay.info/files/cgdc.pdf.

—— (2003a) 'The Gendering of Computer Gaming: experiences and space', in S. Fleming and I. Jones (eds) *Leisure Cultures: investigations in sport, media and technology*, Eastbourne: Leisure Studies Association, 3–22.

—— (2003b) 'Gender Dynamics and the Social and Spatial Organization of Computer Gaming', *Leisure Studies*, 22, 1–15.

—— (2006) 'Digital Games and the Violence Debate', in Rutter and Bryce (2006), 205–22.

Buchanan, D.D. and Funk, J.B. (1996) 'Video and Computer Games in the 90s: children's time commitment and games preferences', *Children Today*, 24, 12–15.

Buckingham, D. (1991) 'Intruder in the House: the regulation of children's viewing in the home', paper presented at the Fourth International Television Studies Conference, London, July.

Burn, A. (2006) 'Reworking the Text: online fandom', in D. Carr, D. Buckingham, A. Burn and G. Schott (eds) *Computer Games: text, narrative and play*, Cambridge, Polity, 88–102.

Burn, A. and Carr, D. (2006) 'Motivation and Online Gaming', in D. Carr, D. Buckingham, A. Burn and G. Schott (eds) *Computer Games: text, narrative and play*, Cambridge: Polity, 103–18.

Byrne, D. N. (2008) '"The Future of (the) 'Race'": identity, discourse and the rise of computer-mediated public spheres', in K. Salen (ed.) *The Ecology of Games: connecting youth, games and learning*, Cambridge, MA: MIT Press, 15–38.

Caillois, R. (1962) *Man, Play and Games*, London: Thames and Hudson.

Calhoun, C. (2002) *Dictionary of the Social Sciences*, Oxford: Oxford University Press, 2002.

Calvert, S.L. and Tan, S. (1994) 'Impact of Virtual Reality on Young Adults' Physiological Arousal and Aggressive Thoughts: interaction versus observation', *Journal of Applied Developmental Psychology*, 15, 125–39.

Carr, D. (2006a) 'Games and Narrative', in D. Carr, D. Buckingham, A. Burn and G. Schott (eds) *Computer Games: text, narrative and play*, Cambridge: Polity, 30–44.

—— (2006b) 'Play and Pleasure', in D. Carr, D. Buckingham, A. Burn and G. Schott (eds) *Computer Games: text, narrative and play*, Cambridge: Polity, 45–58.

Carroll, L. ([1871] 2007) *Through the Looking Glass and What Alice Found There*, Scituate, MA: DSI Publishing.

Cassell, J. and Jenkins, H. (2000) 'Chess for Girls: feminisms and computer games', in J. Cassell and H. Jenkins (eds) *From Barbie to Mortal Kombat: gender and computer games*, Cambridge, MA: MIT Press, 2–45.

Castronova, E. (2005) *Synthetic Worlds: the business and culture of online games*, Chicago: University of Chicago Press.

Cavin, S. and Noguchi, R. (2006) 'Video Game Sub-Culture and Addiction in Japan and in the US', paper presented at the annual meeting of the American Sociological Association, Montreal, Quebec, Canada, 10 August. Online. Available HTTP: http://www.allacademic.com/meta/p96527_index.html.

Chan, D. (2005) 'Playing with Race: the ethics of racialized representations in e-games', *International Review of Information Ethics*, 4, 25–30.

Chatman, S. (1978) *Story and Discourse: narrative structure in fiction and film*, Ithaca, NY: Cornell University Press.

Chayko, M. (1993) 'What is Real in the Age of Virtual Reality? "Reframing" frame analysis for a technological world', *Symbolic Interaction*, 16 (2), 171–81.

Clark, A. and Chalmers, D. (1998) 'The Extended Mind', *Analysis*, 58, 10–23.

Cohen, A. (1955) *Delinquent Boys: the culture of the gang*, London: Macmillan.

Cogburn, J. and Silcox, M. (2009) *Philosophy through Video Games*, London: Routledge.

Colwell, J., Grady, C. and Rhaiti, S. (1995) 'Computer Games, Self-Esteem and Gratification of Needs in Adolescents', *Journal of Communication and Applied Social Psychology*, 5 (3), 195–206.

Colwell, J. and Payne, J. (2000) 'Negative Correlates of Computer Game Play in Adolescents', *British Journal of Psychology*, 91, 295–310,

Consalvo, M. (2003) 'Hot Dates and Fairy-Tale Romances: studying sexuality in video games', in Wolf and Perron (2003), 171–94.

—— (2007) *Cheating: gaining advantage in video games*, Cambridge, MA: MIT Press.

Conway, S. (2010) '"If It's in the Game, It's in the Game": an analysis of the football digital game and its players', unpublished PhD thesis, University of Bedfordshire.

Copier, M. (2005) 'Connecting Worlds: fantasy role-playing games, ritual acts and the magic circle', in *Changing Views – Worlds in Play: proceedings of the DiGRA 2005 conference, Vancouver, Canada, 16–20 June*. Online. Available HTTP: http://www.digra.org/dl/db/06278.50594.pdf.

Couldry, N. (2005) 'The Extended Audience: scanning the horizon', in M. Gillespie (ed.) *Media Audiences*, Maidenhead: Open University Press/McGraw-Hill, 184–222.

Cover, R. (2006) 'Audience Inter/Active: interactive media, narrative control and reconceiving audience history', *New Media and Society*, 8 (1), 139–58.

Crawford, C. (1984) *The Art of Computer Game Design*, New York: McGraw-Hill

Crawford, G. (2003) 'The Career of the Sport Supporter: the case of the Manchester Storm', *Sociology*, 37 (2), 219–37.

—— (2004) *Consuming Sport: sport, fans and culture*, London: Routledge.

—— (2005a) 'Digital Gaming, Sport and Gender', *Leisure Studies*, 24 (3), 259–70.

—— (2005b) 'Sensible Soccer: sport fandom and the rise of digital gaming', in J. Magee, A. Bairner and A. Tomlinson (eds) *The Bountiful Game? Football, identities and finance*, London: Meyer and Meyer, 249–66.

—— (2006) 'The Cult of Champ Man: the culture and pleasures of *Championship Manager/Football Manager* gamers', *Information, Communication and Society*, 9 (4), 496–514.

—— (2009) 'Forget the Magic Circle (or Towards a Sociology of Video Games)' keynote presentation to the Under the Mask 2 conference, University of Bedfordshire, UK, 5 June 2009. Online. Available HTTP: http://underthemask.wikidot.com/key-note.

Crawford, G. and Gosling, V.K. (2005) 'Toys for Boys? The continued marginalization and participation of women as digital gamers', *Sociological Research Online*, 10 (1). Online. Available HTTP: http://www.socresonline.org.uk/10/1/crawford.html.

—— (2008) 'Freak Scene? Narrative, audience and scene', *[Player] Conference Proceedings, Copenhagen: IT University of Copenhagen, 26–29 August 2008*, Copenhagen: IT University of Copenhagen, 113–43.

—— (2009) 'More Than a Game: sports-themed video games and player narratives', *Sociology of Sport Journal*, 26, 50–66.

Crawford, G., Gosling, V.K. and Light, B. (2011a) 'The social and cultural significance of online games', in G. Crawford, V.K. Gosling and B. Light (eds) *Online Gaming in Context: the social and cultural significance of online games*, London: Routledge.

—— (2011b) 'It's Not Just a Game: contemporary challenges for games research and the Internet', in G. Crawford, V.K. Gosling and B. Light (eds) *Online Gaming in Context: the social and cultural significance of online games*, London: Routledge.

Crawford, G. and Rutter, J. (2006) 'Cultural Studies and Digital Games', in Rutter and Bryce (2006), 148–65.

—— (2007) 'Playing the Game: performance in digital game audiences' in J. Gray, C. Sandvoss, and C.L. Harrington (eds) *Fandom: identities and communities in a mediated world*, New York: New York University Press, 271–84.

Csikszentmihalyi, M. (1988) *Optimal Experience: psychological studies of flow in consciousness*, Cambridge: Cambridge University Press.

Curran, S. (2010) 'Smoke and Mirrors: the illusion of interactivity', keynote presentation at Under the Mask 3 conference, University of Bedfordshire, UK, 2 June 2010.

de Certeau, M. (1984) *The Practice of Everyday Life*, Berkeley: University of California Press.

—— (1986) *Heterologies: discourse on the other*, Minneapolis: University of Minnesota Press.

de Certeau, M., Giard, L. and Mayol, P. (1998) *The Practice of Everyday Life*, vol. 2, *Living and Cooking*, Minneapolis: University of Minnesota Press.

Debord, G. (1967) *The Society of the Spectacle*, Detroit: Black and Red.

Delamere, F.M. (2011) '*Second Life* as a Digitally Mediated Third Place: social capital in virtual world communities', in G. Crawford, V.K. Gosling and B. Light (eds) *Online Gaming in Context: the social and cultural significance of online games*, London: Routledge.

Devlin, K. (2009) 'Computer Game Players "more likely to drink, ignore family and have low self-esteem"', *Telegraph*, 23 January. Online. Available HTTP: http://www.telegraph.co.uk/technology/news/4323067/Computer-game-players-more-likely-to-drink-ignore-family-and-have-low-self-esteem.html.

Dietz, T.L. (1998) 'An Examination of Violence and Gender Role Portrayals in Video Games: implications for gender socialization and aggressive behaviour', *Sex Roles*, 38 (5–6), 426–42. Online. Available HTTP: http://videogames.procon.org/sourcefiles/Dietz.pdf.

Dill, K.E. and Dill, J.C. (1998) 'Video Game Violence: a review of the empirical literature', *Aggression and Violent Behaviour*, 3, 407–28.

Dormans, J. (2010) 'Understanding fan practices: a study into videos, role-play and fanfiction based on pervasive gameworlds', paper presented at the Under the Mask 3 conference, University of Bedfordshire, UK, 2 June. Online. Available HTTP: http://underthemask.wdfiles.com/local--files/papers-2010/Judith%20Dormans.pdf.

Dourish, P. (2001) *Where the Action Is: the foundations of embodied interaction*, Cambridge, MA: MIT Press.

Dovey, J. and Kennedy, H. (2006) *Games Cultures: computer games as new media*, Maidenhead: Open University Press.

Dring, C. (2010) 'Black Ops Smashes UK Day 1 Record', *MCV Online*. Online. Available HTTP: http://www.mcvuk.com/news/41776/Black-Ops-sets-new-UK-day-1-record.

Drotner, K. (1992) 'Modernity and Media Panics', in M. Skovmand and K.C. Schroder (eds) *Media Cultures: reappraising transnational media*, London: Routledge.

du Sautoy, M. (2010) 'Liked the Book? Try the App', *Guardian Online*. Online. Available HTTP: http://www.guardian.co.uk/books/2010/jul/03/marcus-du-sautoy-apps-books.

Eco, U. (1979) *The Role of the Reader: explorations in the semiotics of texts*, Bloomington: Indiana University Press.

Elias, N. (1978) *The Civilising Process*, vol. 1, *The History of Manners*, Oxford: Blackwell.

ELSPA (2008) 'European Video Gamers 2008 – Research Revealed', Entertainment and Leisure Software Publishers Association. Online. Available HTTP: http://www.elspa.com/?i=7555&s=1111&f=49&archive=.

—— (2009) 'Games Industry Welcomes Findings of New Study on Interactive Gaming', Entertainment and Leisure Software Publishers Association. Online. Available HTTP: http://www.elspa.com/?i=8002&s=1111&f=49&archive=.

Emes, C.E. (1997) 'Is Pac Man Eating Our Children? A review of the effects of video games on children', *Canadian Journal of Psychiatry*, 42, 409–14.

Enevold, J. and Hagström, C. (2008) 'My Momma Shoots Better Than You! Who is the female gamer?', *[Player] Conference Proceedings, Copenhagen: IT University of Copenhagen, 26–29 August 2008*, Copenhagen: IT University of Copenhagen, 144–67.

—— (2009) 'Time to Play: ethnographic perspectives on mothers' digital gaming', presentation to the Under the Mask 2 conference, University of Bedfordshire, UK, 5 June.

—— (2010) 'Modifying the Methods: player research reconsidered', presentation to the Under the Mask 3 conference, University of Bedfordshire, UK, 2 June.

Erickson, B. (1996) 'Culture, Class and Connections', *American Journal of Sociology*, 102, 217–51.

ESA (2010) *Essential Facts about the Computer and Video Game Industry 2010*, Entertainment Software Association. Online. Available HTTP: http://www.theesa.com/facts/pdfs/ESA_Essential_Facts_2010.PDF.

Eskelinen, M. (2001) 'The Game Situation', *Game Studies*, 1 (1). Online. Available HTTP: http://gamestudies.org/0101/eskelinen/.

Eskelinen, M. and Tronstad, R. (2003) 'Video Games as Configurative Performances', in Wolf and Perron (2003), 195–220.

Everett, A. and Watkins, C. (2008) 'The Power of Play: the portrayal and performance of race in video games', in K. Salen (ed.) *The Ecology of Games: connecting youth, games and learning*, Cambridge, MA: MIT Press, 141–66.

Everett, R. (2003) *The Diffusion of Innovations*, 5th edn, New York: Free Press.

Facer, K. and Furlong, R. (2001) 'Beyond the Myth of the "Cyberkid": young people at the margins of the information revolution', *Journal of Youth Studies* 4 (4), 451–69.

Facer, K., Furlong, J., Furlong, R. and Sutherland, R. (2001) 'Home is Where the Hardware is: young people, the domestic environment and "access" to new technologies', in I. Hutchby and J. Moran-Ellis (eds) *Children, Technology and Culture*, London: Falmer Press, 13–27.

Falcão, T. and Ribeiro, J.C. (2011) 'The Whereabouts of Play, or How the Magic Circle Helps Create Social Identities in Virtual Worlds', in G. Crawford, V.K. Gosling and B. Light (eds) *Online Gaming in Context: the social and cultural significance of online games*, London: Routledge.

Farmer, F.R. (1992) 'Social Dimensions of Habitat's Citizenry', in C.E. Loeffler and T. Anderson (eds) *The Virtual Casebook*, New York: Van Nostrand Reinhold, 118–22.

Filiciak, M. (2003) 'Hyperidentities: postmodern identity patterns in massively multiplayer online role-playing games, in Wolf and Perron (2003), 87–102.

Fine, G.A. (1983) *Share Fantasy: role-playing games as social worlds*, Chicago: University of Chicago Press.

Fiske, J. (1987) 'Cagney and Lacey: reading characters structurally and politically', *Communication*, 9 (3/4), 399–426.

—— (1989a) *Understanding Popular Culture*, London: Unwin Hyman.

—— (1989b) *Reading the Popular*, London: Unwin Hyman.

—— (1992) 'The Cultural Economy of Fandom', in L.A. Lewis (ed.) *The Adoring Audience*, London: Routledge, 30–49.

Foucault, M. (1979) *Discipline and Punish: the birth of the prison*, Harmondsworth: Penguin Books.

—— (1984) *The History of Sexuality Volume 1*, Harmondsworth: Penguin Books.

Frasca, G. (2003) 'Simulation versus Narrative: introduction to ludology', in Wolf and Perron (2003), 221–35.

Fromme, J. (2003) 'Computer Games as a Part of Children's Culture', *Game Studies*, 3 (1). Online. Available HTTP: http://www.gamestudies.org/0301/fromme/.

Fuller, M. and Jenkins, H. (1995) 'Nintendo and New World Travel Writing: a dialogue' in S.G. Jones (ed.) *Cyber Society: computer-mediated communications and community*, London: Sage, 57–72.

Gansing, K. (2003) 'The Myth of Interactivity? Interactive films as an imaginary genre', paper presented at the Melbourne DAC 2003 conference, RMIT University, Melbourne, Australia, 19–23 May. Online. Available HTTP: http://hypertext.rmit.edu.au/dac/papers/Gansing.pdf.

Gardiner, M.E. (2000) *Critiques of Everyday Life*, London: Routledge.

Garfinkel, H. (1967) *Studies in Ethnomethodology*. Englewood Cliffs, NJ: Prentice-Hall.

Genette, G. (1980) *Narrative Discourse*, Oxford: Blackwell.

—— (1997) *Paratexts: thresholds of interpretation*, Cambridge: Cambridge University Press.

Genvo, S. (2009) 'Understanding Digital Playability', in B. Perron and M.J.P. Wolf (eds) *The Video Game Theory Reader 2*, London: Routledge, 133–50.

Gerbner, G. (1967) 'Mass media and human communication theory', in F.E.X. Dance (ed.) *Human Communication Theory*, New York: Rinehart & Winston.

Giddens, A. (1991) *Transformation of Intimacy: sexuality, love and eroticism in modern society*, Stanford, CA: Stanford University Press.

Giulianotti, R. (1991) 'Scotland's Tartan Army in Italy: the case for the carnivalesque', *Sociology Review*, 39 (3), 503–30.

Glaser, B.G. (ed.) (1968) *Organizational Careers*, Chicago: Aldine.

Goffman, E. (1961) *Encounters: two studies in the sociology of interaction*, London: Allen Lane.

—— (1968) *Asylums*, Harmondsworth: Penguin Books.

—— (1969) *The Presentation of Self in Everyday Life*, Harmondsworth: Penguin Books.

—— (1974) *Frame Analysis: an essay on the organization of experience*, New York: Harper and Row.

Goldstein, J., Cajko, L., Oosterbroek, M., Michielsen, M., Van Houten, O. and Salverda, F. (1997) 'Video Games and the Elderly', *Social Behavior and Personality*, 25 (4), 345–52.

Gosling, V.K. and Crawford, G. (2011) 'Game Scenes: theorizing digital game audiences', *Games and Culture*, 6 (2), 135–54.

Gramsci, A. (1971) *Selections from the Prison Notebooks*, London: Lawrence and Wishart.

Green, C.S. and Bavelier, D. (2006) 'Action-Video-Game Experience Alters the Spatial Resolution of Vision', *Psychological Science*, 18 (1), 88–94. Online. Available HTTP: http://www.fed.cuhk.edu.hk/~lchang/material/Evolutionary/vision%20and%20 video%20games.pdf.

Green, E. (2001) 'Technology, Leisure and Everyday Practices', in E. Green and A. Adam (eds) *Virtual Gender: Technology, Consumption and Identity*, London: Routledge, 173–88.

Greenfield, P.M. (1996) 'Video Games as Cultural Artefacts', *Journal of Applied Developmental Psychology*. Special issue: effects of interactive environment technologies on development, 15, 3–12.

Greenfield, P.M. and Cocking, R.R. (1996) *Interacting with Video*, New York: Greenwood Publishing.

Griffiths, M.D. (2002) *Gambling and Gaming Addictions in Adolescence*, Oxford: British Psychological Society/Blackwell.

Griffiths, M.D., Davies, M.N.O. and Chappell, D. (2003) 'The Breaking of Stereotypes: the case of online gaming', *CyberPsychology and Behaviour*, 6 (1), 81–91.

—— (2004) 'Demographic Factors and Playing Variables in Online Computer Games', *CyberPsychology and Behaviour*, 7 (4), 479–87.

Griffiths, M.D. and Hunt, N. (1997) 'Dependence on Computer Games by Adolescents', *Psychological Reports*, 82, 475–80.

Griffiths, J.L., Voloschin, P., Gibb, G.D. and Bailey, J.R. (1983) 'Differences in Eye-Hand Motor Coordination of Video-Game Users and Non-Users', *Perceptual and Motor Skills*, 57 (1), 155–8.

Grodal, T. (2003) 'Stories for Eye, Ear, and Muscles: video games, media, and the embodied experience', in Wolf and Perron (2003), 129–56.

Grossberg, L. (1992a) *We Gotta Get Out of This Place*, London: Routledge.

—— (1992b) 'Is there a Fan in the House? The affective sensibility of fandom', in L.A. Lewis (ed.) *The Adoring Audience: fan culture and popular media*, London: Routledge, 50–65.

Grossman, D. (2000) 'Teaching Kids to Kill', *Phi Kappa Phi National Forum*. Online. Available HTTP: http://www.killology.org/article_teachkids.thm.

—— (2001) 'Trained to Kill', *Journal des Professoren Forum*, 2 (2), 3–10.

Guttman, A. (1986) *Sports Spectators*, New York: Columbia University Press.

Haddon, L. (2004) *Information and Communication Technology in Everyday Life: a concise introduction and research guide*, Oxford: Berg.

Hall, S. (1980) 'Encoding/Decoding', in S. Hall, D. Hobson, A. Lowe and P. Willis (eds) *Culture, Media, Language: working papers in cultural studies, 1972–79*, London: Hutchinson, 197–208.

Hand, M. and Moore, K. (2006) 'Community, Identity and Digital Games', in Rutter and Bryce (2006), 166–82.

Haraway, D. (1991) *Simians, Cyborgs and Women: the reinvention of nature*, London: Free Association Press.

Hebdige, D. (1979) *Subculture: the meaning of style*, London: Methuen.

—— (1988) *Hiding in the Light: on images and things*, London, Routledge.

Henderson, W.M. (1997) *I, Elvis: confessions of a counterfeit king*, New York: Boulevard Books.

Hesmondhalgh, D. (2005) '"Subcultures, Scenes or Tribes?" None of the above', *Journal of Youth Studies*, 8 (1), 21–40.

Higgin, T. (2009) 'Blackless Fantasy: the disappearance of race in massively multiplayer online role-playing games', *Games and Culture*, 4 (1), 3–26.

Highmore, B. (2011) *Ordinary Lives: studies in the everyday*, London: Routledge.

Hills, M. (2002) *Fan Cultures*, London: Routledge.

Hodge, R. and Tripp, D. (1986) *Children and Television*, Cambridge: Polity.

Hodkinson, P. (2002) *Goth: identity, style and subculture*, Oxford: Berg.

Huizinga, J. ([1938] 1949) *Homo Ludens: a study of the play-element in culture*, London: Routledge.

Interactive Software Federation of Europe (2010) *Video Gamers in Europe 2010*. Online. Available HTTP: http://www.isfe-eu.org/tzr/scripts/downloader2.php?filename=T003/F0013/d6/1a/3401b53qaghqd4j25b2ullin3&mime=application/pdf&originalname=ISFE_Consumer_Survey_2010.pdf.

Jackson, L., Gauntlett, D. and Steemers, J. (2008) *Virtual Worlds: an overview and study of BBC Children's "Adventure Rock"*. Online. Available HTTP: http://www.bbc.co.uk/blogs/knowledgeexchange/westminsterone.pdf.

Jenisch, J. (2008) *The Art of Video Games*, New York: Quirk Books.

Jenkins, H. (1992) *Textual Poachers*, Routledge: London.

—— (1993) '"X logic": repositioning Nintendo in children's lives', *Quarterly Review of Film and Video*, 14 (4), 55–70.

—— (2004) 'Game Design as Narrative Architecture', in N. Wardrip-Fruin and P. Harrigan (eds) *First Person: new media as story, performance and game*, Cambridge, MA: MIT Press, 118–30.

—— (2005) 'Games, the Lively Art', in J. Raessens and J. Goldstein (eds) *Handbook of Video Games Studies*, Cambridge, MA: MIT Press, 175–89.

—— (2006a) *Fans, Bloggers and Gamers: exploring participatory culture*, New York: New York University Press.

—— (2006b) *Convergence Culture: where old and new media collide*, New York: New York University Press.

Jenkins, R. (1992) *Pierre Bourdieu*, Routledge: London.

Jones, S.E. (2008) *The Meaning of Video Games: gaming and textual strategies*, London: Routledge.

Juul, J. (2001) 'Games Telling Stories?', *Game Studies*, 1 (1). Online. Available HTTP: http://www.gamestudies.org/0101/juul-gts/.

—— (2003) 'Half-Real: video games between real rules and fictional worlds', unpublished PhD thesis, IT University Copenhagen.

—— (2005) *Half-Real: video games between real rules and fictional worlds*, Cambridge, MA: MIT Press.

—— (2008) 'The Magic Circle and the Puzzle Piece', in S. Günzel, M. Liebe and D. Mersch (eds) *Conference Proceedings of the Philosophy of Computer Games 2008*, DIGAREC Series 1, Potsdam: Potsdam University Press, 56–69. Online. Available HTTP: http://opus.kobv.de/ubp/volltexte/2008/2007/pdf/digarec01.pdf.

—— (2009) 'Fear of Falling? The many meanings of difficulty in video games', in M.J.P. Wolf and B. Perron (eds) *The Video Game Theory Reader 2*, London: Routledge, 237–52.

Kafai, Y.B. (1996) 'Electronic Play Worlds: gender differences in children's construction of video games', in Y.B. Kafai and M. Resnick (eds) *Constructionism in Practice: designing, thinking and learning in a digital world*, Mahwah, NJ: Lawrence Erlbaum Associates, 97–111.

Katsell, J.H. (2005) 'Review of *Limits to Interpretation: the meanings of "Anna Karenina"* by Vladimir E. Alexandrov', *Slavic and East European Journal*, 49 (3), 497–8.

Katz, E., Blumer, J.G. and Gurevitch, M. (1974) 'Utilization of Mass Communication by the Individual', in J.G. Blumer and E. Katz (eds) *The Uses of Mass Communication*, London: Sage, 11–35.

Kelman, N. (2005) *Video Game Art*, New York: Assouline.

Kendall, L. (2002) *Hanging Out in the Virtual Pub: masculinities and relationships online*, Berkley: University of California Press.

Kerr, A. (2006) *The Business and Culture of Digital Games: gamework/gameplay*, London: Sage.

—— (2011) 'Player Production and Innovation in Online Games: time for new rules?', in G. Crawford, V.K. Gosling and B. Light (eds) *Online Gaming in Context: the social and cultural significance of online games*, London: Routledge.

Kerr, A., Brereton, P., Kücklich, J. and Flynn, R. (2004) *New Media: new media pleasures?*, STeM Working Paper: Final Research Report of a Pilot Research Project, Dublin City University. Online. Available HTTP: http://www.stem.dcu.ie/reports/NMNP.pdf.

Kestenbaum, G.I. and Weinstein, L. (1985) 'Personality, Psychopathology, and Development Issues in Male Adolescent Video Game Use', *Journal of the American Academy of Child Psychiatry*, 24, 329–37.

Kinder, M. (1991) *Playing with Power in Movies, Television and Video Games: from Muppet Babies to Teenage Mutant Ninja Turtles*, Berkeley: University of California Press.

King, A. (2001) 'Violent Pasts: collective memory and football hooliganism', *Sociological Review*, 49 (4), 569–85.

King, B. and Borland, J. (2003) *Dungeons and Dreamers: the rise of computer game culture, from geek to chic*, New York: McGraw-Hill.

King, G. and Krzywinska, T. (2006) *Tomb Raiders and Space Invaders: videogame forms and contexts*, London: I.B. Tauris.

Kirkpatrick, G. (2004) *Critical Technology: a social theory of personal computing*, Aldershot: Ashgate.

—— (2011) *Aesthetic Theory and the Video Game*, Manchester: Manchester University Press.

Kirshenbaum, M. (2009) 'War Stories: board wargames and (vast) procedural narratives', in P. Harrigan and N. Wardrip-Fruin (eds) *Third Person: exploring and authoring vast narratives*, Cambridge, MA: MIT Press, 357–72.

Klein, M.H. (1984) 'The Bite of Pac-Man', *Journal of Psychology*, 11, 395–401.

Kline, S., Dyver-Witherford, N. and De Peuter, G. (2003), *Digital Play: the interaction of technology, culture, and marketing*, London: McGill-Queen's University Press.

Kristeva, J. (1969) *Semeiotikè*, Paris: Points.

Krotoski, A. (2004) *Chicks and Joysticks: an exploration of women and gaming*, ELSPA White Paper. Online. Available HTTP: http://www.elspa.com/about/pr/elspawhite-paper3.pdf.

Kücklich, J. (2006) 'Literary Theory and Digital Games', in Rutter and Bryce (2006), 95–111.

Kuhlman, J.S. and Beitel, P.A. (1991) 'Videogame Experience: a possible explanation for different anticipation of coincidence', *Perceptual and Motor Skills*, 72, 483–8.

Lally, E. (2002) *At Home with Computers*, Oxford: Berg.

Lantz, F. (2009) 'Games Are Not Media', *Games Design Advance*. Online. Available HTTP: http://gamedesignadvance.com/?p=1567.

Lamerichs, N. (2010) 'All Dressed Up: conceptualizing "cosplaying" as a fan practice', paper presentation to the Under the Mask 3 conference, University of Bedfordshire, UK, 2 June.

Lefebvre, H. ([1947] 1991) *Critique of Everyday Life*, vol. 1, *Introduction*, London: Verso.

Leonard, D. (2004) 'High Tech Blackface – Race, Sports Video Games and Becoming the Other', *Intelligent Agent*, 4 (2). Online. Available HTTP: http://www.intelligentagent.com/archive/Vol4_No4_gaming_leonard.htm.

Leonard, D. (2006) 'An Untapped Field: exploring the world of virtual sports', in A.A. Raney and J. Bryant (eds) *Handbook of Sports and Media*, London: Lawrence Erlbaum, 393–407.

—— (2009) 'Young, Black (and Brown) and Don't Give a Fuck: virtual gangstas in the era of state violence', *Cultural Studies/Critical Methodologies*, 9, 248–72.

Lévy, P. (1997) *Collective Intelligence: mankind's emerging world in cyberspace*, Cambridge: Perseus.

Liebe, M. (2008) 'There Is No Magic Circle', in S. Günzel, M. Liebe and D. Mersch (eds) *Conference Proceedings of the Philosophy of Computer Games 2008*, DIGAREC Series 1, Potsdam: Potsdam University Press, 324–40.

Liebes, T. and Katz, E. (1990) *The Export of Meaning: cross-cultural readings of "Dallas"*, New York: Oxford University Press.

Lin, H. and Sun, C.T. (2008) 'Invisible Gameplay Participants: the role of onlookers in arcade gaming', paper presented at the Under the Mask conference, University of Bedfordshire, UK, 7 June. Online. Available HTTP: http://underthemask.wikidot.com/linandsun.

—— (2011) 'Thrift Players in a Twisted Game World? A study of private online game servers', in G. Crawford, V.K. Gosling and B. Light (eds) *Online Gaming in Context: the social and cultural significance of online games*, London: Routledge.

Ling, R. and Haddon, L. (2003) 'Mobile Telephony, Mobility and the Coordination of Everyday Life', in J. Katz (ed.) *Machines that Become Us: the social context of personal communication technology*, New Brunswick, NJ: Transaction.

Lister, M., Dovey, J., Giddings, S., Grant, I. and Kelly, K. (2009) *New Media: a critical introduction*, 2nd edn, London: Routledge.

Livingstone, S. (2005) 'Media Audiences, Interpreters and Users', in M. Gillespie (ed.) *Media Audiences*, Maidenhead: Open University Press/McGraw-Hill, 184–222.

Loftus, G.R. and Loftus, E.F. (1983) *Mind at Play: the psychology of video games*, New York: Basic Books.

Lombard, M. and Ditton, T. (1997) 'At the Heart of It All: the concept of presence', *Journal of Computer-Mediated Communication*, 3 (2). Online. Available HTTP: http://www.ascusc.org/jcmc/vol3/issue2.

Long, G. (2009) '(Some) Games Are Media: a response to Frank Lantz', Gambit: Singapore-MIT Gambit Game Lab blog. Online. Available HTTP: http://gambit.mit.edu/updates/2009/09/some_games_are_media_a_respons.php.

Longhurst, B. (2007) *Cultural Change and Ordinary Life*, Maidenhead: McGraw-Hill.

—— (2009) *Popular Music and Society*, 2nd edn, Cambridge: Polity.

Longhurst, B., Smith, S., Bagnall, G., Crawford, G. and Ogborn, S. (2008) *Introducing Cultural Studies*, 2nd edn, London: Prentice-Hall.

Lury, C. (1996) *Consumer Culture*, Cambridge: Polity.

MacCallum-Stewart, E. (2011) '"You No Take Candle". Online games as different social spaces', in G. Crawford, V.K. Gosling and B. Light (eds) *Online Gaming in Context: the social and cultural significance of online games*, London: Routledge.

Mackay, H. (1997) *Consumption and Everyday Life: culture, media and identities*, London: Sage.

McMillan, S. (2002) 'A Four-Part Model of Cyber-Interactivity: some cyber-places are more interactive than others', *New Media and Society*, 4 (2), 271–91.

McNamee, S. (1998) 'The Home: youth, gender and video games: power and control in the home', in T. Skelton and G. Valentine (eds) *Cool Places: geographies of youth cultures*, London: Routledge, 195–206.

Mactavish, A. (2008) 'Licensed to Play: digital games, player modifications, and authorized production', in S. Schreibman and R. Siemens (eds) *A Companion to Digital Literary Studies*, Oxford: Blackwell, 349–86.

Maffesoli, M. (1996) *The Time of the Tribes: the decline of individualism in mass society*, London: Sage.

Malaby, T. (2007) 'Parlaying Value: capital in and beyond virtual worlds', *Games and Culture*, 1 (2), 141–62.

Mauss, M. (1934) 'Les Techniques du corps', *Journal de Psychologie*, 32 (3–4), 365–86. Reprinted in M. Mauss (1936) *Sociologie et anthropologie*, Paris: PUF.

Marsh, P. (1978) 'Life and Careers on the Football Terraces', in R. Ingham (ed.) *Football Hooliganism*, London: Inter-Action Trust.

Marshall, P.D. (2002) 'The New Intertextual Commodity', in D. Harries (ed.) *The New Media Book*, London: BFI, 69–81.

Martin, B. (1981) *A Sociology of Contemporary Cultural Change*, Oxford: Blackwell.

Martin, J.P., Ruiz, J.I. and Martinez, S.P. (2006) *Women and Videogames: habits and preferences of the video gamer*, Madrid: Universidad Europea de Madrid and Observatorio del Videojuego y de la Animación. Online. Available HTTP: http://www.womeningamesinternational.org/resources/content/perez_2006_womenandgames.pdf.

Massie, K. (2011) 'Representations of Race and Gender within the Gamespace of the MMO *EverQuest*', in G. Crawford, V.K. Gosling and B. Light (eds) *Online Gaming in Context: the social and cultural significance of online games*, London: Routledge.

Mathiesen, T. (1997) 'The Viewer Society: Michel Foucault's "Panopticon" revisited', *Theoretical Criminology*, 1 (2), 215–34.

May, C. (2002) *The Information Society: a sceptical view*, Cambridge: Polity.

Mäyrä, F. (2008) *An Introduction to Game Studies: games in culture*, London: Sage.

——(2009) 'Getting into the Game: doing multidisciplinary game studies', in B. Perron and M.J.P. Wolf (eds) *The Video Game Theory Reader 2*, London: Routledge, 313–30.

—— (2010) 'Gaming Culture at the Boundaries of Play', *Game Studies*, 10 (1). Online. Available HTTP: http://gamestudies.org/1001/articles/mayra.

——(2011) 'Games in the Mobile Internet: towards contextual play in *Flickr* and *Facebook*', in G. Crawford, V.K. Gosling and B. Light (eds) *Online Gaming in Context: the social and cultural significance of online games*, London: Routledge.

Meek, J. (2010) 'Calling on the Audience to Live the Dream', *Guardian*, 21 August, 29.

Moores, S. (2004) 'The Doubling of Place: electronic media, time–space arrangements and social relationships', in N. Couldry and A. McCarthy (eds) *Mediaspace: place, scale and culture in a media age*, London: Routledge, 21–36.

Moorhouse, H.F. (1991) *Driving Ambitions: an analysis of the American hot rod enthusiasm*, Manchester: Manchester University Press.

Morley, D. (2006) 'What's Home Got to Do with It? Contradictory dynamics in the domestication of technology and the dislocations of domesticity', in Berker *et al.* (2006), 19–36.

Morley, D. and Silverstone, R. (1990) 'Domestic Communication: technologies and meanings', *Media, Culture and Society*, 12 (1), 31–56.

Murray, J.H. (1997) *Hamlet on the Holodeck: the future of narrative in cyberspace*, New York: Free Press.

—— (2000) *Hamlet on the Holodeck: the future of narrative in cyberspace*, 3rd edn, Cambridge, MA: MIT Press.

Murray, J.H. and Jenkins, H. (n.d.) *Before the Holodeck: translating Star Trek into digital media*. Online. Available HTTP: http://web.mit.edu/21fms/wwww/faculty/henry3/holodeck.html.

Myers, D. (2009) 'The Video Game Aesthetic: play as form', in B. Perron and M.J.P. Wolf (eds) *The Video Game Theory Reader 2*, London: Routledge, 45–64.

Neumann, J.V. and Morgenstern, O. (1944) *Theory of Games and Economic Behaviour*, Princeton, NJ: Princeton University Press.

Newman, J. (2004) *Videogames*, London: Routledge.

—— (2008) *Playing with Videogames*, London: Routledge

Nieborg, D.B. and Hermes, J. (2008) 'What Is Game Studies Anyway?', *European Journal of Cultural Studies*, 11 (2), 131–46.

Nielsen (2010) *Three Screen Report*, 7 (4th quarter). Online. Available HTTP: http://in.nielsen.com/site/documents/3Screens_4Q09_US_rpt.pdf.

Nielsen, S.E., Smith, J.H. and Tosca, S.P. (2008) *Understanding Video Games: the essential introduction*, London: Routledge.

Nintendo (2009) 'Nintendo DS Product Line Sells More Than 1.04 Million, Sets Industry Record for April Hardware Sales', *Nintendo.com*. Online. Available HTTP: http://www.nintendo.com/whatsnew/detail/B0Y9wB_G8BGLqmxaaoPisAOqm0__PhEJ.

Nitsche, M. (2008) *Video Game Spaces: image, play, and structure in 3D game worlds*, Cambridge, MA: MIT Press.

Nutt, D. and Railton, N. (2003) '*The Sims*: Real Life as Genre', *Information, Communication and Society*, 6 (4), 577–607.

Oldenburg, R. (1999) *The Great Good Place: cafés, coffee shops, community centers, beauty parlors, general stores, bars, hangouts, and how they get you through the day*, New York: Marlowe and Company.

Orosy-Fildes, C. and Allan, R.W. (1989) 'Videogame Play: human reaction time to visual stimuli', *Perceptual and Motor Skills*, 69, 243–7.

Padilla-Walker, L.M., Nelson, L.J., Carroll, J.S. and Jensen, A.C. (2008) 'More Than Just a Game: video game and Internet use during emerging adulthood', *Journal of Youth and Adolescence*, 39, 103–13. Online. Available HTTP: http://www.springerlink.com/content/w487673k5415k142/fulltext.pdf.

Palmer, D. (2003) 'The Paradox of User Control', paper presented at the Melbourne DAC 2003 Conference, RMIT University, Melbourne, Australia, 19–23 May. Online. Available HTTP: http://hypertext.rmit.edu.au/dac/papers/Palmer.pdf .

Pargman, D., and Jakobsson, P. (2008) 'Do You Believe in Magic? Computer games in everyday life', *European Journal of Cultural Studies*, 11 (2), 225–43.

Parker, S. (2000) 'EverQuest Fan Fiction Controversy', *GameSpot.com*. Online. Available HTTP: http://uk.gamespot.com/news/2637913.html.

Pearce, C. (2009) *Communities of Play: emergent cultures in multiplayer games and virtual worlds*, Cambridge, MA: MIT Press.

—— (2011) 'Identity-as-Place: Trans-Ludic Identities in Mediated Play Communities: the case of the *Uru* diaspora', in G. Crawford, V.K. Gosling and B. Light (eds) *Online Gaming in Context: the social and cultural significance of online games*, London: Routledge.

Pearson, G. (1993) 'Talking a Good Fight: authenticity and distance in the ethnographer's craft', in D. Hobbs and T. May (eds) *Interpreting the Field: accounts of ethnography*, Oxford: Clarendon Press, vii–xx.

Peirce, C.S. ([1909] 1998). *The Essential Peirce: selected philosophical writings*, vol. 2 (1893–1913), Peirce Edition Project, Indianapolis: Indiana University Press.

Perron, B. and Wolf, M.J.P. (2009) 'Introduction', in B. Perron and M.J.P. Wolf (eds) *The Video Game Theory Reader 2*, London: Routledge, 1–22.

Peterson, R. and Kern, R. (1996) 'Changing Highbrow Taste: from snob to omnivore', *American Sociological Review*, 6 (1), 900–7.

Pinch, T. and Bijker, W.E. (1987) 'The Social Construction of Facts and Artifacts: or how the sociology of science and the sociology of technology might benefit each other', in W.E. Bijker, T.P. Hughes and T. Pinch (eds) *The Social Construction of Technological Systems*, Cambridge, MA: MIT Press, 17–50.

Poster, M. (1990) *The Mode of Information: poststructuralism and social context*, Cambridge: Polity.

Pratchett, R. (2005) *Gamers in the UK: digital play digital lifestyles*, London: BBC Creative Research and Development. Online. Available HTTP: http://open.bbc.co.uk/newmediaresearch/files/BBC_UK_Games_Research_2005.pdf.

Prensky, M. (2003) 'Digital Game-Based Learning', *ACM Computers in Entertainment*, 1 (1), Book 02. Online. Available HTTP: http://210.240.189.212/Dctelearning/Type_Resources/01_Papers/9612_Digital_Papers/2_English/BIT095103/Digital%20game-Based%20learning.pdf.

Provenzo, E. (1991) *Video Kids*, Cambridge, MA: Harvard University Press.

Putman, R. (2000) *Bowling Alone: the collapse and revival of American community*, New York: Simon & Schuster.

Rakow, L. (1998) 'Women and the Telephone: the gendering of a communications technology', in C. Kramarae (ed.) *Technology and Women's Voices: keeping in touch*, London: Routledge, 207–28.

Radway, J. (1984) *Reading the Romance: women, patriarchy and popular literature*, Chapel Hill, NC: University of North Carolina Press.

Rambusch, J., Jakobsson, P. and Pargman, D. (2007) 'Exploring E-Sports: a case study of gameplay in counter-strike', in *Situated Play: proceedings of DiGRA 2007 conference, Tokyo*. Online. Available HTTP: http://www.digra.org/dl/db/07313.16293.pdf.

Randall, N. (2011) 'The Boardgame Online: Simulating the Experience of Physical Games', in G. Crawford, V.K. Gosling and B. Light (eds) *Online Gaming in Context: the social and cultural significance of online games*, London: Routledge.

Rehak, B. (2003) 'Playing at Being: psychoanalysis and the avatar', in Wolf and Perron (2003), 103–28.

Ricoeur, P. (1988) *Time and Narrative*, vol. 3, Chicago: University of Chicago Press.

Rodriguez, H. (2006) 'The Playful and the Serious: an approximation to Huizinga's *Homo Ludens*', Game Studies, 6 (1). Online. Available HTTP: http://gamestudies.org/0601/articles/rodriges.

Rogers, E.M. (2003) *The Diffusion of Innovations*, 5th edn, New York: Free Press.

Rojek, C. (2001) *Celebrity*, London: Reaktion.

Rosewater, M. (2002) 'Timmy, Johnny and Spike', *Making Magic*, 11 March. Online. Available: www.wizards.com/Magic/Magazine/Article.aspx?x=mtgcom/daily/mr11.

—— (2006) 'Timmy, Johnny and Spike Revisited', *Making Magic*, 18 December. Online. Available: www.wizards.com/Magic/Magazine/Article.aspx?x=mtgcom/daily/mr258.

—— (2007) 'Melvin and Vorthos', *Making Magic*, 7 May. Online. Available: www.wizards.com/Magic/Magazine/Article.aspx?x=mtgcom/daily/mr278.

Ross, K. and Nightingale, V. (2003) *Media Audiences: new perspectives*, Maidenhead: Open University Press.

Rossi, L., Mortensen, T., Jørgensen, K. and Glas, R. (2011) 'Framing the Game: four game-related approaches to Goffman's frames', in G. Crawford, V.K. Gosling and B. Light (eds) *Online Gaming in Context: the social and cultural significance of online games*, London: Routledge.

Rushkoff, D. (1999) *Playing the Future: what we can learn from digital kids*, New York: Riverhead Trade.

Rutter, J. and Bryce, J. (eds) (2006) *Understanding Digital Games*, London: Sage.

Salen, K. and Zimmerman, E. (2004) *Rules of Play: game design fundamentals*, Cambridge, MA: MIT Press.

Sandvoss, C. (2003) *A Game of Two Halves: football, television and globalization*, London: Routledge.

—— (2005) *Fans: the mirror of consumption*, Cambridge: Polity.

Savage, M., Bagnall, G. and Longhurst, B. (2005) *Globalization and Belonging*, London: Sage.

Saxe, J. (1994) 'Violence in Videogames: what are the pleasures?', paper presented at the International Conference on Violence in the Media, St. John's University, New York, 3–4 October. Online at http://web.archive.org/web/20000815110856/http://www.media-awareness.ca/eng/issues/violence/resource/reports/gamedoc.htm.

Schell, J. (2010) 'Design outside the Box', presentation to the annual DICE (Design Innovate Communicate Entertain) summit, 17–19 February. Online. Available HTTP: http://www.g4tv.com/videos/44277/dice-2010-design-outside-the-box-presentation/.

Schleiner, A.M. (2001) 'Does Lara Croft Wear Fake Polygons? Gender and gender-role subversion in computer adventure games', *Leonardo*, 34 (3), 221–6.

Schott, G. (2006) 'Agency in and around Play', in D. Carr, D. Buckingham, A. Burn and G. Schott (eds) *Computer Games: text, narrative and play*, Cambridge: Polity, 133–48.

Schott, G. and Burn, A. (2004) 'Art (Re)production as an Expression of Collective Agency within Oddworld Fan-Culture', *Works and Days*, 43/44, 22 (1/2), 1–24.

Schott, G. and Horrell, K.R. (2000) 'Girl Gamers and Their Relationship with the Game Culture', *Convergence*, 6 (4), 36–54.

Schott, G. and Kambouri, M. (2006) 'Social Play and Learning', in D. Carr, D. Buckingham, A. Burn and G. Schott (eds) *Computer Games: text, narrative and play*, Cambridge: Polity, 199–32.

Schutz, A. (1973) 'On Multiple Realities', in *Collected Papers*, vol. 1, The Hague: Martinus Nijhoff, 207–59.

Schwartz, B. (2003) 'Jesse Schell Interview', *Game Journal*, October. Online. Available HTTP: http://www.thegamesjournal.com/articles/JesseSchell.shtml.

Shank, B. (1994) *Dissonant Identities: the rock 'n' roll scene in Austin, Texas*. Hanover, NH: Wesleyan University Press.

Shaw, A. (2010) 'What Is Video Game Culture? Cultural studies and game studies', *Games and Culture*, 5 (4), 403–24.

Shaw, S.M. (1994) 'Gender, Leisure and Constraint: towards a framework for analysis of women's leisure', *Journal of Leisure Research*, 26, 8–22.

Shields, R. (1996a) 'Virtual Spaces, Real Histories and Living Bodies', in R. Shields (ed.) *Cultures of Internet*, London: Sage.

—— (1996b) 'Introduction', in Maffesoli (1996), ix–xii.

Siisiäinen, M. (2000) 'Two Concepts of Social Capital: Bourdieu vs. Putnam', paper presented at the ISTR fourth international conference, The Third Sector: for what and for whom?, Trinity College, Dublin, Ireland, 5–8 July. Online. Available HTTP: http://www.suz.uzh.ch/fux/lehre/Sozialkapital/siisiainen.pdf.

Silverman, R.E. (2009) 'Xbox to Exile? Videogames linked to antisocial behavior', *Wall Street Journal*, 23 January. Online. Available HTTP: http://blogs.wsj.com/juggle/2009/01/23/xbox-to-exile-new-study-links-videogames-with-antisocial-behavior/.

Silverstone, R. (1994) *Television, Technology and Everyday Life: an essay in the sociology of culture*, London: Routledge.

Silverstone, R., Hirsch, E. and Morley, D. (1992) 'Economy of the Household', in R. Silverstone, E. Hirsch and D. Morley (eds) *Consuming Technologies: media and information in domestic spaces*, London: Routledge.

Sjöblom, B. (2008) 'Gaming as a Situated Collaborative Practice', *Human IT*, 9 (3), 128–65.

Smith, G.W.H. (2006) *Erving Goffman*, London: Routledge.

Steinkuehler, C.A. and Williams, D.S. (2006) 'Where Everybody Knows Your (Screen) Name: online games as "third places"', *Journal of Computer-Mediated*

Communication, 11, 885–909. Online. Available HTTP: http://onlinelibrary.wiley.com/doi/10.1111/j.1083-6101.2006.00300.x/pdf.

Stone, A.R. (1995) *The War of Desire and Technology at the Close of the Mechanical Age*, Cambridge, MA: MIT Press.

Strathern, M. (1992) 'Foreword: the mirror of technology', in Silverstone *et al.* (1992), vi–ix.

Straw, W. (1991) 'System of Articulation, Logics of Change: communities and scenes in popular music', *Cultural Studies*, 15 (3), 368–88.

Subrahmanyam, K. and Greenfield, P.M. (1994) 'Effect of Video Game Practice on Spatial Skills in Girls and Boys', *Journal of Applied Developmental Psychology*, 15 (1), 13–32.

Sundén, J. (2009) 'Hot Gaming: a queer eye on *World of Warcraft*', paper presented at the Informatics Research Institute, University of Salford, 29 April.

Sutton-Smith, B. (1997) *The Ambiguity of Play*, Cambridge, MA: Harvard University Press.

Tavinor, G. (2009) *The Art of Videogames: new directions in aesthetics*, Oxford: Wiley-Blackwell.

Taylor, I., Walton, P. and Young, J. (1973) *The New Criminology: for a social theory of deviance*, London: Routledge.

Taylor, K.E. (2011) '*Wordslinger*: visualising physical abuse in a virtual environment', in G. Crawford, V.K. Gosling and B. Light (eds) *Online Gaming in Context: the social and cultural significance of online games*, London: Routledge.

Taylor, T.L. (2003) 'Multiple Pleasures: women and online gaming', *Convergence*, 9 (1), 21–46.

—— (2006) *Play between Worlds: exploring online game culture*, Cambridge, MA: MIT Press.

—— (2007) 'Pushing the Boundaries: player participation and game culture', in J. Karaganis (ed.) *Structures of Participation in Digital Culture*, New York: SSRC, 112–30.

Thompson, G. (1981) *Popular Culture and Everyday Life*, Buckingham: Open University Press.

Thornton, S. (1995) *Club Cultures: music, media and subcultural capital*, Cambridge: Cambridge University Press.

Tomas, D. (2000) 'The Technophilic Body', in D. Bell and B.M. Kennedy (eds) *The Cybercultures Reader*, London: Routledge, 113–29.

Trend, D. (2007) *The Myth of Media Violence: a critical introduction*, Oxford: Blackwell.

Tulloch, J. (1999) *Performing Culture: stories of expertise and the everyday*, London: Sage.

Tulloch, J. and Jenkins, H. (1995) *Science Fiction Audiences: watching Dr Who and Star Trek*, London: Routledge.

Turkle, S. (1995) *Life on the Screen: identity in the age of the Internet*, New York: Simon & Schuster.

—— (1996) 'Constructions and Reconstructions of the Self in Virtual Reality', in T. Druckrey (ed.) *Electronic Culture: technology and representation*, New York: Aperture, 354–65.

—— (2005) *The Second Self: computers and the human spirit*, 20th anniversary edn, Cambridge, MA: MIT Press.

Van der Voort, T. H.A., Beentjes, J.W.J., Bovill, M., Gaskell, G., Koolstra, C.M., Livingstone, S. and Marseille, N. (1998) 'Young People's Ownership and Uses of New and Old Forms of Media in Britain and the Netherlands', *European Journal of Communication*, 13 (4), 457–78.

Van Gennep, A. (1908) *Les Rites de passage*, Paris, trans. M. Vizedom and G. Caffee as *The Rites of Passage*, Chicago: University of Chicago Press, 1960.

Wacquant, L. (2004) 'Habitus', in J. Beckert and M. Zafirovski (eds) *International Encyclopedia of Economic Sociology*, London: Routledge, 315–19.

Walsh, C.S and Apperley, T. (2008) 'Gaming Capital: rethinking literacy', in *Changing Climates: education for sustainable futures. Proceedings of the 2008 AARE conference, Brisbane*. Online. Available HTTP: http://www.aare.edu.au/08pap/wal08101.pdf.

Warde, A. (1990) 'Introduction to the Sociology of Consumption', *Sociology*, 24, 1–4.

—— (1992) 'Notes on the Relationship between Production and Consumption', in R. Burrows and C. Marsh (eds) *Consumption and Class: divisions and change*, London: Macmillan, 15–31.

Warde, A., Martens, L. and Olsen, W. (1999) 'Consumption and the Problem of Variety: cultural omnivorousness, social distinction and dining out', *Sociology*, 33 (1), 105–27.

Wearing, B. (1998) *Leisure and Feminist Theory*, London: Sage.

Webb, J., Shirato, T. and Danaher, G. (2002) *Understanding Bourdieu*, London: Sage.

Welsh, T.J. (2006) 'Everyday Play: cruising for leisure in San Andreas', in N. Garrelts (ed.) *The Meaning and Culture of 'Grand Theft Auto': critical essays*, London: McFarland and Co., 127–42.

Westecott, E. (2008) 'Bringing the Body Back into Play', *[Player] Conference Proceedings, Copenhagen: IT University of Copenhagen, 26–29 August 2008*, Copenhagen: IT University of Copenhagen, 379–92.

Williams, R. (1974) *Television: technology and cultural form*, London: Fontana.

—— (1976) *Keywords: a vocabulary of culture and society*, London: Fontana.

Willis, P. (1977) *Learning to Labour*, London: Saxon House.

Wolf, M.J.P and Perron, B. (eds) (2003) *The Video Game Theory Reader*, London: Routledge.

Wright, T., Boria, E. and Breidenbach, P. (2002) 'Creative Player Actions in FPS On-Line Video Games: playing *Counter-Strike*', *Game Studies*, 2 (2). Online. Available HTTP: http://www.gamestudies.org/0202/wright/.

Yates, S.J. and Littleton, K.L. (2001) 'Understanding Computer Game Culture: a situated approach' in E. Green and A. Adam (eds) *Virtual Gender: technology, consumption and identity*, London: Routledge, 103–23.

Yee, N. (2006) 'The Demographics, Motivations, and Derived Experiences of Users of Massively Multi-User Graphical Environments', *Presence*, 15 (3), 309–29.

Index

Printed in the USA/Agawam, MA
August 15, 2011

560697.025